THE
TEACHING PORTFOLIO

THE
TEACHING PORTFOLIO

*A Practical Guide to Improved Performance
and Promotion/Tenure Decisions*

SECOND EDITION

Peter Seldin

Lubin School of Business
Pace University
Pleasantville, NY

ANKER PUBLISHING COMPANY, INC.
Bolton, MA

The Teaching Portfolio

A Practical Guide to Improved Performance
and Promotion/Tenure Decisions

Second Edition

ISBN 1-882982-15-0

Composition by Deerfoot Studios
Cover design by Deerfoot Studios

Anker Publishing Company, Inc.
176 Ballville Road
P.O. Box 249
Bolton, MA 01740-0249

ABOUT THE AUTHOR

Peter Seldin is Distinguished Professor of Management at Pace University, Pleasantville, New York. A specialist in the evaluation and development of faculty performance, he has been a consultant to more than two hundred and fifty colleges and universities throughout the United States and in twenty-five countries around the world.

Peter is a frequent speaker at national and international conferences and regularly serves as a faculty leader in programs offered by the American Council on Education and the American Assembly of Collegiate Schools of Business.

His well-received books include: *Improving College Teaching* (1995, with associates), *Successful Use of Teaching Portfolios* (1993, with associates), *The Teaching Portfolio* (1991), *How Administrators Can Improve Teaching* (1990, with associates), *Evaluating and Developing Administrative Performance* (1990), *Coping With Faculty Stress* (1987, with associates), *Changing Practices in Faculty Evaluation* (1984), *Successful Faculty Evaluation Programs* (1980), *Teaching Professors to Teach* (1977), and *How Colleges Evaluate Professors* (1975).

He has contributed numerous articles on the teaching profession, student ratings, and academic culture to such publications as *The New York Times, The Chronicle of Higher Education,* and *Change* magazine.

Peter has won awards both as an educator and as a grower of cherry tomatoes.

CONTENTS

About the Author   *v*

Contributors   *viii*

Preface to the Second Edition   *xi*

1. The Teaching Portfolio   1

2. Choosing Items for the Portfolio   4

3. Preparing the Portfolio   10

4. Using the Portfolio   15

5. Answers to Common Questions About the Teaching Portfolio   19

6. Some Final Thoughts   25

7. Preparing the Portfolio: A Personal View   28
   Joseph A. Weber

8. Developing an Institutional Portfolio Program:
   A Step-by-Step Report   32
   Karen E. Mura

9. Improving Teaching Through Portfolio Revisions   37
   John Zubizarreta

10. The Electronically Augmented Teaching Portfolio   46
    Devorah A. Lieberman & John Rueter

11. Sample Portfolios From Across Disciplines   58

12. Afterword   252
    Linda Annis

Appendix: Key Points on Revising a Portfolio   255
   Peter Seldin & John Zubizarreta

Index   265

CONTRIBUTORS

Donna W. Angarano is Professor at the College of Veterinary Medicine, Auburn University, where she teaches in the Department of Small Animal Surgery and Medicine.

Linda Annis is Professor of Educational Psychology and former Director of the Center for Teaching and Learning at Ball State University. She is actively involved as writer, presenter, and mentor in the teaching portfolio movement.

Judith M. Arnold is Instructional Services Librarian at Western Michigan University where she coordinates the instructional program and provides instruction and reference service for the university libraries.

Indira Chatterjee is Associate Professor of Electrical Engineering at the University of Nevada, Reno. Formerly she held academic positions at the University of Utah and the University of Alabama, Tuscaloosa.

Diane M. Clark is Associate Professor of Music at Rhodes College where she teaches vocal music, music theory, and public speaking.

Daria T. Cronic is a faculty member in the Department of Foundations and Special Education at Clemson University. Her teaching and research interests are in the areas of special education, teacher preparation, and educational leadership.

Anthony P. Ferzola is Associate Professor of Mathematics at the University of Scranton. He has been teaching mathematics and computer science for eighteen years.

Daniel M. Gropper is Associate Professor of Economics and the Director of the MBA Program in the College of Business at Auburn University.

Ellen H. Hendrix is Instructor of English at Georgia Southern University where she teaches English literature and composition.

Colleen Kennedy is Associate Professor of English and Assistant to the President at the College of William and Mary. She is former Director of the Writing Program.

Stephanie L. Kenney is Assistant Professor of Special Education at Georgia Southern University where she trains students to teach children and adults with special learning needs.

Devorah Lieberman is Director of Teaching and Learning in the Center for Academic Excellence at Portland State University. Her interests include intercultural communication, diversity in business, and communication and aging.

Robert R. Llewellyn is Associate Professor of Philosophy at Rhodes College. He recently returned to full-time teaching after being Associate Dean of Academic Affairs at Rhodes for thirteen years.

R. Heather Macdonald is Dean of Undergraduate Studies and Associate Professor of Geology at the College of William and Mary.

R. M. MacQueen is Professor of Physics at Rhodes College. Previously, he spent twenty-two years with the National Center for Atmospheric Research in Boulder, Colorado.

Oliver J. Morgan, S. J. is Associate Professor of Counseling and Human Services at the University of Scranton. He also works as Pastoral Psychologist at the University Counseling Center.

Karen E. Mura is Assistant Professor of English at Susquehanna University. While trained as a medievalist, she is a committed generalist, teaching courses which emphasize student writing, portfolios, and community service learning.

Charles P. Rose is Professor of Law at Wake Forest University's School of Law where his teaching responsibilities include a course in each of the three years of law school.

John Rueter is Professor of Biology at Portland State University. He has been involved with educational technology since 1993 and in 1995 was the "Faculty in Residence" in the Center for Academic Excellence.

James M. Ryan is Associate Professor of Biology at Hobart and William Smith Colleges. His teaching and research interests are in vertebrate morphology, cellular neurobiology, and conservation biology.

Kenneth L. Stanley is Dean and Professor of Finance at Valdosta State University's College of Business Administration.

Maggie M. Sullivan is a second-year Ph.D. student at Southern Illinois University. She teaches as a graduate assistant in the Department of Speech Communication.

Tammy Tobin-Janzen is Assistant Professor of Biology at Susquehanna University where her teaching and research interests are in genetics, microbiology, and immunology.

Joseph A. Weber is Director of the Oklahoma State University Gerontology Institute and Professor in the Department of Family Relations and Child Development.

Clyde E. Willis is Associate Professor of Political Science at Valdosta State University where he teaches American government and courses in public law.

Janie H. Wilson is Assistant Professor of Psychology at Georgia Southern University where she teaches psychological statistics, research methods, physiological psychology, and introduction to psychology.

John Zubizarreta is Professor of English and Director of Honors at Columbia College. In 1994 he was selected as the South Carolina Carnegie Professor of the Year.

PREFACE
TO THE SECOND EDITION

Since 1991, I have visited more colleges and universities and talked with more faculty members and administrators than during any five-year period since I began teaching and writing in 1968. Much of this visiting was a consequence of the nationwide renewed interest in teaching which continues to the present time. Some was the result of the first edition of this book.

During that period, I talked with promotion and tenure committees, department chairs, deans, and faculty groups about the portfolio and its place in the improvement and evaluation of teaching. And I had the pleasure of working one-on-one as mentor to more than three hundred faculty members as they prepared their personal teaching portfolios.

This extensive involvement with portfolios, not just as a theorist but also as a practitioner, has enabled me to pick up new ideas, gain new perspectives, and refine and modify what has already been learned about portfolios. This new edition of *The Teaching Portfolio* puts many of these into print.

This second edition also includes contributed chapters by prominent educators who have prepared their own exemplary teaching portfolios, worked with others who have done so, and engaged in seminal work in the development and use of portfolios.

The Teaching Portfolio, Second Edition, offers college and university faculty and administrators the kind of practical, research-based information necessary to foster the most effective use of portfolios. It is written for presidents, provosts, academic vice-presidents, deans, department chairs, instructional development specialists, and faculty—the essential partners in evaluating and improving teaching. Graduate students, especially those planning careers as faculty members, should also find this book stimulating and helpful.

Earlier books exploring the teaching portfolio have taken a broad how-to approach and have been geared primarily to describing the kinds of documents and material that could go into a portfolio. This book is different.

- It offers practical suggestions for getting started and then maintaining the most effective use of portfolios.

- It identifies key issues, red-flag dangers and benchmarks for success.

- It provides helpful answers to common questions.

- It discusses how portfolio revisions improve teaching.

- It describes the design of a technologically enhanced portfolio.

- It offers twenty-three actual teaching portfolios from across disciplines and institutions.

OVERVIEW OF THE CONTENTS

Chapter One discusses the teaching portfolio concept, what it is, why professors might want to prepare one, and the explosive growth of the concept at colleges and universities across America.

Chapter Two examines the wide range of items that might be included in a portfolio and discusses how to integrate them into a fair and accurate representation of one's teaching and how to select appropriate appendix items.

Chapter Three describes the key role of the mentor, spells out alternative approaches to structure the collaboration, provides practical advice on what to do and what not to do as a mentor, and presents a seven-step approach to create a portfolio.

Chapter Four outlines in important detail how to use portfolios to improve teaching and how to use them for personnel decisions for tenure, promotion, and retention. It also spells out portfolio use for other purposes, such as in grant applications and by graduate students seeking to enter the job market.

Chapter Five offers pragmatic answers to questions commonly raised about developing and using portfolios. Here are guidelines on the background mentors need, how to do self-mentoring if there are no trained mentors available, how faculty members can demonstrate efforts to improve their teaching, how much time it takes to produce a portfolio. Also, suggestions for getting started, why all portfolios don't look alike, why an impressive looking portfolio cannot gloss over poor teaching.

Chapter Six summarizes key lessons learned about teaching portfolios. It also contains the bibliography for Chapters One through Five.

Chapter Seven is a personal report by an Oklahoma State University professor on his portfolio preparation, how he looked critically at his own teaching, what he found out, and why he is such a strong advocate of the portfolio.

Chapter Eight describes the step-by-step development of the teaching portfolio program at Susquehanna University, how an existing group of committed faculty moved the process forward, and how important balance was maintained between administrative support and faculty ownership of the program.

Chapter Nine is a personal case study by a professor of English on how and why portfolio revisions improve teaching. It offers tips on maintaining revisions and contains detailed instructions and clear references which enable readers to see how a draft changes over time and to understand the key role of the mentor in identifying potential changes.

Chapter Ten discusses the advantages and potential drawbacks of a technologically enhanced teaching portfolio. It spells out specific ways to enhance a portfolio and offers a step-by-step description of how various components can be augmented using technology.

Chapter Eleven contains the actual teaching portfolios of twenty-three faculty members from different disciplines and institutions.

Chapter Twelve is a personal report by an experienced portfolio mentor on the gratifying and sometimes surprising reports she has received on the ways in which portfolios are being used by faculty members she mentored.

Peter Seldin
Pleasantville, New York
October 1996

ACKNOWLEDGEMENTS

I am grateful to the many, many faculty members and administrators who have written or phoned to tell me that the first edition of *The Teaching Portfolio* indeed was a practical guide to improved instructional performance and promotion/tenure decisions.

Special thanks to the writers who contributed to this new edition for their good-humored acceptance of deadlines and revisions. I am particularly grateful to John Zubizarreta. In addition to being a steady source of advice and encouragement, John read an early draft of this manuscript in the hope of guarding the English language from too obvious discord. His ear for the music of good language improved the text.

THE TEACHING PORTFOLIO

An historic change is taking place in higher education: Teaching is being taken more seriously. At long last, after years of criticism and cries for reform, more and more colleges and universities are reexamining their commitment to teaching and exploring ways to improve and reward it.

As for faculty, they are being held accountable, as never before, to provide clear and concise evidence of the quality of their classroom teaching. Why? Perhaps it is the result of the growing chorus of complaints from those who serve on tenure and promotion review committees that they are given little factual information about teaching performance. They argue that the typical curriculum vitae describes publications, research grants, and other scholarly accomplishments but says very little about teaching.

It is no surprise that committee members are pressing for more information about what professors do in the classroom and why they do it. Without such meaningful information, they argue, how can they be expected to judge a professor's performance? And how can they give the teaching function its rightful value?

Is there a way for colleges and universities to respond simultaneously to the movement to take teaching seriously and to the pressures to improve systems of teaching accountability? The answer is yes. A solution can be found by looking outside higher education.

Artists, photographers, and architects all have portfolios in which they display their best work. The portfolio concept can be adapted to higher education. A teaching portfolio would enable faculty members to display their teaching accomplishments for the record. And, at the same time, it would contribute to more sound personnel decisions and to the professional development and growth of individual faculty members.

What is a teaching portfolio? It is a factual description of a professor's teaching strengths and accomplishments. It includes documents and materials which collectively suggest the scope and quality of a professor's teaching performance. It is to teaching what lists of publications, grants, and honors are to research and scholarship.

Why would very busy—even harried—faculty members want to take the time and trouble to prepare a teaching portfolio? They might do so in order to gather and present hard evidence and specific data about their teaching effectiveness to tenure and promotion committees. Or they might do so in order to provide the needed structure for self-reflection about areas of their teaching needing improvement. Are there other purposes for which professors might prepare a portfolio? The answer is yes. They might do so in order to: a) document for themselves how their teaching has evolved over time; b) prepare materials about their teaching effectiveness when applying for a new position or for post-tenure review; c) share their expertise and experience with younger faculty members; d) provide teaching tips about a specific course for new or part-time faculty; e) seek teaching awards or grants relating to teaching; f) leave a written legacy within the department so that future generations of teachers who will be taking over the courses of about-to-retire professors will have the benefit of their thinking and experience.

An important point: The portfolio is not an exhaustive compilation of all of the documents and materials that bear on teaching performance. Instead, it presents *selected information* on teaching activities and *solid evidence* of their effectiveness. Just as statements in a curriculum vitae should be supported by convincing evidence (such as published articles or invitations to present a paper at an academic conference), so claims in the teaching portfolio should be supported by firm empirical evidence.

The teaching portfolio concept has gone well beyond the point of theoretical possibility. It has been used in Canada (where it is called a teaching dossier) for nearly twenty years. Today it is being adopted or pilot-tested in various forms by a rapidly increasing number of American institutions. Although reliable numbers are hard to come by, it is estimated that as many as 1,000 colleges and universities in the United States are now using or experimenting with portfolios. That is a stunning jump from the approximately ten institutions thought to be using portfolios in 1990. Among the many current users or experimenters with portfolios are Hobart and

William Smith Colleges (New York), Clemson University (South Carolina), Georgia Southern University, The College of William and Mary (Virginia), Rhodes College (Tennessee), Valencia Community College (Florida), Wake Forest University (North Carolina), and Rutgers University (New Jersey).

CHOOSING ITEMS
FOR THE PORTFOLIO

Because the portfolio is a highly personalized product, no two are exactly alike. Both content and organization differ widely from one faculty member to another. (See the sample portfolios in Chapter 11.) Different fields and courses cater to different types of documentation. For example, an introductory economics course is worlds apart from a studio arts course. A graduate seminar in organizational theory is far removed from a freshman biology course. The items chosen for the portfolio depend on the teaching style of the professor, the purpose for which the portfolio is prepared, and any content requirements of a professor's department or institution. Individual differences in portfolio content and organization should be encouraged so long as they are allowed by the department and institution.

Based on empirical evidence, certain items clearly turn up in portfolios with much more frequency than others. From personal review of hundreds of portfolios prepared by professors in institutions representing all sectors of higher education, the writer can assert that certain items appear again and again, falling into three broad categories.

MATERIAL FROM ONESELF

- Statement of teaching responsibilities, including course titles, numbers, enrollments, and a brief statement about whether the course is required or elective, graduate or undergraduate

- A reflective statement by the faculty member, describing his or her personal teaching philosophy, strategies and objectives, methodologies
- Representative course syllabi detailing course content and objectives, teaching methods, readings, homework assignments
- Participation in programs on sharpening instructional skill
- Description of curricular revisions, including new course projects, materials, and class assignments
- Instructional innovations and assessment of their effectiveness
- A personal statement by the professor, describing teaching goals for the next five years
- Description of steps taken to evaluate and improve one's teaching, including changes resulting from self-evaluation, time spent reading journals on improving teaching

MATERIAL FROM OTHERS

- Statements from colleagues who have observed the professor in the classroom
- Statements from colleagues who have reviewed the professor's teaching materials, such as course syllabi, assignments, testing and grading practices
- Student course or teaching evaluation data which produce an overall rating of effectiveness or suggest improvements
- Honors or other recognition from colleagues, such as a distinguished teaching or student advising award
- Documentation of teaching development activity through the campus center for teaching and learning
- Statements by alumni on the quality of instruction

THE PRODUCTS OF TEACHING/STUDENT LEARNING

- Student scores on pre- and post-course examinations
- Examples of graded student essays along with the professor's comments on why they were so graded
- A record of students who succeed in advanced study in the field
- Student publications or conference presentations on course-related work

- Successive drafts of student papers along with the professor's comments on how each draft could be improved

- Information about the effect of the professor and his or her courses on student career choices or help given by the professor to secure student employment or graduate school admission

These are the most commonly selected items, but they are not the only ones to appear in portfolios. Some professors, for reasons of academic discipline, teaching style, or institutional preference, choose a different content mix.

SOME ITEMS THAT SOMETIMES APPEAR IN PORTFOLIOS

- Evidence of help given to colleagues leading to improvement of their teaching

- A videotape of the professor teaching a typical class

- Invitations to present a paper on teaching one's discipline

- Self-evaluation of teaching-related activities

- Participation in off-campus activities relating to teaching

- A statement by the department chair, assessing the faculty member's teaching contribution to the department

- Description of how computers, films, and other nonprint materials are used in teaching

- Contributing to, or editing, a professional journal on teaching the professor's discipline

- Performance reviews as a faculty advisor

How much information is needed to represent a professor's teaching performance fairly and completely? Experience suggests that a selective document of eight to ten pages plus supporting appendix materials is sufficient for the vast majority of faculty members. (Some institutions put a ceiling on the number of pages or number of pounds they permit in order to prevent data overkill in the portfolio.)

Being selective does not mean constructing a biased picture of one's teaching but rather providing a fair and accurate representation of it. As Zubizarreta (1994, p. 324) points out, "Even the occasional flop is worthy material for a . . . portfolio if it reveals a process of genuine adjustment and growth, if the teacher has articulated innovation and risk as key components of a teaching philosophy, and if the institution recognizes experimentation and change as signals of vitality in teaching."

INTEGRATING THE ITEMS IN A PORTFOLIO

A sound portfolio integrates documents and materials from oneself and others as well as the products of teaching (student learning). It offers a coherent teaching profile in which all parts support the whole. For example, a statement of philosophy might reflect an emphasis on scholarship in teaching while methods and materials will reveal a complementary focus on scholarship through rigorous library assignments. Another example: Not only will comments from faculty observers bolster a claim of effective active learning strategies but student evaluations will as well (Seldin, Annis, & Zubizarreta, 1995).

THE APPENDIX

Just as information in the narrative part of the portfolio should be selective, so, too, the appendices should consist of judiciously chosen evidence that adequately supports the narrative section of the portfolio. Should the portfolio require additional appendix space—for supplemental descriptions, hard copy disks, or audio or video tapes, for example—then the professor may briefly discuss such materials in the narrative and make them available for review upon request.

Rather than offer a separate, isolated commentary for each appendix item, many professors weave references to appendices within unified essays. Why? Because this approach strengthens coherence. (See sample portfolios in Chapter 11.) Further, many faculty include in their appendices supporting documents such as syllabi, student evaluations, peer reviews, graded student papers, and invitations to speak at a conference on teaching their discipline.

The appendices must be of manageable size if they are to be read. Millis (1995) encourages faculty to organize their appendices with two directives in mind: integrity and lucidity. By integrity, she means that certain key items, such as syllabi and student ratings, are expected and must be included to support the validity of the portfolio. These key supporting documents must be presented in a manner that reflects a discernable pattern, such as all evaluations for one course for the past three years or all syllabi for all courses taught for the past two years. Further, says Millis, a key test of the lucidity of the appendices is if they are clear to potential readers, especially those outside of the department or discipline.

A word of caution: Sometimes faculty preparing portfolios fall into the trap of permitting the appendices—the supporting documents—to determine the portfolio creation. Should that happen, professors may find themselves focusing on a shopping list of possible portfolio items, determining which are easily accessible, and then creating the reflective section of their portfolios around the evidence they have at hand. The result? Unfortunately they end up focusing on the "what" rather than the "why."

A far better approach is to first reflect about one's underlying philosophy of teaching, then describe the teaching strategies and methodologies that flow from that philosophy (*why* you do *what* you do in the classroom), and only then to select documents and materials which provide the hard evidence of one's teaching activities and their effectiveness.

THE VALUE OF SELF-REFLECTION

In truth, one of the most significant parts of the portfolio is the faculty member's self-reflection on his or her teaching. Preparing it can help professors unearth new discoveries about themselves as teachers. The following topics may assist in the process of self-reflection: How do you work with students who are academically struggling? Describe a teaching success from the past year. Why did it work? Describe a teaching flop. Why did it not work? What new strategies have you tried in the last year? What did you learn from them? How has your teaching changed in the last five years? Are these changes for the better? What do your syllabi say about your teaching style? What do they say about your interest in students (Rehnke, 1994)?

A TYPICAL TABLE OF CONTENTS

A table of contents identifies the major headings of the portfolio. When the purpose is to *improve teaching*, a typical table of contents might look like this:

TEACHING PORTFOLIO
Faculty Member's Name
Department/College
Institution
Date

Table of Contents
1. Teaching Responsibilities
2. Statement of Teaching Philosophy
3. Teaching Methodology, Strategies, Objectives

4. Description of Course Materials (Syllabi, Handouts, Assignments)
5. Efforts to Improve Teaching
   a) Conferences/Workshops Attended
   b) Curricular Revisions
   c) Innovations in Teaching
6. Student Ratings on Diagnostic Questions
7. Products of Teaching (Evidence of Student Learning)
8. Teaching Goals: Short- and Long-Term
9. Appendices

One element of the portfolio which may go unnoticed is the date, an item important to any portfolio because it helps the faculty member establish a base line from which to measure actual development in teaching performance. Such growth can be gauged by the degree to which the portfolio demonstrates instructional improvement resulting from the faculty member's reexamination of his or her philosophy, strategies, objectives, and methodologies (Seldin, Annis, & Zubizarreta, 1995).

A typical table of contents for a portfolio prepared for *evaluation* purposes might include the following entries:

TEACHING PORTFOLIO
Faculty Member's Name
Department/College
Institution
Date

Table of Contents
1. Teaching Responsibilities
2. Statement of Teaching Philosophy
3. Teaching Methods, Strategies, Objectives
4. Student Ratings on Summative Questions
5. Colleague Evaluations From Those Who Have Observed Classroom Teaching or Reviewed Teaching Materials
6. Statement by the Department Chair Assessing the Professor's Teaching Contribution
7. Detailed, Representative Course Syllabi
8. Products of Teaching (Evidence of Student Learning)
9. Teaching Awards and Recognition
10. Teaching Goals: Short-Term and Long-Term
11. Appendices

PREPARING THE PORTFOLIO

In theory, a teaching portfolio can be prepared by the professor working alone, but this isolated approach has limited prospects for improving classroom performance or contributing to personnel decisions. Why? Because portfolios prepared by the professor working alone do not include the collegial or supervisory support needed in a program of teaching improvement. And, importantly, there is none of the control or corroboration of evidence that is essential to sustain personnel decisions. That is why portfolio development should involve interaction and mentoring in the same way that a doctoral dissertation reflects both the efforts of the candidate and the advice of the mentor.

THE MENTOR

Collaboration balances the professor's subjectivity with objective criteria. As Zubizarreta (1994, p. 325) points out, "It ensures a fresh, critical perspective that encourages cohesion between the portfolio narrative and supporting appendix evidence." A skillful mentor flushes out objective information that is evident or readily discovered in a faculty member's work.

Since teaching tends to be a private, solitary activity, collaboratively designed portfolios are an antidote to isolation and a way to promote collegial exchange focused on teaching and learning.

Department chairs, colleagues, or teaching improvement specialists on campus can serve as mentors and discuss with professors key guiding questions: Why are they are preparing the portfolio? (This is particularly important because the purpose drives the content and organization.) Which areas of the teaching-learning process do they expect to examine? What do they hope to learn from it? How will the information be gathered, analyzed, and presented?

The resources of a portfolio mentor blessed with wide knowledge of current instruments and procedures to document effective teaching are especially important. The consultant needs to be familiar with multiple approaches and techniques to document effective teaching. In this way the mentor can assist the faculty member by providing suggestions and resources, and by maintaining important support during the preparation of the portfolio (Seldin, 1993).

Is there a "best" way to structure the collaboration? Unfortunately not. But there are several approaches which have proven useful:

- An outside consultant either from one's own discipline or from another

- A buddy system in which two faculty members team up for a semester or year to visit each other's classes, talk to their students, confer on teaching materials, and then assist each other in documenting their teaching in their portfolios

- A trained group of in-house consultants who, in exchange for a course reduction in teaching load, mentor several professors as they prepare their portfolios

- An older, more experienced professor who works directly with a younger colleague from the same or another discipline

In actual practice, the writer has found that it is not necessary for the mentor to be in the same academic discipline as the faculty member whom he or she is mentoring. In fact, it has been my experience that I may be more effective as a mentor when mentoring in a discipline different from my own. Why? Because when I am interacting with a professor in my own teaching area, it is often hard to avoid focusing on the content rather than on the teaching activities. Should that occur, it becomes more difficult to offer fresh and innovative approaches to documenting teaching effectiveness.

Along with several colleagues, I have formed a portfolio mentoring team. We work with individual faculty members at institutions across the country as they prepare their portfolios. Zubizarreta (1996), a member of the mentoring team, says that the genuinely supportive and instructive collegiality that develops as mentors and faculty members work together toward a common goal is a "refreshing, even transforming, experience. Mentors and faculty members have only one real objective: to enhance the quality of teaching and student learning."

One caution: The mentor must bear in mind that the portfolio is owned by the faculty member. Decisions about what goes into it are generally cooperative decisions between the mentor and professor. But the final decision about what to include, its ultimate use, and the retention of the final product all rest with the professor. In short, the mentor must respect the integrity of the faculty member, the process of portfolio development, and the final product. In doing so, the mentor must refrain from imposing his or her own assumptions, purposes, form, or style, no matter how tempting it might be. The mentoring role is that of guide, not director.

MENTORING SEVERAL FACULTY MEMBERS AT THE SAME TIME

Since faculty members who are preparing portfolios often struggle with the same issues, I especially enjoy mentoring several faculty members during the same time period. Why? So that we can also meet as a group to discuss common problems and offer encouragement and support to each other. Oftentimes, these faculty will return to their departments or colleges and themselves become mentors to others in an "each one, teach one" model.

THE ROLE OF THE CHAIR

Although some professors will prepare portfolios in collaboration with their department chair, most will work with someone else. For that reason, when the portfolio is prepared for personnel decisions, it is especially important that a periodic, written exchange of views between the chair and the professor takes place to discuss expectations and how teaching performance is to be reported. Otherwise, there is a danger that the department chair may erroneously conclude that the data submitted may cover up areas of suspected weaknesses and overlook areas of prime concern (Seldin, 1996).

In truth, when used for personnel decisions, a teaching portfolio will have genuine value only when those who make tenure, promotion, and retention decisions learn to trust the approach. Important to the development of such trust is the periodic exchange of views between the department chair and faculty member.

SEVEN STEPS TO CREATE A TEACHING PORTFOLIO

Most faculty members rely on the following step-by-step approach in creating their portfolios. It is based on the work of Shore and others (1986), O'Neil and Wright (1993), Rodriguez-Farrar (1995), and Seldin (1996).

Step 1. Summarize teaching responsibilities

Portfolios often begin with a two- or three-paragraph statement covering such topics as courses currently taught or those taught in the recent past, whether the courses are graduate or undergraduate, required or elective. It might also cover teaching-related activities such as serving as faculty advisor to student organizations, or advising individual graduate or undergraduate students. The focus here is on what the faculty member is responsible for as a teacher.

Step 2. Describe your approach to teaching

Bearing in mind the summary of teaching responsibilities described in Step 1, the faculty member prepares a two- to two-and-one-half-page reflective statement describing his or her teaching philosophy, strategies, methodologies, and objectives. This statement addresses the issue of how the professor carries out teaching responsibilities from the standpoint of why they do what they do in the classroom. The most effective reflective statements reveal the faculty member's knowledge of pedagogy and subject area specializations by presenting their beliefs about teaching and their aims for students and an explanation of why they believe these aims are important. Further, the most effective reflective statements provide detailed examples of classroom practices which show how the faculty member's teaching methods fit his or her aims and the context of the course.

Step 3. Select items for the portfolio

From the list of possible items for a portfolio, the professor selects those items for inclusion which are most applicable to his or her teaching responsibilities and approach to teaching. Choice of items should also reflect the faculty member's personal preferences, style of teaching, academic discipline, and particular courses. Being creative and inclusive in itemizing teaching accomplishments and presenting reflections on teaching will help faculty members to create a personalized portfolio.

Step 4. Prepare statements on each item

Statements are prepared by the professor on activities, initiatives, and accomplishments on each item. Among key questions that might be considered: Do the syllabi of courses coalesce around a specific theme about your teaching? Have you participated in programs, colloquia, or seminars designed to improve teaching? Do you have a variety of measures of your teaching effectiveness? Back-up documentation and appendices are referenced, as appropriate.

Step 5. Arrange the items in order

The sequence of the accomplishments in each area is determined by their intended use. For example, if the faculty member intends to demonstrate teaching improvement, entries that reflect that goal (such as participating in seminars and workshops designed to enhance classroom performance) would be stressed.

Step 6. Compile the supporting data

Evidence supporting all items mentioned in the portfolio is retained by the professor and made available for review. These would include, for example, original student evaluations of teaching, samples of student work, invitations to contribute articles on teaching in one's discipline, colleague evaluation. Such evidence is not part of the portfolio but is back-up material placed in the appendix or made available upon request.

Step 7. Incorporate the portfolio into the curriculum vitae

Although the portfolio can stand as a separate document, the faculty member may choose to insert it into his or her curriculum vitae under the heading of "teaching." The intent is to provide a formal record of teaching accomplishments so they can be accorded their proper weight along with other aspects of a professor's role.

It is best to present all of the portfolio material in a single container. A three-ring binder is well-suited for the purpose. It is secure and flexible, encouraging the efficient arrangement of materials in separate sections labeled with identification tabs (Zubizarreta, 1994).

For a more technologically sophisticated portfolio, Zubizarreta (p. 325) urges the faculty member to write part or all of the portfolio contents on computer disk: "The advantage of having at least the narrative portion . . . on disk is that if a teacher needs part of the portfolio—for example, a statement of philosophy for a teaching award, a description of methods and goals for a grant or fellowship . . . then the appropriate section is easily printed from the disk." (See Chapter 10 by Lieberman and Rueter for a detailed look at designing a technologically enhanced teaching portfolio.)

Keep in mind that the portfolio is a living collection of documents and materials which changes over time. New items are added. Others are dropped. Updating a portfolio becomes a simple matter of placing items pertaining to teaching in a file drawer or large envelope just as professors now do for research and service. Once each year, when the research and service sections of the curriculum vitae are updated, the same is done for the teaching section. (See Chapter 9 by Zubizarreta for a close look at how his portfolio has evolved over time.)

USING THE PORTFOLIO

The teaching portfolio is a vital tool for faculty; it provides tangible evidence of classroom instruction and can be used to improve teaching performance or personnel decisions.

USING THE PORTFOLIO TO IMPROVE TEACHING

Just as students need feedback to correct errors, professors need factual and philosophical data to improve teaching performance. The portfolio is a particularly effective tool for instructional improvement because it is grounded in discipline-based pedagogy. That is, the focus is on teaching a particular subject to a particular group of students at a particular time.

When used for improvement purposes, the portfolio includes no required items. Instead, it contains only items chosen by the professor. For example, a professor might decide to target in his or her portfolio one particular course for improvement and might include such items as: 1) a summary of instructional methods used; 2) specific course objectives and the degree of student achievement of those objectives; 3) innovative teaching practices; 4) student ratings of course and instructor; 5) classroom observation reports. Whether teaching improvement actually occurs depends largely on the kind of information that turns up in the portfolio. The process of improvement won't work unless the instructional elements to be strengthened are specifically singled out.

When written for improvement, a portfolio may shift some priority away from the category of "material from others" and concentrate on reflective analysis, action planning, and assessment of products of student learning. Yet, "material from others" is still important, especially if the faculty member can incorporate the benefits of detailed, written collegial reviews of teaching into comprehensive and specific strategies for improvement.

The preparation of a portfolio provides the stimulus and structure for self-reflection about areas of teaching which need improvement. The process of selecting and organizing material for a portfolio often results in thinking about teaching in new ways. More specifically, the process encourages the professor to: 1) reconsider teaching activities; 2) rethink teaching strategies and objectives; 3) reorganize priorities; 4) plan for the future. Oftentimes, it triggers formative discoveries that lead to philosophical shifts, curricular changes, revision of materials, methodological innovations, and reconsidered goals (Seldin, Annis, & Zubizarreta, 1995).

Consider these comments:

A mathematics professor in Indiana: "As a new faculty member, I profited greatly from preparing a portfolio. It sharpened my teaching philosophy, my methods, my goals."

A history professor in Massachusetts: "If this concept had been around twenty years ago, all of the students I've taught would have benefited because I would have been a better teacher."

A political science professor in Nebraska: "Assembling a portfolio was a real learning experience for me. Though I've taught for ten years, this was the first time I really stopped to step back to reflect on my teaching and how to improve it."

One thing is clear: Improvement in teaching is more likely to occur if the faculty member discusses the portfolio items with a sympathetic and knowledgeable colleague or a teaching improvement specialist. Professors, like everyone else, need assurance that their shortcomings are neither unusual nor insurmountable; they can also use wise counsel in overcoming them.

USING THE PORTFOLIO FOR PERSONNEL DECISIONS

In the past, factual information about teaching has been skimpy at best. Typical professors have had little solid evidence about what they do in the classroom and how they do it. The result: Teaching has been evaluated almost exclusively on the basis of student ratings.

The use of portfolios is the best way that I know to get at the complexity and individuality of teaching. Because the content and organization of portfolios differ from one professor to another, experience suggests that the problem can be best laid to rest by requiring portfolios used for tenure and promotion decisions, or for teaching excellence awards, to include certain mandated items along with the elective ones. Such mandated items might include, for example, a reflective statement on the professor's teaching, summaries of student ratings on global questions, representative course syllabi, and the chair's assessment of the faculty member's teaching contribution to the department. All additional items included in the portfolio would be selected by individual professors. Among the institutions adopting this approach are Washington State University, Marquette University (Wisconsin), the University of Colorado at Boulder, and the Medical College of Georgia.

Since teaching is now being taken more seriously, Seldin (1993, p. 8) says that "... professors seeking recognition as superior teachers stand to benefit by providing tenure and promotion committees with their teaching portfolios. It provides evaluators with hard-to-ignore information on what they do in the classroom and why they do it. And by so doing, it avoids looking at teaching performance as a derivative of student ratings."

Does the teaching portfolio approach really make any difference? Consider these typical comments from professors whose portfolios were used for purposes of personnel decisions:

A marketing professor in New York: "My promotion to associate professor was largely due to my portfolio. It gave the evaluation committee in-depth information set in the context of my teaching responsibilities, objectives, strategies, and methodologies."

A biology professor in California: "I was just named teacher of the year! My portfolio took 15 hours to put together. But there is no other way that the selection committee would have known the details of what I do and why I do it in my classroom."

A philosophy professor in Florida: "Portfolios provide a very effective way for our T & P committee to get beyond the ubiquitous student ratings in assessing teaching effectiveness."

USING PORTFOLIOS FOR OTHER PURPOSES

Although most portfolios are prepared for teaching improvement or personnel decisions, some are prepared for different purposes. Among others, they include the following:

- Portfolios are used to help determine winners of awards for outstanding teaching or for merit pay consideration.

- Excerpts from portfolios are used in successful grant applications.

- Colleges and universities are requesting portfolios from finalists for teaching positions.

- Portfolios are being taken on the road by professors seeking a different teaching position.

- Graduate students are preparing portfolios to bolster their credentials as they enter the job market.

- Professors nearing retirement are preparing portfolios in order to leave a written legacy in their department so that other faculty who will be taking over their courses will have the benefit of their experience.

ANSWERS TO COMMON QUESTIONS ABOUT THE TEACHING PORTFOLIO

Since 1989, I have discussed the teaching portfolio concept at nearly 200 colleges and universities of differing sizes and missions. I've talked with countless faculty groups and administrators about the portfolio and its place in the improvement and evaluation of teaching. And I've had the distinct pleasure of serving as mentor to more than three hundred professors across disciplines as they have prepared their portfolios.

In the course of this activity, certain questions were raised by faculty members and administrators with much greater frequency than others. Those questions and my answers to them follow.

HOW TIME CONSUMING IS THE PREPARATION OF A PORTFOLIO?

Although it may appear that putting together a portfolio might take more time than teaching itself, in practice this is not the case. Most professors can complete their portfolio in twelve to fifteen hours spread over several days. They already have much of the material on hand, such as student ratings, letters of invitation or thanks, departmental annual reports. These items represent the basics of the portfolio. Keeping up-to-date files of supporting documents (course syllabi, copies of student work) makes preparation of the portfolio much easier. As faculty we are trained to document our research and publication activities. But we don't document our teaching. Doesn't it make sense to do so with the same care and completeness we exercise to document research and scholarship outside the classroom?

IS THE PORTFOLIO RESTRICTED
TO TRADITIONAL CLASSROOM TEACHING?

The answer is no. I interpret the word "teaching" to include all professional activity that provides direct support for student learning. In addition to traditional classroom teaching, that would include instruction in laboratories or in the field, advising students, serving as reader or mentor on theses.

CAN AN IMPRESSIVE PORTFOLIO
GLOSS OVER TERRIBLE TEACHING?

No, because the preparer could not document effective teaching performance. The evidence is just not there. Fancy covers, computer graphics, and attractive printer fonts cannot disguise weak performance for a professor any more than it can for a student. On the other hand, for an excellent teacher, the portfolio offers an unmatched opportunity to document classroom practices that have previously gone unrecognized and unrewarded.

WHAT KIND OF BACKGROUND DO MENTORS NEED?

They must have wide knowledge of current instruments and procedures used to document teaching performance. Faculty development specialists are particularly well-qualified for the role because they are trained in multiple approaches and techniques to demonstrate teaching effectiveness; they can also provide valuable suggestions and resources as well as important support during portfolio preparation.

IS THERE A WAY TO SELF-MENTOR
IF THERE ARE NO TRAINED MENTORS AVAILABLE?

Although I strongly recommend that portfolios be developed collaboratively, I am keenly aware that sometimes there are no willing and able mentors available to faculty members. In that case, even though the important collaborative aspect of portfolio development will be lost, it is still possible to prepare a portfolio. The following self-assessment questions identified by Eison (1996) and Seldin (1996) may help:

- Does the portfolio clearly identify what you teach, how you teach it, why you teach it as you do?

- Is a descriptive table of contents included?

- Is every claim made in the narrative supported by hard evidence in the appendices?

- Does the portfolio present reflective observations?

- Is any departmental/institutional factor that influenced your teaching effectiveness reported?

- Are creative or innovative teaching approaches described?

- Is the portfolio sufficiently selective?

- Does it include a balance of items from oneself, from others, and from student learning?

- Have efforts at growth and improvement been cited?

- Should any nonprint items such as photos, reviews, or videos of student work or your own work be included?

HOW CAN PREPARATION OF A PORTFOLIO HELP NEW TEACHERS?

It can help them learn the culture of the institution, its mission and standards, and its criteria for evaluating teaching performance. At the same time, preparation of a portfolio encourages formative development as well as innovation and experimentation in teaching.

DON'T ALL PORTFOLIOS LOOK ALIKE?

Not at all. In truth, the portfolio is a highly personalized product. Both the content and the organization differ widely from one professor's draft to another. Varying importance is assigned by different professors to different items. (See the sample portfolios in Chapter 11.) Different disciplines and courses cater to different types of documentation. For example, an introductory freshman composition class is far removed from a senior seminar in organizational behavior. And a graduate research design course is worlds apart from an undergraduate course in private voice instruction. Such differences in portfolio content and organization should be encouraged so long as they are allowed by the department and institution.

EVEN THOUGH PORTFOLIOS DIFFER CONSIDERABLY FROM EACH OTHER, ARE THERE CERTAIN ITEMS WHICH SEEM TO APPEAR CONSISTENTLY?

A review of more than three hundred portfolios suggests that the following items are most often selected for inclusion: 1) student evaluation data; 2) statement of current teaching responsibilities; 3) syllabi for all courses taught; 4) reflective statement by the faculty member discussing his or her teaching objectives, strategies, and methodologies; 5) participation in seminars and workshops intended to improve teaching.

ARE STUDENT RATINGS ACTUALLY INSERTED INTO THE PORTFOLIO?

The actual material normally is placed in the appendices but some highlights of the ratings typically appear in the body of the portfolio. Here is one example of what such highlights would look like:

My student ratings are consistently higher than the department average. For the Fall 1996 semester, the thirty students in my Introduction to Psychology class (Psych. 101) rated my teaching as follows:

Criteria	My Rating	Dept. Average
Explains Clearly	4.60	4.14
Organization of Course	4.32	3.98
Respect for Students	4.55	4.23
Best Course in Department	4.26	4.02
Best Instructor in Department	4.30	4.12

[Scale: one is low and five is high.]

If the portfolio is being prepared for purposes of tenure or promotion, it is especially important to include highlights in the body of the portfolio. Why? Because promotion and tenure committee members—who are often pressed for time and are frequently overworked—may skim the appendices. Highlights cannot be easily overlooked.

HOW CAN FACULTY MEMBERS DEMONSTRATE CONTINUOUS EFFORTS TO IMPROVE THEIR INSTRUCTION?

They can document and explain recent course innovations and the reasons for those innovations. They can also describe the positive impact of professional development activities (workshops, conferences) on their teaching. The following list suggests the kinds of evidence that might be presented:

- Applying for and receiving a grant related to teaching and describing resulting changes in instruction

- Describing changes in assignments and the reasons for those changes

- Describing innovative instructional practices and the reasons for introducing those practices
- Attending or participating in professional conferences focused on teaching the professor's discipline and detailing what was learned, how it was applied in the classroom, and how it impacted on teaching and learning
- Providing two syllabi for the same course from different years and suggesting reasons for the changes over time
- Detailing changes in teaching that resulted from careful analysis of student evaluations

SHOULD ALL EVIDENCE IN THE PORTFOLIO BE EXPLAINED?

Unexplained evidence is difficult for readers to understand and interpret. For example, including two course syllabi from different years provides evidence of instructional change over time. But the significance of the change and why it took place are not apparent. That is why the addition of a commentary explaining why specific changes were made as well as the impact of those changes on student learning provides more convincing evidence about the professor's efforts to improve instruction.

HOW IMPORTANT IS A SECTION ON STUDENT LEARNING IN A TEACHING PORTFOLIO?

The products of student learning are an integral part of a valid, complete portfolio. Without it, the reliability of the portfolio, its capacity to address the rigorous demands of assessment, and its effectiveness as a means for improvement are seriously impaired. Good teaching must be connected to good student learning. How can the impact of teaching on students' progress be demonstrated? It can be seen in: a) student projects; b) fieldwork reports; c) laboratory reports; d) successful practicums; e) essays in draft form with instructor comments; f) pre- and post-testing; g) coached student presentations at conferences and student publications; h) documentation of students' success in higher level courses or post-graduate careers; i) results of juried exhibitions of students' work; and j) theater or music performance reviews of students' performance (Seldin, Annis, & Zubizarreta, 1995).

The process of preparing a portfolio raises a professor's awareness of the importance of student learning and the ways to document it. Such reflection and strategy can improve learning as a consequence of the portfolio's process of discovery, documentation, and planning.

CAN GRADUATE TEACHING ASSISTANTS
DEVELOP WORTHWHILE PORTFOLIOS?

The answer is yes. Even though they lack extensive teaching experience from which to draw materials and evaluations, graduate teaching assistants can write detailed portfolios that include substantive information on their teaching goals and objectives for achieving those goals. At Brown University, Harvard University, and Southern Illinois University, the portfolio programs are, in fact, designed to assist graduate students to document what they taught, why they taught it that way, and how well they taught it to give them a leg up when entering the job market. (See the portfolio by Sullivan, this volume.)

WHAT GUIDELINES WOULD YOU SUGGEST
FOR GETTING STARTED WITH PORTFOLIOS?

If the portfolio is ultimately to be embraced, a climate of acceptance must first be created. The following guidelines should be helpful in doing so: 1) start small; 2) involve the institution's most respected professors from the start; 3) include faculty who are new to teaching and others who are new to the institution; 4) field-test the portfolio process at the institution; 5) rely on faculty volunteers but don't force anyone to participate; 6) obtain top-level academic administrative support for the portfolio concept and an institutional commitment to provide the necessary resources to launch the program successfully; 7) allow sufficient time—a year or even two—for acceptance and implementation; 8) keep everyone fully informed every step of the way about what is going on.

SOME FINAL THOUGHTS

Equipped with hindsight and the benefit of experience, we've learned a good deal about teaching portfolios. Among other things:

We know that portfolios are being used—and being used successfully—in a variety of different ways. They are being used to improve teaching; to determine salary increases, merit pay, teaching awards, grants, fellowships, and released time; to make tenure and promotion decisions. They are also being used by professors and graduate teaching assistants to get teaching positions and by institutions to screen applicants for teaching jobs.

We know that preparing and maintaining a portfolio do not consume an excessive amount of time. Experience has taught that most professors can prepare their portfolios in about 15 hours spread over several days. And a large part of that time is spent in thinking, planning, and gathering the documentation for the appendices. Updating the material takes about a day and demands no more than keeping files on everything relating to one's teaching in the same way that files are kept on everything relating to a professor's research and scholarship outside of the classroom.

We know that an impressive portfolio cannot gloss over weak teaching. Why? Because the evidence needed for a portfolio is just not there. An elegant cover and fancy typeface cannot disguise weak performance in the classroom for a professor any more than it can for a student. On the other hand, for an excellent teacher, the portfolio offers an unmatched opportunity to get beyond the ubiquitous student ratings to document classroom practices that have previously gone unrecognized and unrewarded.

We know that preparing a portfolio helps to improve teaching. It often triggers formative discoveries that lead to philosophical shifts, curricular changes, revision of materials, innovations in methodology, and reconsidered teaching goals. The very process of creating the collection of documents and materials which comprises the portfolio stimulates professors to reflect on what has worked in a particular class, what has not, and what might be done to improve the quality of their instruction. (See the chapters by Mura and by Weber, this volume, for further detail.)

We know that the portfolio is best prepared in consultation with a mentor. Since most faculty members come to the portfolio concept with no previous experience with the concept, the resources of a mentor should be made available to them. The mentor must have wide knowledge of current instruments and procedures to document teaching effectiveness. In this way, the mentor can assist the faculty member by providing suggestions and resources, and by maintaining important support during the preparation of the portfolio.

We know that open communication regarding the use of portfolios is vital to gaining faculty acceptance. The concept must be presented candidly, clearly, and completely to all faculty members, department chairs, and other relevant academic administrators before its implementation. The utility of the teaching portfolio as an additional, not replacement, source of information on teaching must be crystal clear.

We know that the subjectivity of the portfolio does not interfere with its use for personnel decisions. Those who raise the issue of subjectivity have probably not personally engaged in the collaborative effort between a faculty member and a mentor. It is the mentor who helps steer the direction of the evidence-based documentation and insists that all information in the narrative be substantiated in the appendix. If, for example, a faculty member claims in a portfolio that student evaluations rate his or her high scholarly expectations as outstanding, then rating forms in an appendix must contain such evidence. The mentor's task is not one of assisting the professor to fabricate (or present culled) information. On the contrary, the mentor's task is to flush out objective data, provide balance and control, and corroborate evidence (Seldin, Annis, & Zubizarreta, 1995).

We know that the benefits derived from preparing a portfolio are well worth the time and energy required. That is the conclusion from the experience of tens of thousands of faculty in many colleges and universities in preparing portfolios. The fact is, it usually takes no more than a few days to put together. And, on the plus side, the benefits are considerable.

Many faculty members find that the very process of collecting and sorting documents and materials that reflect their teaching performance serves as a springboard for self-improvement.

But the portfolio concept does more than that. It provides an opportunity for professors to describe their teaching strengths and accomplishments for the record and offers hard-to-ignore evidence upon which to make judgments about teaching effectiveness. And, importantly, many colleges and universities find that portfolios are a useful means to underscore teaching as an institutional priority.

BIBLIOGRAPHY

Eison, J. (1996). *Creating a teaching portfolio: The SCRIPT model.* Tampa, FL: University of South Florida, Center for Teaching Enhancement.

Millis, B. Private discussion, (1995).

O'Neil, M. C., & Wright, W. A. (1993). *Recording teaching accomplishment: A Dalhousie guide to the teaching dossier,* 4th ed. Halifax, NS: Office of Instructional Development and Technology, Dalhousie University.

Rehnke, M. A. (1994) Teaching and learning. *The Independent.* Washington, DC: Council of Independent Colleges. October 1994. p. 7.

Rodriguez-Farrar, H. B. (1995). *Teaching portfolio handbook.* Providence, RI: Center for the Advancement of College Teaching, Brown University.

Seldin, P. (1991). *The teaching portfolio: A practical guide to improved performance and promotion/tenure decisions.* Bolton, MA: Anker.

Seldin, P., & Associates. (1993). *Successful use of teaching portfolios.* Bolton, MA: Anker.

Seldin, P., Annis, L., & Zubizarreta, J. (1995). Answers to common questions about the teaching portfolio. *Journal on Excellence in College Teaching 6* (1).

Seldin, P. (June 1996). The teaching portfolio. Paper presented for the American Council on Education, Department Chairs Seminar, Washington, DC.

Shore, M. B., & others. (1986). *The teaching dossier,* revised edition. Montreal: Canadian Association of University Teachers.

Zubizarreta, J. (1994). Teaching portfolios and the beginning teacher. *Phi Delta Kappan,* December 1994: 323–326.

Zubizarreta, J. Private discussion, (1996).

PREPARING THE PORTFOLIO:
A PERSONAL VIEW

Joseph A. Weber

Developing a teaching portfolio and classroom teaching share a similar process. Both lead to student excellence.

As I began to think about my own classroom teaching and developing a teaching portfolio, it became apparent that I was going to have to step back and reflect on my personal views of teaching. Many questions came to mind. How does a teacher encourage student excellence? How are students motivated to learn? Have I encouraged students to excel?

I quickly realized that teaching is an adventure. Many people claim to teach, but only a true explorer helps students uncover and discover new insights into the self and one's surroundings. I began to view the process of teaching as a safari. This adventure is continuous and never ending, always revealing new knowledge, cutting down old myths, and building strong bridges over rocky terrain. The process of developing my teaching portfolio became an adventure for me as I realized I was the one guiding students on an adventure which would last a lifetime.

Planning a safari can be very difficult. The safari guide (teacher) must develop a survival package with all the necessary equipment to help travelers (students) through the jungle of discovery. Of course, they are not all going to the same place. As travelers decide on their destination, the guide assists in identifying an appropriate strategy to help students reach their goals. Some guides are very wise but overload the traveler with too much equipment and not enough supplies. Other guides are quick to recognize dangerous areas inhabited by wild beasts but are inexperienced and often get lost themselves or eaten in unexplored territories. Luckily, most safari guides are experienced explorers and have developed a well-organized adventure package for travelers.

Developing a teaching portfolio was a way I could look critically at my own teaching and determine if I was meeting my goal of fostering student excellence. When assembling my portfolio I realized three major areas of discussion were necessary. These areas include 1) reflecting on my teaching, 2) gathering documentation of personal and student excellence, and 3) planning future directions in my own career.

Reflecting on my teaching philosophy was very difficult. I had never sat down to evaluate, much less critique, my performance. At first, I was apprehensive and scared at what I might find. Why did I love teaching? Why had I developed a certain teaching style? What would I find or uncover about my teaching? These were hard questions I needed to answer for myself. I realized fear of the hidden and the unknown could ultimately prevent me from moving forward.

As my starting point, I spent several hours reviewing in my mind aspects of classroom strategies, student challenges, teaching methods, and student excellence. Thoughts raced through my mind as I began to conceptualize my teaching philosophy. Taking out a note pad, I began jotting down words, ideas, and phrases which described my teaching. At first, the words started coming slowly but within a few minutes I could hardly stop generating ideas. I wrote down everything and anything related to my lecturing, assignments, student involvement, and course objectives. The list was long, but a picture quickly emerged that identified my teaching philosophy.

I realized my philosophy was one which incorporates aspects to stimulate thinking, demand excellence in myself and my students, and ultimately prepare students for a future world we can hardly imagine today. Much of the information we learn today is outdated in fewer than three to five years. For example, many of us who learned PC computer skills a few years ago are woefully behind third and fourth graders who have become computer technowizards who are very comfortable surfing in cyberspace and searching the Internet by clicking a mouse and making links on the World Wide Web.

Operationalizing my teaching philosophy was challenging and rewarding. I viewed my teaching as a process of educating and encouraging future scholars. In order to help prepare future professionals in a rapidly changing world, I realized my teaching philosophy was one of interdisciplinary integration. This philosophy, which I discuss in my portfolio, incorporates this concept into the classroom and encourages students to 1) learn from the past, 2) understand the present, and 3) reach out into the future.

After clarifying my teaching philosophy, the second major challenge was to document representations of teaching excellence. It was one of the most time-consuming and rigorous exercises I have ever undertaken. It was also frustrating because I knew the types of items I wanted to include but had not kept files or had forgotten where they were. I started by selecting two areas I wanted to incorporate into the body of my portfolio. These included 1) evidence of instructional effectiveness, and 2) measures of student achievement.

Evidence of instructional effectiveness refers to my scholarship in the classroom while measures of student achievement report student successes. To document instructional effectiveness, I summarized course evaluations. Feedback from students is one method of understanding an instructor's classroom scholarship. Reporting evaluation scores for the last three years gives a picture of student reactions to a course. In an appendix, I included selected written comments by students on the evaluation forms. Students need to be heard and their comments critically evaluated. Luckily, I had kept past student course evaluation forms for the last ten years. It was an easy task to pull the file and summarize the evaluation data.

Sometimes you will receive a note, card, or letter from students who comment on their college career and how valuable your course was in helping them to decide on an occupation. Student comments are a valuable way to document instructional success. Over the years I have received numerous cards from former students; these I included in an appendix.

Faculty are often rewarded by colleagues or students for their efforts in the classroom. In a subsection on teaching honors and awards I included several awards I had received at the departmental and college level. The award I am most proud of is the 1995 Graduate Student Mentor Award. This is a student-generated award for teaching excellence and student support.

Measures of student achievement are an important way to benchmark instructional effectiveness. As an instructor, you can co-present classroom projects at professional meetings and co-author journal articles with students in your class. I strongly believe in extending the classroom beyond traditional structural boundaries. The student learns that scholarship is a continuing process. More importantly, I continue to learn from my students. They extend and stretch my thoughts and give me new insights into gerontological issues. In this section I included student papers, abstracts, presentations, and articles generated from class projects. Also included is a listing of student career placement and success.

The third major section of my portfolio was a discussion of professional development of teaching activities. Participating in teaching seminars, workshops, and professional meetings are ways to continue teaching excellence. I have made it a professional and personal goal to participate in teaching improvement activities. It is extremely important to evaluate present teaching goals in relationship to future directions. Are your teaching goals and objectives going to stay the same next year? How can you make your teaching scholarship keep pace with changing social events, changing student interests, and changing technological advances?

The answer lies in critical evaluation of self and your teaching scholarship. The portfolio process was an excellent vehicle for me to step back and reflect on my teaching philosophy, analyze my teaching methods, and consider new and innovative objectives and goals for the future.

Let us now return to the safari we started. We are coming to the end of our journey. The guide has fulfilled the objectives of taking travelers on an exciting adventure, exploring uncharted territories. Before another adventure begins, the guide reviews the past trip, makes necessary changes, and starts making plans for another adventure for new travelers. Travelers give feedback to the guide as they put together scrapbooks, pictures, and notes from the finished adventure. Many travelers are ready for another adventure with the same or a different guide.

The safari never ends as there are always unexplored and new territories to research. The guide is the key to any safari. You are the key to the success of your teaching scholarship. The portfolio process gave me the tools necessary to evaluate my teaching. The adventure is just beginning.

(See the portfolio by Joseph A. Weber in Chapter 11.)

8

Developing an Institutional Portfolio Program: A Step-by-Step Report

Karen E. Mura

The teaching portfolio momentum at Susquehanna University (S.U.) has gone hand in hand with the development of what we call "Teaching Cells." Since many of the participants in the first Teaching Portfolio Workshop held on our campus in January 1996 were also Teaching Cell members, it is hard to talk separately about either group.

Shortly after four S.U. faculty attended the Council of Independent Colleges–run workshop on teaching portfolios in June 1994, the first Teaching Cell was formed. In August 1994, five faculty from different disciplines (Accounting, Biology, English, History, Human Resource Management) agreed to meet weekly to talk about teaching. Initially, our first year of meetings was devoted to sharing our current successes and failures, as we tried new and innovative approaches and projects in our classes. Over time we were able to build a deep sense of trust while we discussed a wide range of topics, including class committees, evaluating group work, mid-semester student evaluations, and grading essay exams, to name a few.

Gradually we began to do peer visitation of each other's classes: one visit to several different colleagues by the end of the first year, increasing to a goal in the second year of three visits to the same class by the same professor. We became more focused about the purpose for these visitations, discussing beforehand our primary objectives for the class and using a Classroom

Observation Report provided by Peter Seldin. This systematic feedback over a period of time affirmed something that many of us discovered in the process of compiling our portfolios: Many of our classroom methods and interactions were effective and worked well. It was not until we tried to articulate our classroom strategies and methods and demonstrate student learning concretely (for the portfolios) or received consistent, specific feedback from peers (from the Observation Reports) that we were able to acknowledge the real strengths in our teaching. Recognizing the presence of our teaching strengths along with identifying our goals for improving teaching effectiveness has proven to be one of the greatest rewards of the teaching portfolio process.

Early in the fall of 1994, two of us from the original CIC workshop began to strategically plan a teaching portfolio workshop on our campus. The first step in this process was to meet with the Vice President for Academic Affairs to garner support from the administration. She was enthusiastic about the workshop idea and impressed by the strong interest among a core of faculty in enhancing and improving teaching on campus. Not only did she pledge continued support, but she assured us that our effort would remain faculty driven. We stated clearly our belief that this teaching portfolio initiative should come from the faculty and be strictly voluntary.

As with any new initiative, there is always the question of funding. The Vice President for Academic Affairs offered to provide funds for several Friday sessions where faculty could gather to talk about teaching innovations and the teaching portfolio project. In addition, she steered us toward the Aid Association for Lutherans Higher Education Grant as the most likely source for outside funding to pay for the workshop and related expenses. In the spring of 1995, we drafted a grant proposal entitled "Improving Teaching Through Self-Assessment Portfolios," which was awarded to the university in June 1995.

In July 1995, Susquehanna University hired a new Vice President for Academic Affairs. We met several times with him during his first months on the job, describing the growing interest among faculty for more opportunities to talk about teaching on campus as well as outlining our plans for the upcoming teaching portfolio workshop. The fact that the teaching portfolio momentum on campus did not falter or slow down with a change in administrators attests to the level of faculty support and commitment to this project.

In anticipation of the January 1996 Teaching Portfolio Workshop, in August 1995 the first teaching cell planned a "Teaching Fair" focusing on teaching initiatives and innovations at S.U. for the entire faculty. During this "teaching fair" several faculty members discussed in more detail both the teaching cells and the teaching portfolio process as well as topics such as service learning, technology in the classroom, and collaborative learning. As another teaching cell got underway (one in fall 1995 and another in spring 1996), we began talking more seriously with colleagues about teaching portfolios and held several informal sessions to describe the portfolio process and answer questions. The eventual outcome of these efforts and interest was that fifteen out of 100 full-time faculty members devoted one week of their semester break to designing their portfolios.

During conversations early in the workshop week, it became clear that there were widely varying reasons for completing this portfolio project. One participant chose to focus on how to avoid burnout as a teacher. Another pair of participants selected a specific team-taught course as the focus of their portfolio. This aided them in setting common goals, objectives, and strategies for their course and led to a presentation at a national conference on "Medieval Studies as an Interdisciplinary Program for Undergraduates" later that semester. Some participants decided to focus on core courses that they teach every year, while others preferred to concentrate on upper division courses within their major. Then there were those who hoped to use portfolio material as part of their third-year review or tenure file. One faculty member was strongly urged to apply for promotion based on the evidence of excellent teaching provided in her portfolio.

Two months after the workshop, the fifteen participants met again as a group to share ways in which the portfolio process had made an impact on their current classes. Faculty made comments such as, "more aware of classroom atmosphere," "I very much relied on a mid-course assessment that I gave to my class," "I particularly examined the information I used for assessment," and "I've thought more about the overall structure and goals of my courses." Overall, there was general consensus that our assessment of student learning was matching more closely our expectations set out at the beginning of the semester. Our enthusiastic response to this discussion of teaching portfolio outcomes led many of us to ask "Where can we go from here?"

Once again, we met with the Vice President for Academic Affairs to describe current faculty reactions to the portfolio process and to outline some of our future goals. We were assured of continued administrative support for teaching portfolio development on campus and promised that participation in the project would remain voluntary. We discussed at length the desire of some faculty to use teaching portfolio material for promotion and tenure reviews. The Vice President proposed that we examine together the existing faculty handbook guidelines to determine if teaching portfolios could be included or if the guidelines might have to be amended.

In May 1996, we made a presentation to the faculty at the last faculty meeting of the year describing how the teaching portfolio process has made an impact on our current classes. One assistant professor in her second year of teaching and one associate professor with a long record of outstanding university teaching presented their differing perspectives on this reflective process. We proposed to the faculty a second (faculty-led) teaching portfolio workshop in May 1997, when individual faculty members would mentor a partner through the process of developing a portfolio. In addition, we designed a number of short-term goals:

- Present the teaching portfolio concept and process at new faculty orientation in August 1996.

- Meet with department heads in fall 1996 to discuss how departments can make use of and facilitate portfolios among their faculty. (One department head who participated in the workshop even suggested that a department could compile its own teaching portfolio for the core courses that are shared among department members. This would require a collaborative departmental effort of reflecting on teaching goals, objectives, and strategies for core classes and would be a great resource for newly hired teachers.)

- Sponsor a series of Friday afternoon faculty sessions called "portfolio posters." We would highlight several different faculty portfolios at each session and have faculty prepare a type of poster for display and discussion.

- Use portfolios to track newly designed courses over time to see how they develop and evolve.

- Conduct research on the relationship between teaching portfolio preparation and the life stages of teaching.

Reflecting on the past two years of teaching initiatives at Susquehanna University, it is clear that the success of the teaching portfolio on campus results in part from an existing group of faculty who were ready and eager to talk about ways to improve teaching and student learning. The teaching portfolio and teaching cells were welcomed as vehicles to channel this interest and energy. In addition, we have been able to maintain an important balance between administrative support and faculty ownership of this project, both of which are essential to sustain our momentum. I also suspect that this project dovetailed nicely with a broader university vision to encourage growth and learning among S.U. faculty and students.

(I wish to thank Peggy Holdren for suggestions to improve this report.)

IMPROVING TEACHING THROUGH PORTFOLIO REVISIONS

John Zubizarreta

Developing a teaching portfolio is hard but gratifying work. From a purely practical standpoint, the benefits of engaging in portfolio writing with a mentor include

- Building a sound method of documentation of teaching performance

- Directing more scrupulous attention to diverse types of supportive information

- Placing stronger emphasis on how teaching affects the quality and amount of student learning

- Realizing the potential for renewal and shared professional respect in collaboration.

Such concrete advantages are corollaries to the central value of how portfolios improve teaching by promoting close, careful, recorded, and timely reflection about teaching and learning. Rooted in the notion of reflective practice as articulated by Schön (1983), portfolios demonstrate that good teaching is constantly in flux, challenging us to reexamine what and how we teach but more importantly why. Portfolios provide a means to question the assumptions, methods, materials, and goals of our teaching in order to test continually the extent of their influence on student learning.

Model professors remain successful teachers probably because in large part they recognize the process nature of their craft. Seeking regularly to strengthen their impact on learning by engaging in meticulous, intentional research about their labor in the classroom, such professors demonstrate what Boyer (1990) calls the scholarship of teaching; they take seriously the call to improve practice through reflection and action.

The teaching portfolio offers a process document that promotes continual improvement of the teaching enterprise if it is revised conscientiously and regularly. The portfolio provides a vehicle for recorded evidence of performance and, more importantly, for analysis and detailed goal setting, indispensable steps in a revisionary process of teaching enhancement. Revisions of a portfolio should go beyond routine replacement of evidential materials in a file folder, a simple act that reduces the portfolio to not much more than an elaborate, time-consuming filing system. Instead, revisions should stress current, concise, written review of the relationship of teaching performance to student learning, measured and recorded over time.

Equally important, faculty must realize that a genuine focus on improvement demands as much attention to evidence as preparation for various personnel decisions if the steps taken to strengthen practice are to have any significant, lasting effect on teacher behavior or student learning. The imperative of taking seriously the scholarship of teaching and the benefits of ongoing classroom research is crucial to revising portfolios. As Wolf says in an early study of schoolteachers' portfolios, "Taken together . . . classroom artifacts, framed by the teacher's explanations and reflections, could provide an authentic and multitextured view of the actual teaching that took place, as well as some insight into the thinking behind the teaching" (1991, p. 132). Improvement occurs from tying reflection—what we think or say happens in our classes and what we want to happen—to evidence of what really happens. In the act of writing critically about current, actual teaching efforts and in constructing a rhetorical framework that compels the teacher to gather supporting materials, analyze information, draw substantial conclusions, and posit action plans for better practice, the teacher develops a habit of intentional improvement based on periodic, timely revisions of a portfolio.

TWO BASIC PREREQUISITES FOR SUCCESS

Mentor support

One of the keys to the conciseness and efficacy of a successful process of portfolio revision is the involvement of a knowledgeable, supportive mentor who serves as formative coach and peer reviewer in prompting useful and creative strategies for revision without the high stakes of summative evaluation. Collaboration offers significant opportunities for strengthening the quality of teaching and learning by engaging professors in open discourse on pedagogical substance, making teaching a more public and peer-reviewed activity. When collaboration involves a colleague from another discipline or from outside the instructor's institution, the focus of portfolio development is more readily kept on teaching enhancement through meticulous, objective inspection of evidence.

Institutional support

Institutional support is also a crucial dimension of the process of revision, and faculty are more willing to maintain momentum and continue to use the portfolio as a living document and a tool for improvement when they know that such teaching development activities are valued and rewarded. Faculty need the encouragement and support of a formal institutional commitment to instructional development and must trust administrators' recognition of the scholarship of teaching as exemplified by rigorous revisions of portfolios. Four or five days devoted to concentrated writing and collaboration with a mentor provide the optimum occasion for development of an initial portfolio draft, and institutions should provide the resources needed to allow faculty to continue the process successfully and revise portfolios not only for periodic personnel decisions but for continual improvement.

HOW PORTFOLIO REVISIONS IMPROVE TEACHING: AN INDIVIDUAL CASE

The initial act of writing a portfolio has its own intrinsic merits in encouraging faculty to discover potential areas for development which escape notice in the daily paces of the academic life. Writing also provides an indelible record of current performance, a baseline for renewal, a challenge to revise practice and its impact on student learning. My own experience has validated that writing flushes out the unseen and crystallizes the seen, making known in clear terms where the teacher has been most successful and where efforts need redoubling. Using my portfolio revisions as a model, I offer two examples of how written portfolio revisions improve teaching. Significantly, both illustrations, written in this chapter as personal reflections, demonstrate the importance of collaboration in shaping revisions. For an in-depth view of a mentor's detailed analysis of revisions to one of my portfolio drafts, see the Appendix in this volume.

Revising form and content

When I first produced a draft of my portfolio after working out preliminary issues on a carefully designed "Getting Started" questionnaire, I was pleased that my mentor approved of my emphasis on diverse sources of information about my teaching which went beyond the usual student ratings and year-end self reports of most evaluation-of-teaching systems. Yet, my draft comingled responsibilities, philosophy, strategies, and methods, a naive decision I made deliberately because, as I argued then, I believe that what and how I teach are inseparably tied to why I teach as I do and to my values in teaching. My mentor pressed that I should extract my teaching values from the lengthy section and examine them more carefully as a distinct statement of philosophy.

After a careful revision, taking into account the mentor's suggestions on several key items, I began to notice that despite my disciplinary emphasis as an English professor on assigning essays, conferencing with students on successive drafts, and spending countless hours providing feedback on student writing, I had no real evidence in the form of student products that my efforts actually improved student learning. I had never systematically and intentionally paid attention to assessing the outcomes of my teaching. My initial portfolio draft said much about my teaching ventures, but I had not addressed student learning.

At a later meeting, the mentor capitalized on my discovery and returned to the theme of writing a distinct philosophy. As I revisited my portfolio, I saw that my values were all in teaching as performance. No word about learning. No word about assessment. No deliberate inclusion of student products. The revelation was stunning but invigorating. As a consequence of using the efficacious power of writing as a recorded process of discovery and criticism in updating my portfolio, I devised an action plan to study selected student works as a means of researching the effects of my methods, materials, and grading on strengthening course outcomes. My portfolio soon looked substantially different, separating philosophy as a distinct core that connected theoretically and practically to all the other components of the portfolio. The appendix at the end of this book includes a detailed, keyed summary of revisions completed on an early draft of my portfolio.

Revision and practice:
Course portfolios as classroom research

Since the first example, my portfolio has taken many turns. In adapting general teaching portfolio strategies to composing individual course portfolios, I have focused on the particular philosophy, methods, materials, evaluations, outcomes, and goals of one course to help me refine the teaching and learning in a single subject. In my efforts, I have opted for devising a compact and structured instrument (Zubizarreta, 1995), relying on Seldin's (1991, 1993) model of portfolio development.

Using the portfolio as a vehicle for recorded evidence of teaching performance and extent of student learning, I recently discovered over time that my objective examinations in an upper-level literary critical theory course were not fairly gauging the students' knowledge. In informal journal entries, most students were thoughtful, engaged, and reasonably secure in understanding the difficult course content, but the same students would perform poorly on examinations.

After compiling sample test questions, selected assignment sheets, and summaries of grades, I sent copies of two successive drafts of my reflective analysis of the dilemma along with intentionally collected student products to a colleague who taught a similar course at another institution. Enlisting the insights of a collaborator, I learned to combine take-home exams with in-class exams to provide students with an informal but still graded venue for "studying" for objective tests. The take-home exams helped bridge the students' enthusiasm for reflective writing with the imperative of factual content knowledge. Varied types of questions provided students with more opportunities to recall, synthesize, and/or apply their knowledge creatively. The portfolio enabled me to understand how different kinds of written assignments and tests can help tap the various learning styles and potentials of diverse students. Student performance, according to the most recent revision of my course portfolio and the selected products in the appendix, improved markedly.

Portfolio revisions, therefore, involve faculty in a method of earnest research about their individual teaching goals, objectives, and outcomes. Such a mechanism for improvement demonstrates a broad, genuine scholarship of teaching which recognizes that exemplary teaching perhaps only begins with inspiration and talent; the rest is hard work and systematic reevaluation. The process also reveals that conscientious and self-aware teaching is not separate from the intellectual, scholarly development of professors. The portfolio reconciles the perceived polarities of teaching and research but only if it is engaged as a motivating contract for ongoing reflective practice rather than as a one-time hurdle for evaluation. Revision, to be sure, is central to improvement.

TIPS ON MAINTAINING PORTFOLIO REVISIONS

Keeping up the momentum of improvement begun by the initial act of writing a teaching portfolio is not as easy as it seems, especially once the consuming duties of the semester take over. Yet, conscientious teachers can and do make time for crucial development activities as part of their commitment to exemplary teaching and their responsibility to student learning. Here are some suggestions that may make the important step of regular and timely revisions of a portfolio more manageable and productive:

- Use the appendix as a convenient, self-defined filing system for hard-copy information and documentation. For example, the portfolio probably already has an appendix for materials such as examinations or handouts. As new materials are developed for the purpose of trying to improve student learning, pitch them into the appropriate appendix for future assessment. As evaluations come in at midterm or at the end of the course, store them in the corresponding appendix, where they can later be analyzed for patterns of improvement or areas of concern.

- Don't reinvent the wheel. If year-end self reports are part of one's evaluation of teaching system, then combine the narrative revision of the portfolio and its assessment of quantitative information in the appendix with the required report. Find ways of making required assessment and evaluation activities integral dimensions of portfolio revisions which, unlike most forms and data-driven reports, prompt genuine growth and intellectual engagement because of the power of reflective writing combined with the benefits of rigorous documentation.

- Focus on selected areas for enhancement. Narrow the scope of improvement efforts and the amount of information analyzed in a revision. Identify, for instance, one particular assignment in one course and the role of the teacher's periodic, written feedback on the work of three students of varying abilities.

- Keep revisions detailed and specific. Conceiving of revision as a complete reshaping of all the fundamental components of a portfolio as document is intimidating and unnecessary. Rarely do we undergo such dramatic revelations about philosophy and practice that the entire portfolio must be recast. Remember that the portfolio is a *process of continual analysis and improvement.* Revise deliberately, a step at a time, for clearer evidence of steady, systematic renewal.

- Take advantage of faculty development staff to help identify areas for improvement and to suggest specific revisions of portions of the portfolio. Trained in implementing videotapes of teaching, peer review systems, teaching and learning styles inventories, classroom assessment techniques, and other strategies for improvement, faculty developers can introduce new modes of research into teaching that may prompt ideas for further revisions.

- Entrust a mentor to help guide the development of a portfolio through its various revisions. While collaboration with an experienced colleague outside one's institution is often best in the initial stage of writing a draft of a portfolio, teaming with a colleague within or outside the department or with a department chair can help create a useful perspective on the portfolio which stimulates worthwhile revision. The allied benefit of such collaboration is that teaching begins to grow in value across disciplines because of the cross-fertilization of serious commitment to ongoing improvement.

The final tip provides a useful, instructive venue for collaboration on several important issues that should be addressed in evaluating the content, documentation, and format of a teaching portfolio both in the initial development of a draft and in the revision process. A mentor and a professor should discuss such issues throughout the process of writing and revising a portfolio, perhaps using the following checklist as a guide for collaboration:

Suggested Checklist for Evaluation of Teaching Portfolio

- ✓ Does the portfolio include current information?
- ✓ Does the portfolio balance information from self, from others, and from products of student learning?
- ✓ Is there coherence among the various components of the portfolio, revealing demonstrated effectiveness in practice tied to an articulated philosophy?
- ✓ Does the portfolio demonstrate teaching consistent with departmental and institutional strategic priorities and missions?
- ✓ What constitutes valid documentation and evidence?
- ✓ Are multiple, selective sources of information included, offering a diverse and objective assessment of teaching?

✓ Does the portfolio adequately supplement narrative description, analysis, and goals with empirical evidence in the appendix?

✓ How clearly and specifically does the portfolio reveal the relevance of professional development, research, and scholarship to the teaching enterprise?

✓ Does the portfolio include a core of agreed-upon seminal statements with accompanying evidence?

✓ Do products of student learning reveal successful teaching?

✓ Does the portfolio provide evidence of efforts to improve teaching? Is there evidence of improvement in methods, materials, evaluations, goals?

✓ Is the portfolio the *only* source of information on teaching effectiveness? Or is it complemented by additional materials and corroborative information about a professor's complex and varied roles?

✓ How does the portfolio profile individual style, achievements, discipline? Is a strong case made in both narrative and documentation in the appendix for the complexity and individuality of a professor's particular teaching effort in a particular discipline with a particular group of students?

✓ Does the portfolio meet established length requirements?

If we take seriously the current call in higher education for more emphasis on accountability, assessment, and productivity, the model of reflective practice demonstrated by the teaching portfolio emerges as one compelling solution to the need for professors to improve the standards of teaching and learning in the academy. Of course, other methods of strengthening the connection between teaching and learning exist and should be implemented just as carefully and widely as portfolio strategies. As I have posited earlier, periodic portfolio revisions challenge us consistently to reexamine what and how we teach but more importantly why, with the aim of improving the impact of our practice on student learning. Is the labor of keeping up portfolio revisions worth the effort? I believe it is because portfolios are a small investment in creating a climate in higher education where teaching is valued and rewarded because professors can document on a regular and timely basis their commitment to enhancing the quality of education in our institutions.

REFERENCES

Boyer, E. L. (1990). *Scholarship reconsidered: Priorities of the professoriate.* Princeton, NJ: Carnegie Foundation for the Advancement of Teaching.

Schön, D. (1983). *The reflective practitioner.* New York, NY: Basic Books.

Seldin, P. (1991). *The teaching portfolio: A practical guide to improved performance and promotion/tenure decisions.* Bolton, MA: Anker.

Seldin, P., & Associates. (1993). *Successful use of teaching portfolios.* Bolton, MA: Anker.

Wolf, K. (1991). The Schoolteacher's Portfolio: Issues in Design, Implementation, and Evaluation. *Phi Delta Kappan,* October 1991: 129–36.

Zubizarreta, J. (1995). Using teaching portfolio strategies to improve course instruction. In P. Seldin and Associates, *Improving college teaching* (pp. 167–79). Bolton, MA: Anker.

THE ELECTRONICALLY AUGMENTED TEACHING PORTFOLIO

Devorah A. Lieberman and John Rueter

There is consistent evidence that teaching portfolios are becoming more pervasive throughout higher education. It is imperative that the highest quality of teaching is captured in the portfolio and that multiple strategies are used to do this. The purpose of this chapter is to offer alternate strategies for creating an electronically augmented teaching portfolio (EATP). The electronically enhanced portfolio augments the traditional print portfolio with electronic materials that can strengthen particular portfolio components. This also allows display of materials that cannot otherwise be reviewed in a portfolio. Since the premise of the teaching portfolio is that it should be a solid reflection of teacher development, quality of teaching, student learning, and quality teaching process and products, a selective inclusion of electronic media can aid in meeting these teaching portfolio goals.

Consider for a moment what items are included in the traditional portfolio: materials from oneself, materials from others, products of good teaching, and miscellaneous items that do not fit in with the above categories (Seldin, 1993). Technological capabilities offer three avenues for augmenting and enhancing these categories. First, there may be ways to display the print materials electronically that the reader finds easier to understand and more enjoyable to read or view. Second, technology allows us to capture information about our teaching that previously was not part of our teaching frame of reference. Third, the technology allows efficient means of storing and critiquing the portfolio. This chapter provides suggestions both for augmenting that which would have been presented through a print medium and for capturing "scholarship of teaching" through electronic means that previously would have been impossible to capture.

ADVANTAGES AND DISADVANTAGES OF THE EATP

Electronic enhancement may at first appear quite appealing, but there are both advantages and disadvantages of the electronically augmented teaching portfolio.

Advantages

More types of information about the individual and his/her teaching can be included and displayed. The traditional teaching portfolio includes print materials and various forms of "pictures" that may be included between the front and back covers of a selected notebook. Information about the individual in the EATP may be included from sources such as the Internet (teaching materials posted on his/her home page, learning outcomes or products produced by students and posted on their own home page and easily hotlinked to the teacher's home page), CD-ROM displaying projects created for his/her own class, or interactive software designed as learning tools for students.

Materials presented can be animations, simulations or videoclips. Many types of electronic materials can be presented in the EATP. A few of these include simulations, animations, video clips, sound clips, story boards, multimedia projects and presentations, or full color graphics.

Appendices can be stored on disk. Materials that may be bulky for the traditional teaching portfolio can be stored on a disk and easily accessed by reviewers. An electronic index can be included to help the reviewer access sections that interest him/her most.

Electronic publications on the Internet by the professor can be easily accessed. With the appropriate address provided for the reviewer in print form (Uniform Resource Location: URL), he/she can easily access the Internet site.

Portfolio materials are not lost during transport between reviewers. Documents included in the traditional portfolio may be misplaced or lost when they are examined by many reviewers over a period of time. Included disks or CD-ROMS are much more likely to remain in the pocket of the portfolio, and back-up copies for all electronic inclusions are easily made. Internet access to class home pages and materials need not have any additional paperwork or disks; it merely must include the home page Internet address.

The ability to model in the portfolio that which a professor embeds in the course. Universities are including computer literacy in their student learning outcome objectives. What better way of modeling the value-added abilities of technology in presentation of materials than through the EATP. If a professor either uses technology to present information in class or requires that students use technology as a tool for their own learning, then this can be modeled and displayed in the presentation of the portfolio. We feel it is a contradiction to describe with print medium only an electronic project or presentation embedded in a teaching situation designed for helping achieve student learning goals and objectives.

Disadvantages

There may be too much emphasis on the "bells and whistles" of the portfolio rather than on using technology to support the portfolio and meet the objectives of the designer. At a recent portfolio workshop the facilitator described a portfolio that was presented entirely through an electronic medium. She described how ineffective it was because it seemed to draw the reviewers' attention away from the content. The table of contents was presented as clouds that the reviewer would click on and it would link you to that section. If you clicked on something incorrectly a voice from the computer said, "oops, try again" with no other instructions. It is examples like this that remind us that the technological elements of the portfolio should add value to its content and objectives or make it easier to use.

Recommendation: Portfolios should be well-designed with intuitive or very simple navigation aids to the reviewer. It might be advantageous for institutions to draft format guidelines to help both the author and the reviewers.

Potentially the readers of the portfolio may need to be provided with appropriate hardware and software in order to access information on a disk or on Internet provided by the portfolio designer. Both Macintosh and Microsoft Windows platforms can access information on the Internet. However, floppy or CD-ROM disks may be formatted so that they cannot be viewed by both types of machines.

Recommendation: All disks should indicate clearly if they are formatted for both players or only one. Minimum system requirements must be specified.

Portfolio readers and/or reviewers may need to be educated about the importance of reviewing diverse portfolio components, e.g., electronic media. Some reviewers may not be versed in the electronic medium included in the portfolio. If this is the case, the portfolio developer needs to evaluate the necessity for including the technology in the portfolio or provide a means to help the reviewer view the materials. Another element is that reviewers need to be able to competently assess the merits of the electronically augmented teaching portfolio.

Recommendation: Reviewers should be given guidance on how electronic media can be used to meet specific institutional criteria. These guidelines should be developed and distributed before portfolios are widely used.

It may be inconvenient for the readers/reviewers to access the electronic information presented. It can be off-putting to reviewers if they do not have ready access to a computer or the computer that is most appropriate for the medium needed. It also can be argued that this might be more convenient than visiting the classroom during a particular lesson, or watching a complete videotape in order to view a few minutes of highlighted material.

Recommendation: Both portfolio authors and reviewers should be made aware that the purpose of the EATP is to make review more inclusive and not more extensive. Also, reviewers can be reminded that several minutes of video might substitute for several hours of classes.

EXAMPLES OF MATERIAL AND FORMAT

Electronic materials can be most easily and effectively displayed in the sections of the teaching portfolio that contain "materials from self" and "materials that are products of good teaching." The remaining portion of this chapter will suggest ways to display various items of the teaching portfolio and where possible will display, in print form, a representation of the electronic example. As you view the print form, keep in mind how much more effective it would be if it were electronically presented, dynamic and potentially interactive. Most importantly we are describing through written word and traditional print medium that which we are suggesting you might explore electronically. Please keep in mind that the limitations you may perceive in our written presentation are exactly what might be improved by use of an electronic medium. Also, throughout this section of the chapter, we may recommend a genre of software capabilities as opposed to a particular brand name or company. For example, we may suggest a "presentation software" without identifying specific companies. Offices of instructional technology or faculty development on each campus can provide readers with specific software that meet the needs suggested in this chapter. The software suggested here are all common commercially available tools for both Macintosh and Windows.

Suggestions for "materials from self"

The curriculum vitae. Include on hard (paper) copy within the portfolio as well as on disk. On disk, teaching-related publications, associations, conference presentations, advising, grant activities, and innovative teaching activities can be highlighted by colors or fonts which draw the reviewers' attention to these items.

Some word processing programs include an annotation function. It allows the reviewers, while viewing the electronic curriculum vitae, to make comments on the vitae which are easily shared among viewers on a shared file. This avoids Post-it notes on the document or potentially lost papers among reviewers. The annotations can be shared with the teaching portfolio owner or filed for later use.

Figure 1

A portion of a Curriculum Vitae with examples of annotations

Employment

Faculty in Residence, Spring 1995–Spring 1996, Center for Academic Excellence, PSU

Professor of Biology, 1988 to present, Portland State University

Director, Environ. Sci. and Res. Program, 1991 to 1993, Portland State University

Associate Professor of Biology, 1984–1988, Portland State University

Assistant Professor of Biology, 1979–1984, Portland State University

Refereed Publications or Other Creative Achievements
Articles and chapters

Lieberman, D. A., & Rueter, J. G. (1996). Designing, Implementing, and Assessing a University Technology-Pedagogy Institute. Submitted to *To Improve the Academy,* Volume 15. Stillwater, OK: New Forums Press.

Reuter, J. G. (1993). Limitation of primary production in the oceans by light, nitrogen, and iron. In *Photosynthetic Responses to the Environment.* H. Yamamoto and C. Smith, (Eds.), American Society Plant Physiologist Series. 126–135.

Note: This excerpts a Microsoft Word document version of a curriculum vitae. The reviewer's annotations are inserted in the text. Each reviewer's machine will automatically stamp the annotation with the source. For example, see reviewer A and reviewer B stamped within the text.

Figure 2

Reviewers' annotations from the Curriculum Vitae excerpt in Figure 1

[REV-A1] What is the split appointment?

[REV-B2] It was a .5 FTE split in Biology and CAE.

[REV-A3] Interesting publication that relates to the Center for Academic Excellence job.

[REV-A4] This is a general paper that discusses the implications of his research.

Annotations are listed in the order in which they appear in the text and can be listed for any particular reviewer. Printing a list of the annotations is an option in the print dialog box.

Figure 3

Notes embedded within the Curriculum Vitae document

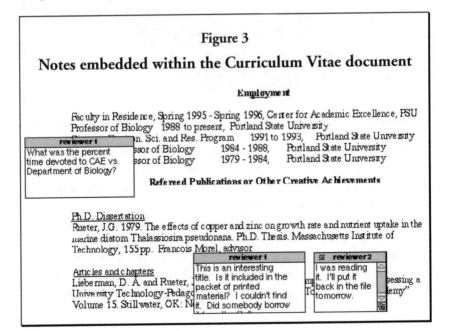

Note: A screen shot (picture) with what an Adobe PDF document would look like for the same page. The original document was "printed" to the pdf format using Adobe Acrobat Exchange and notes added later. The notes can be collapsed or summarized for the reviewers' convenience.

Quantitative teaching evaluations. An electronic display can be more effective than a traditional presentation of quantitative rankings term by term. A dynamic display of teaching evaluations using histograms in which each year is built on the year before allows the viewer to compare yearly dimension rankings. There are no pages to turn or averages to review. Visually, the viewer can see how a dimension has increased or decreased as it dynamically overlays the previous year or term.

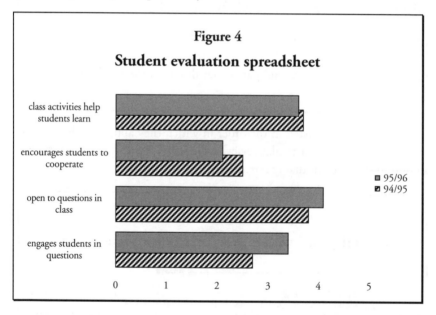

Figure 4

Student evaluation spreadsheet

Note: An example of how a spreadsheet is used to represent the relative response of students from one year to the next. This can highlight weaker areas and trends in improvement. In this example, the lower rating and improvement in that area are highlighted.

Course syllabi. Syllabi can easily and more efficiently be displayed electronically than traditionally. Syllabi can be placed on disk as part of the appendices or as presentation of "one's own materials." The professor can draw attention to particular parts of the syllabus through special fonts and colors. The syllabus in Figure 5 is an example of how this might appear.

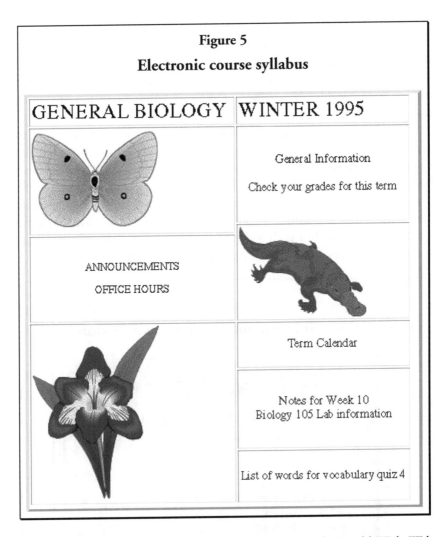

Figure 5

Electronic course syllabus

GENERAL BIOLOGY WINTER 1995

General Information

Check your grades for this term

ANNOUNCEMENTS

OFFICE HOURS

Term Calendar

Notes for Week 10
Biology 105 Lab information

List of words for vocabulary quiz 4

Note: An electronic syllabus might take the form of a World Wide Web page that provides links to the different activities or a calendar that provides newly added information each week.

Suggestions for "products of good teaching"

Electronic mail. Include examples of how electronic mail (e-mail) has been used as a tool for innovative teaching. Many teachers use an electronic listserv as a way not only to distribute information to all students, but also as a way for students to interact with each other on a specific topic in a manner that actually enhances their learning while concurrently teaching them how to use technology.

Presentation software. Materials presented in class via presentation software can be displayed in the EATP. There are numerous presentation software programs that are available for use to enhance traditional classroom information communicated in class. The class component can be contained on disk and viewed by the reviewers. This information can be prepared prior to class and used dynamically as it is presented during class.

Presentation software can be adapted to foster student interaction or to serve as a class discussion tool. Figure 6 represents a discussion that the teacher "diagrammed" as the students created the threads. This is innovative because the teacher was able to document the thread of the discussion as the students created it. Also, the teacher was able to lead the discussion while concurrently capturing student contributions. Following the discussion, the teacher was able to close each level of bubbles and reveal them again as she reviewed the discussion "path" contained in that session.

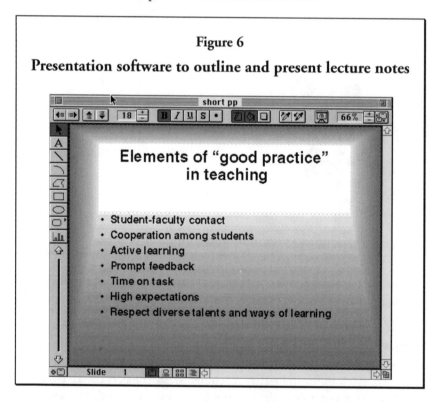

Figure 6

Presentation software to outline and present lecture notes

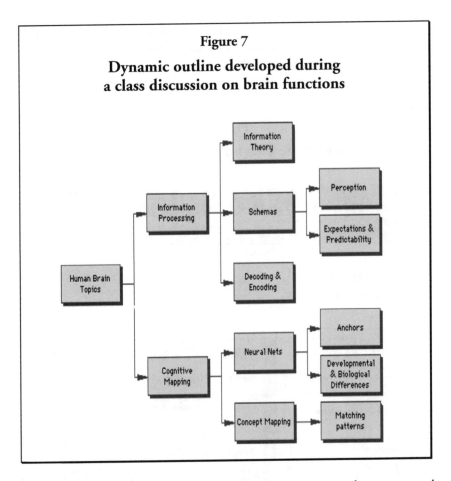

Figure 7

Dynamic outline developed during a class discussion on brain functions

A small group discussion decision-making process can be represented electronically to accompany the traditional portfolio. This process (as displayed in Figure 7) would display for the reviewer the decision-making sequence that students initiated with the software actually capturing that process and simultaneously giving the students feedback on their decisions so that they can view the process and receive information to inform their future decision-making action.

Many teachers are requiring students to participate in self-paced learning to accompany their classes. Teachers design self-paced learning modules on disk or on the Internet which allow the student to complete lessons for the class independent of the scheduled class. The self-paced tools document how a student is progressing with the particular lesson and give students feedback on a particular concept. The disk may include readings, interactive tools, test taking which scores students and does not allow them to progress to the next unit until the test is completed correctly, etc. These tools can easily accompany the traditional portfolio and allow the portfolio reviewers to interact with the same tools that the students are required to use for the class.

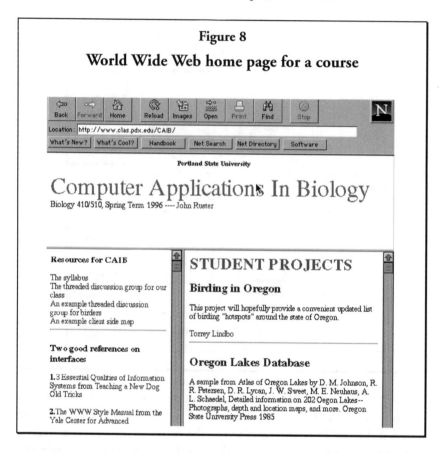

Figure 8

World Wide Web home page for a course

Teachers are using the Internet home pages to provide students with information about class (see Figure 8). The teaching portfolio can easily include a home page address to which portfolio reviewers can log on. The home page can contain class notes, links to other pages which are used in class, displays of class projects, etc. There is no need to include an accompanying disk or graphics, merely the home page address.

An increasing number of professors are publishing on the World Wide Web. Instead of containing a hard copy of a publication, which may never appear in hard copy but merely on the Web, the professor can include the Internet address on which the publication appears. Also, many World Wide

Web sites are able to document the number of individuals who have logged on to the site. A common complaint of hard copy journal publication is that one cannot document how many individuals actually read a particular article. By documenting the number of individuals logged on to a particular site, one is more reliably able to ascertain potential interest in a specific article.

The following address of the Biology Education Review is an example of one such website: [http://biology.uoregon.edu/biology-www/workshop-biol/newsletters/spr96.html].

For many faculty, the electronic portion of a portfolio can be indispensable for a fair representation of their accomplishments. Technology may be embedded in a course in order to meet student learning objectives. Consequently, the traditional print-only portfolio precludes an authentic representation of what the instructor is bringing to the course. Please note that even within this particular chapter, representation of media in a print form may not be grasped as readily as if it were viewed through electronic means. The way to guarantee the best reflection of good teaching practices is to encourage diverse forms of media to be included in the teaching portfolio.

REFERENCES

Seldin, P. (1993). *Successful use of teaching portfolios.* Bolton, MA: Anker.

SAMPLE PORTFOLIOS FROM ACROSS DISCIPLINES

Thi chapter is comprised of twenty-three sample teaching portfolios from across disciplines. They have been prepared by faculty at Auburn University (Alabama), Clemson University (South Carolina), College of William & Mary (Virginia), Georgia Southern University, Hobart & William Smith Colleges (New York), Oklahoma State University, Rhodes College (Tennessee), Southern Illinois University, Susquehanna University (Pennsylvania), University of Nevada, University of Scranton (Pennsylvania), Valdosta State University (Georgia), Wake Forest University (North Carolina), and Western Michigan University.

The appendix material referred to, though part of the actual portfolios, is excluded because of its cumbersome nature.

Because each portfolio is an individual document, varying importance has been assigned by different professors to different items. Some professors discuss an item at length, others dismiss it with just a sentence or two, or even omit it.

The portfolios are arranged in alphabetical order by author. The accompanying list groups them by discipline areas and shows page numbers for easy reference.

Important: Reading sample portfolios in other disciplines provides helpful information and insights applicable to your own discipline.

Biology
James M. Ryan
Hobart and William
Smith Colleges 193

Tammy Tobin-Janzen
Susquehanna University 214

Counseling and Human Services
Oliver J. Morgan, S. J.
University of Scranton 167

Economics
Daniel M. Gropper
Auburn University 109

Education
Daria T. Cronic
Clemson University 93

Stephanie L. Kenney
Georgia Southern University 132

Electrical Engineering
Indira Chatterjee
University of Nevada, Reno 78

English
Ellen Hendrix
Georgia Southern University 116

Colleen Kennedy
College of William and Mary 123

Karen E. Mura
Susquehanna University 174

Finance
Kenneth L. Stanley
Valdosta State University 204

Geology
R. Heather Macdonald
College of William and Mary 150

Gerontology
Joseph A. Weber
Oklahoma State University 223

Law
Charles P. Rose
Wake Forest University 183

Library
Judith M. Arnold
Western Michigan University 70

Mathematics
Anthony P. Ferzola
University of Scranton 102

Music
Diane M. Clark
Rhodes College 85

Philosophy
Robert R. Llewellyn
Rhodes College 141

Physics
R. M. MacQueen
Rhodes College 159

Political Science
Clyde E. Willis
Valdosta State University 231

Psychology
Janie H. Wilson
Georgia Southern University 243

Speech Communication
Maggie M. Sullivan
Southern Illinois University 210

Veterinary Surgery and Medicine
Donna Walton Angarano
Auburn University 60

TEACHING PORTFOLIO
Donna Walton Angarano
Department of Small Animal Surgery and Medicine
Auburn University
Spring 1996

Table of Contents
1) Teaching responsibilities
2) Teaching philosophy, strategies and objectives
3) Areas and means of teaching improvement
4) Peer assessment of teaching
5) Student assessment of teaching
6) Recognition of teaching effectiveness
7) Mentoring others
8) Goals and future plans
9) Appendices

Teaching Responsibilities
My teaching responsibilities involve both professional and post-graduate veterinary students. All courses are required except for VM 463, which is an elective clinical rotation.

I team teach the dermatology section of VM 427, Veterinary Medicine and Surgery I. This involves several lectures to a class of 90 second-year veterinary students.

I share clinical responsibilities with one other faculty dermatologist for VM 440, 441, 442, 443 and 463, Small Animal Clinics I, II, III, IV, and V. Clinical rotations are conducted year round with students (5–6 at a time) spending 2.5 weeks on the dermatology/community outpatient service. Students spend most of their day on the clinical rotation. The teaching is conducted in several ways, but focuses on the use of clinical cases. When not working with actual cases, time is spent in rounds, or other small group activities.

As a clinical veterinary dermatologist, I am also involved with post graduate veterinarians who are in internship and residency training programs. All small animal interns and many residents spend time as individuals on my clinical rotation. I work closely with the dermatology resident, supervising his clinical responsibilities, his teaching efforts, and his understanding of veterinary dermatology. In addition to clinics, we spend several hours a week in informal interactions including journal club and dermatohistopathology sessions. Journal club is an informal discussion of recent articles related to veterinary dermatology. Both the dermatology resident and the faculty dermatologist participate. Dermatohistopathology is a one-on-one session involving the resident and myself. We examine, interpret, and discuss microscope slides of cutaneous biopsies.

Teaching Philosophy, Strategies, and Objectives
Didactic course
Dermatology is usually the first clinical subject the professional students encounter. This is both exciting and frustrating for them. While the format is lecture and slide presentation, I use a problem-based approach and try to get students to use things they know as a foundation. (See Course syllabi VM 427—Appendix A.) I encourage them to think. For example, I'll show a dog with hairloss and ask the students to tell me what types of things can cause hairloss. I'm not looking for diseases, but mechanisms. I use an overhead and write down their suggestions. We talk about the types of things we should look for in different situations. We briefly review the relevant anatomy and physiology. Then I introduce various dermatological diseases.

Students are often frustrated because of the similar clinical appearance of many dermatological diseases. I encourage students to learn as we go, often with the use of pop quizzes. As we establish the foundation, I try to build upon it.

At the end of each of the first few lecture sessions, I ask the students to turn in a list of three things they learned during the class and three additional things they plan to review or study. This helps me relate to their level of understanding, and encourages them to pursue learning on their own.

Several take-home paper cases are used, where students are encouraged to work with friends and a variety of other resources to develop a differential diagnosis, diagnostic plan, or potential treatment regime. (See Paper cases, second-year veterinary students—Appendix B.) These are often used as a foundation for the next lecture. I also ask students to identify the source of their information. This may lead to frustration as students realize that different books/articles often say different things. This helps students make the transition from basic science to clinical science where life is not a multiple-choice test, but where sometimes there are multiple correct answers and sometimes there is no answer. Many students find this transition very difficult.

I have also developed a series of cases for students to review that use computer-assisted learning. Students are encouraged to work in groups of two to three as they discuss and thus learn more as they go through the cases. The program uses a random-access slide projector and a computer. Students respond to questions that are primarily multiple choice or fill-in-the-blank. They get feedback as they work.

Clinical courses
In the clinical situation, students see actual dermatology cases. After talking to the owner and examining the patient, the student comes to me and we discuss what they've found and what they think. I try to build on what they know and to help them develop confidence in their own observations and deductions. I then see the case (with the student observing). Depending on the complexity of

the case, we later discuss why I handled it the way I did. For cases that are hospitalized, we look at them again as a group. The student on the case reviews the history, and the rest of the students examine the case and share their thoughts. When they get stumped, I ask the original student to share what he/she now knows. (This is a refection of the general teaching strategy of "see one, do one, and teach one.")

There are a variety of other learning exercises that I use with clinical students depending on the interest of the group and the volume of the caseload. If our caseload happens to be low, I may utilize paper cases, where students work the case based on the information that is provided to them. They may get several pieces of information (paper) during the course of the case. (See Paper cases, senior veterinary students—Appendix C.)

Sometimes I give informal lectures on topics chosen by the students, or areas where they seem confused. For example, a topical therapy lecture may involve a series of slides depicting various clinical cases. I have a sample box of 25–30 bottles of shampoos and dips. We look at the case, briefly discuss the problem and diagnosis and then I ask what shampoos will be helpful. Students can read the labels, smell the products, and assess cost. Sometimes the dialogue gets exciting as we discuss various options and the reasons one product might be used instead of another.

For the senior students, I also have a series of computer cases. These are more complicated cases and almost all choices are fill-in-the-blank. As students work up the case and decide to do a diagnostic test, instead of a report, they may see a slide or a test result that they must interpret. The program also keeps track of the amount of money they are spending. (This is an attempt to remind them of the financial realities of the real world.) Finally, as they treat the case, sometimes they make mistakes. For instance, if they choose a drug that is contraindicated, the animal may get worse or even die. Some wrong answers may even lead to a lawyer's involvement. The students seem to enjoy these cases. Sometimes they go back through the cases picking the wrong answers to see what happens. I believe they learn a lot either way. (My frustration comes from trying to keep up with advances in technology and in medicine. I try to revise the cases as new treatment options are discovered. Also, today's students want slick computer programs, and it takes a long time to re-do cases using new authoring programs. I find that I often spend more time revising old cases than writing new ones.)

During some rotations, I distribute a dermatology crossword puzzle that I developed. Students can work it if they wish. (See Dermatology crossword puzzle—Appendix D.) I ask some groups to write an article that would be suitable for their hometown newspaper in a column called "ask the vet." The only requirement is that it relate to veterinary dermatology. I hope to expand on this project in the future and see if some articles can actually be published locally.

During most rotations, I try to set aside one to two hours for Dermatology Jeopardy. I divide the students into three groups of two. There are numerous topics, including shampoo therapy, large animal dermatological diseases, ear products, and infectious agents. We have fun and review a lot of information. Some of the information is trivial. Some may be present on the national board examination. Some students who don't do well in other settings really shine in this setting (and visa versa). Overall, it's a fun way to review. The setting is very informal. If needed, I sometimes do a short review.

My overall philosophy is that dermatology cases are common in the real world, and that dermatology is fun. When asked a question, students give very few "wrong" answers. The trick is to challenge them to think and to use what they know. I ask a lot of questions. If they don't know the answer, I usually try to lead them to the answer rather than just giving it directly. I may follow up the next day with a similar or even the same question. I try to smile and joke with them so they're not embarrassed, but I also try to emphasize things they should know. I brag about my students to clients, and talk about how close they are to graduation and how I'm just along to do the paperwork. These are future colleagues, and I try to remind everyone of that.

The dermatology resident

The most challenging and rewarding teaching is that of serving as a mentor to my resident. I expect a lot from this individual. As (s)he matures, I often step back, watch, and evaluate him in the role of clinician and teacher. I interject when necessary, but we do most of our discussion one-on-one later. We discuss not only the clinical duties, but also his role as a teacher. I try to walk the line of challenging my resident without causing him to lose confidence. We also do a lot of discussion (histopath sessions, journal club, etc.) as colleagues. I share my knowledge and expect him to share information he is learning from graduate courses and outside reading.

Areas and Means of Teaching Improvement

During the last few years, I have had the opportunity to attend several workshops and symposia related to teaching. (See List of teaching workshops/symposia attended—Appendix E.) Each of these have provided ideas and motivated me to improve my teaching. I have had support from students and the administration, allowing me to experiment with various teaching methods and techniques. At first I found these "experiments" to be frustrating, especially since I didn't usually have an expert available to give me advice. Then I realized I had access to the best feedback available: the students. I try to be honest with them when I am trying something new. I ask for their opinions and suggestions which are sometimes critical, usually constructive, and almost always helpful.

Problem-based learning (PBL) workshops have reinforced the idea that all students have the knowledge and the wherewithal to learn. I have attended multiple PBL workshops, in Toronto, North Carolina, and Mississippi, conducted by Drs. LuAnn Wilkerson and Gwendie Camp. Both of these dynamic educators are associated with medical schools using PBL. It was pointed out that many of us approach students as being like empty buckets, and we think it is up to us to try to pour information into them. In reality, none of the buckets are empty, and our job is to show students how to add to and interpret what they know. We must constantly look for ways to motivate and encourage our students to become independent learners. While our professional curriculum is not entirely problem-based, I have incorporated many PBL techniques into my teaching. For example, rather than lecture on demodicosis, I lead a discussion on hairloss. (*Demodex canis* is a mite that lives in the hair follicle.) In the course of the discussion, we cover several diseases which result in hairloss. At the end of the lecture, when I ask the students what they plan to review, I am actually addressing learning issues. An increased use of paper cases is another direct result of attending PBL workshops.

In 1991, I attended a workshop on computer-assisted learning (CAL). Dr. Fred Smith, at the University of Georgia, is a pioneer in this area, as is Dr. Charles Branch, at the Auburn University College of Veterinary Medicine. Since that time, I have worked with colleagues within the college to establish a student computer laboratory. As a group, we have conducted multiple demonstrations/workshops at the college on computer-assisted learning for faculty and practitioners.

Modern technology is providing a whole new way (unlimited ways!) to enhance teaching. Some students are more comfortable with a computer than with their peers and instructors. Computer-assisted learning offers these individuals a way to gain confidence as well as knowledge. Our profession, however, involves a tremendous amount of human interaction and communication. As a teacher, part of my responsibility is to help students become comfortable in different types of situations.

Once CAL lessons are developed, they allow for more efficient use of a faculty member's time. Hopefully, they encourage independent study and cause students to ask more advanced questions. They also provide additional learning opportunities for the self-motivated student.

As I became interested in teaching methodology, I discovered an entire new world of literature regarding higher education. There are associations, journals, books, and electronic listserves that I never knew existed. As I have explored these sources of information, my interest in experimenting with different teaching methods has increased. Techniques such as listing what you've learned at the end of a lecture, or selecting three students in the class to be in charge of hearing, speed, and boredom, are ideas that I've read. Recently, I've given a lot of thought to the importance of communicating clear and precise goals and objectives. It's an area that needs to be addressed, particularly in light of the current information explosion.

Peer Assessment of Teaching

In 1987, the Auburn University Board of Trustees mandated that student and peer evaluation of instruction be used. Student evaluations were being obtained, but peer review was much less formal. Since that time, our department has used assorted ways of obtaining peer evaluation. In some disciplines, such as dermatology, we attempt to attend each others' lectures. This has been particularly helpful when experimenting with different teaching methods. Some years, faculty within the department were assigned to evaluate a colleague. In addition, all departmental faculty were asked to submit a numeric evaluation of other faculty. Past peer evaluation of my teaching is shown in the following chart. Rating is based on a 10 point scale with 10 being the highest. (See Peer assessment of teaching—Appendix F.)

Academic Year	My rating	Dept. range
93–94 *		
92–93	9.3	7.1–9.4
91–92	9.2	7.2–9.6
90–91	9.5	7.0–9.5

* More recent ratings are not available because the faculty within the department elected to modify the format to a more formal and consistent method of peer review. In 1994, I chaired a committee which developed a proposal that was subsequently adopted by a vote of the faculty in the department. The new format is being used for the first time this year. (See Departmental proposal for peer review process—Appendix G.)

Sample statements from peers are included in Appendix F. Examples include:

- *Dr. A is superior in all facets! Wonderful teacher and mentor for interns and students.*

- *The feeling among the committee members is that she should continue doing what she does well: everything. She is enthusiastic, organized, articulate, and concerned about her subject and her students. Dr. Angarano is to be commended for her skills as an educator.*

Student Assessment of Teaching

Evaluation by clinical students is depicted in the following chart. The overall evaluation of teaching includes ratings (on a 5 point scale, with 5 the highest) by didactic and clinical students. (See Student assessment of teaching—Appendix H.)

Academic Year	Student	Dept. range	Overall	Dept. range
94–95	4.84	2.38–4.89	4.74	2.38–4.74
93–94	4.96	3.00–5.00	4.78	3.00–4.80
92–93	4.81	3.83–5.00	4.80	3.85–5.00
91–92	4.94	3.42–4.94	4.74	3.42–4.74
90–91	4.83	3.79–4.92	4.33	2.95–4.69

Sample statements from students are included in Appendix I. Examples include:

Didactic course

- *Great and very effective teacher. Energetic, enthusiastic, and made a very positive influence on learning.*

- *Dr. Angarano's approach and presentation to the class was very good, interesting, and entertaining. She has an easy and comfortable manner in front of the class.*

Clinical rotation

- *Your manner is encouraging for learning and occasionally guessing (!) without fear of ridicule. It is also very nice that you let us deal with clients and support us to the clients. Thanks!*

- *Thank you for such a good rotation. It is nice to hear the term "we" used (clinician and student) instead of leaving the student out of the picture.*

- *Very creative and informative. Dr. A has great client communication skills; I hope I can mimic her professionalism in the future. A great inspiration for the students. Definitely deserving of AVMA Woman of the Year.*

- *The innovative styles of teaching are very educational, but most of all interesting. Dr. A has a wonderful style of teaching and makes me feel good about myself. You can truly tell that she enjoys teaching.*

Recognition of Teaching Effectiveness
National/international recognition
During 1994–1995, I had the tremendous experience of doing an American Council on Education Fellowship. (See American Council on Education Fellowship—Appendix J.) After completing this program, my perspective will never be the same. In addition to administrative and leadership experience, the ACE fellowship gave me the opportunity to work closely with individuals from a variety of institutional types and disciplines. I gained an appreciation of their challenges and frustrations. Instead of stressing the differences, the program allowed me to recognize the similarities and to realize how all of us in higher education must work together to enhance our educational system.

In 1992, I was chosen by the Association of Women Veterinarians as the Outstanding Woman Veterinarian of the Year. This award is for contributions to veterinary medicine in general, but I feel that in some ways it reflects my teaching, since teaching is so much of who I am. (See Outstanding Woman Veterinarian of the Year—Appendix K.)

In addition to teaching professional students and house officers, I present 10–12 continuing education seminars a year for practitioners. Some of these are 1-hour presentations while others are several hours or days in duration. I have had the opportunity to give 23 international programs on veterinary dermatology to veterinarians in 10 countries. (See Examples of international presentations—Appendix L.)

Institutional recognition

I served as chair of the College of Veterinary Medicine awards and scholarships committee from 1988–1994. As chair, I solicited nominations from professional students and faculty (where appropriate) for the college teaching awards. While not eligible (as committee chair), I was proud to receive several student nominations for the outstanding teacher during those years.

The College of Veterinary Medicine has an annual faculty retreat. In 1991, the retreat covered several topics, and I was invited to give a presentation on "Instructional and Curricular Strategies in Veterinary Medicine." (See text of address in Appendix M.) I was the organizer of the retreat in 1992 on problem-based learning. In 1993, the college curriculum committee organized a retreat to review our entire professional curriculum. I gave the keynote address, entitled "Teach well or perish." (See text of address in Appendix N.)

I have been involved with three funded grants addressing computer-assisted instruction. (See Grants relating to teaching—Appendix O.) On multiple occasions, I have served as a consultant for Provides Veterinary Medical Resource System, IMPROMED Computer Systems, Inc. This company develops diagnostic software for veterinary medicine.

At the 12th Veterinary Medical Educational Symposium in Ames, Iowa, I did a presentation on "Use of computer-assisted lessons to teach veterinary clinical dermatology." Working with Dr. James Noxon (Iowa State University), I have conducted several informal presentations on computer-assisted instruction for veterinary clinical dermatology at the annual meeting of the American College of Veterinary Dermatology/American Academy of Veterinary Dermatology. These have been well-received, and feedback has been helpful during the development process.

In 1995, I was selected to represent the College at an Auburn University workshop on the Use of Teaching Portfolios. The process forced me to review how and why I use various teaching methods. It provided a foundation for tremendous reflection on teaching. In addition, it demonstrated, once again, the importance of enthusiastic mentors in the learning process.

Since the Fall of 1995, I have served as Acting Associate Dean of Student

Affairs at the College of Veterinary Medicine. This job has been in addition to my responsibilities as a faculty member and clinician. In some ways, I feel it has detracted from my teaching, as I have not found the time to continue development of some of my teaching ideas. Overall, however, the opportunity to serve in this position has been fantastic. I have had the chance to interact with students in many different settings dealing with a variety of situations. This has provided me a much broader picture of the stresses and frustrations faced by today's student. Also, in my expanded role as a student advocate, I now have the opportunity to push for faculty development and to recognize and reward teaching excellence. This is a responsibility I do not take lightly.

Mentoring Others

Over the years, I have been fortunate to be associated with many students (professional students and house officers) who have gone on to make wonderful contributions to our profession. (See Former students who are Diplomates of the ACVD—Appendix P.) It is obviously very rewarding to work with individuals who become enthused about my own discipline and who elect to pursue a career within the specialty. Each year at our annual meeting, I am honored by the fact that several junior colleagues ask me if I will have time to talk over lunch or dinner. It reminds me of the importance of mentors and how I still try to catch some one-on-one time with my special mentors. Individual successes motivate not only students but also mentors. It is tremendously gratifying to watch young colleagues develop, to read their work, and listen to their presentations. It's an honor to think that I may have played a part in some of their success.

One of my early mentors was John R. Campbell. He authored a book, *In touch with students*, which to this day reminds me of our numerous roles as a teacher. It's an opportunity and responsibility that we must not take lightly.

Goals and Future Plans

During the next few years, I hope to develop a better method of assessing student learning. This will involve work on both ends: clarifying specific objectives and improving methods of assessment. We also need to assess students at a later date to determine if our instruction truly has made a difference.

I would like to work more closely with colleagues in my discipline discussing teaching. We have often exchanged syllabi demonstrating how many lecture hours we have (We all want more!), but only rarely have we discussed teaching methodology. Two years ago, I organized a breakfast discussion at our annual meeting on the use of computers in teaching veterinary dermatology. I would like to collaborate with colleagues to develop an entire morning session regarding how and why we teach professional students as we do. (Residency training would be an appropriate topic at a later date.)

This type of discussion also needs to occur within the college. A session on teaching portfolios will provide a basis for further discussion. I have already been asked to lead a discussion on the use of teaching portfolios at a departmental seminar. As our department and college begins to formalize our peer review process, teaching portfolios should play an obvious role.

Finally, I plan to work with colleagues from the college to develop a graduate course on veterinary medical education. It's important that we train our graduate students and residents not only how to conduct quality research, but also how to be effective teachers. In the process, we all will benefit.

Appendices

Appendix A: Course syllabi—VM427
Appendix B: Paper cases—second-year veterinary students
Appendix C: Paper cases—senior veterinary students
Appendix D: Dermatology crossword puzzle
Appendix E: List of teaching workshops/symposia attended
Appendix F: Peer assessment of teaching
Appendix G: Departmental proposal for peer review process
Appendix H: Student assessment of teaching
Appendix I: Student assessment of teaching—sample comments
Appendix J: American Council on Education Fellowship
Appendix K: Outstanding Woman Veterinarian of the Year
Appendix L: Examples of international presentations
Appendix M: Faculty address "Instructional and curricular strategies in veterinary medicine"
Appendix N: Faculty address "Teach well or perish"
Appendix O: Grants relating to teaching
Appendix P: Former students who are Diplomates of the American College of Veterinary Dermatology

TEACHING PORTFOLIO
Judith M. Arnold
University Libraries
Western Michigan University
Fall 1996

Table of Contents
1) Teaching and Reference Responsibilities
2) Teaching and Reference Service: Philosophy and Strategies
3) Instructional Methods
4) Teaching Effectiveness
5) Teaching Improvement
6) Goals
7) Appendices

Teaching and Reference Responsibilities
As Instructional Services Librarian at Western Michigan University, I coordinate the library instruction program for the University Libraries. This position requires that I take a leadership role in implementing a systematic program of instruction, including activities such as setting goals for the program, compiling statistics, and encouraging innovation in teaching and regular evaluation of library instruction.

I am a member of a team of reference librarians who offer sessions upon request about using the library effectively for courses taught by faculty from a variety of disciplines. Many of my instruction sessions are at the basic level, primarily the freshman writing courses, ENGL 105 and BIS 142, CELCIS classes for ESL students, and occasionally more advanced subject-specific instruction in courses such as WMS 200 and HIST 190.

The setting for instruction is the electronic classroom in the library, which is equipped with a projection system, theater seating, and fifteen computer stations. The primary audience is traditional-aged undergraduate students. I typically work with a class of 25 students for one hour. Prior to the session I consult with the instructor to agree upon goals, objectives, and content. Strategies for accomplishing these goals and the methods of presentation are left to me.

In 1994–95 I assumed a significant portion of the instructional load. I taught 33 sessions out of the 171 sessions [see Appendix A]. In 1995–96 I taught 28 sessions, including classes of ENGL 105, BIS 142, WMS 200, and HIST 190, which involved over 550 students and over 23 hours of instruction. [A] For Women's Studies, my liaison area, I provided two sessions in WMS 200 (Introduction to Women's Studies) to over 100 students.

The teaching aspects of reference service

Another significant part of my professional responsibilities, providing reference service, involves a more informal, but nonetheless important, setting for instruction. My schedule includes 9.5 to 12 hours of reference desk service weekly during fall, winter, spring, and summer terms. I handle, along with other department members, from 3,000 to 9,000 reference transactions per month. [A] Other unscheduled reference/instruction occurs when I am in the book stacks and approached by a student for help.

The teaching environment during reference resembles tutoring or consultation. A question about resources for a research paper often evolves into instruction on discipline-specific resources such as bibliographies or specialized indexes. Frequently, the question unearths a need for instruction on the online catalog or CD-ROM indexes, or a need to think critically about the topic or the sources. Lessons that are part of traditional classroom instruction become a part of the script for the reference encounter.

Coordinating the instruction program

In my first year as Instructional Services Librarian [see position description in Appendix A], I initiated discussion in the department regarding instruction program goals. We defined competencies and user groups for the program as well as possible methods for providing instruction. [A] Based upon these discussions, I have prepared a draft document "Mission, Goals, Outcomes/Objectives," [A] which will continue to develop as I incorporate the work of the University Libraries' Information Literacy Task Force, which I currently chair. Evaluation of instruction, also a discussion priority, began in Fall 1995 with a standardized form for evaluating instruction sessions. [Appendix C]

In order to streamline reporting instruction sessions and gathering statistics, I revised the *Library Instruction Request Form* [A] and created a database that produces reports for my *Annual Report* on the instruction program [A]. This statistical information will be valuable in assessing growth in the program and identifying areas for development.

Promoting the instruction program is another facet of my role. To publicize the program, I prepared an information sheet for new faculty, [A] which was distributed at their fall orientation session. Using the information in this document, I authored two web pages about the instruction program. [A] The Library Instruction Request Form is also available on the web. Upon request I prepared an article about the instruction program for *Gatherings*, the library's newsletter. [A] Additional efforts to reach faculty have included representing the University Libraries at the InfoFairs for new faculty and graduate teaching assistants and meeting with the graduate teaching assistants for English 105 to promote library instruction for that course. (Instruction for ENGL 105 has increased from 10 sessions in 94–95 to 35 sessions in 1995–96.) I have also coordinated activities with university-wide programs that provide library orientation and instruction, including revising the workbook exercises for University 101 [A] and training the Freshman Orientation leaders.

Teaching and Reference Service: Philosophy and Strategies
My teaching philosophy has evolved significantly since I began library instruction in 1987 as a Public Service/Reference Librarian at Saint Xavier University in Chicago. I started as an information-provider (and still am) but have become more of a facilitator. One of my strongest beliefs is that classroom faculty and librarians share the responsibility for making research and effective library use a part of the student's total educational experience. Information literacy (the ability to find, evaluate, and use information) should be the ultimate goal, and research, like writing and critical thinking, should be integrated across the curriculum—from the beginnings in a course such as University 101 or English 105, through a significant research course in the major. Librarians and classroom faculty should be partners in designing goals for library instruction and in designing effective research assignments. The very best example of this cooperative effort is a fully collaborative and course-integrated approach such as the Senior Seminar for English majors, which I team taught with two English department faculty members at Saint Xavier University in Fall 1991. I am currently working with Women's Studies on an effective integrated library component for WMS 200.

I have also found that instruction and reference service are interrelated, and that my teaching philosophy and strategies operate in the way that I provide reference service. While I always try to discern through the reference interview whether instruction is appropriate for the situation, I do believe that reference service should incorporate some teaching/learning. Whenever time permits, I try to instruct the patron rather than simply give answers; given the volume of requests at the desk, this goal is not always met. I interview the patron to determine level of familiarity, information needs, and willingness to learn. Most patrons are receptive to this approach and are pleased to learn how to use resources that they have not before used. I find, similarly, that I try to bring the elements of the reference interview into the classroom: to teach students ways of defining their information needs for the occasion, to help them decide upon viable and plentiful search options, and to help them critically evaluate what they find. I try to make the classroom instruction resemble the reference encounter by emphasizing personal contact through small group work, and through individual assistance during class time.

I value interaction with students because I believe that students and teachers learn from one another. It is important to me, in teaching and in providing reference service, to relate to the students personally and to encourage their feedback on expectations, learning, and feelings about research and the library.

The library community has identified a phenomenon of "library anxiety" in students, and I have come to recognize the significance of the affective response in the interaction with students. One of the goals for any interaction—whether a class or a reference encounter—is to make students at ease in using the library and to encourage them to ask questions. Sometimes I accomplish this by coming to the session early and chatting informally with them; at other times I ask them about their previous library experience. During reference, I cover this aspect through the beginnings of the reference interview. It is important to relate the sessions to the students' personal interests and topics or the reference question to the assignment or individual's information need. I use examples from the specific assignment and individual topics supplied by the course instructor when talking about the research process and library resources.

Motivation and encouragement are crucial parts of this interaction. I like to think that my enthusiasm for research carries over to the students. When I teach, I work individually with students as much as possible and encourage them as they use the computers. At the reference desk, I try not to send the patron away empty-handed and to be approachable and helpful in order to encourage the patron to return.

Flexibility is an essential trait in teaching. I have learned from teaching a wide range of students that they are individuals and that I must be aware that what moves one student does not necessarily touch another. I constantly try to rethink my approach and to design activities and instructional materials that present key information and strategies in different ways that allow for individual learning styles.

Students learn best when they take responsibility for learning. As much as possible, I try to incorporate cooperative activities or individual tasks for students to enable them to practice strategies for searching for information or to learn to use resources through hands-on practice. Active involvement of and interaction with students are necessary elements which simulate the personal interaction that occurs in the reference transaction. Likewise, small group activities help personalize the teaching, as does one-to-one interaction with students working with hands-on exercises or worksheets.

I value writing as a way of learning. I frequently ask students to do a short writing exercise, responding to the question, "Doing research is like…" This exercise gives me some valuable information about students' understanding of research and reveals attitudes (i.e, many students compare doing research to painful experiences, such as having teeth pulled, or to impossible tasks, such as finding a needle in a haystack). In addition, this writing relates the present occasion (learning about the library and its resources) to students' past experiences with the library. It also provides a topic for opening discussion of the research process, the anxiety it produces, and strategies for a successful researcher.

Instructional Methods

Lecture is a necessary way to present essential information, although I also use printed materials such as guides, bibliographies, or strategy sheets to accompany the lecture. To reduce my information-giving role, I try to keep lecture portions to 15–20 minutes followed by demonstration of the online catalog and relevant databases. With lectures I use *presentation slides,* [B] kept to a minimum so that they do not lose effectiveness. I frequently use a lesson outline overhead which presents a listing of types of information that might be sought and that relates those information needs to the resources in the library. The slide series provides a visual overview of the session for the student and helps me as an instructor to cover the essentials. In the reference setting I am able to use more active information-giving, speaking one-to-one, showing and demonstrating, and supplying supportive printed materials.

I have developed many *teaching materials* (worksheets, guides, Persuasion slides) for ENGL 105, BIS 142, and women's studies classes. Selected examples of these materials can be found in Appendix B. A *letter* from the Director of Women's Studies reflects appreciation for the updated guide to women's studies resources: "Your contributions in the classroom, in individual instruction, and in organizing sources in the brochure, added greatly to our program this year." [E]

Hands-on activities are essential, however, to reinforce the information presented. I spend the remaining twenty to thirty minutes of the session working with students at the reference sources and the classroom terminals, allowing students to practice some strategies and, importantly, to get to know me as a person they can come to for help in the library. Hands-on practice with the technology also eases their anxiety. In the second part of the session I assist students in trying their topics, a strategy which most closely approximates the dynamics of reference service.

I also favor active engagement of the students whenever possible. Using small groups I sometimes try discussion questions to involve them in my lecture. I have also tried using small cooperative groups for topic exploration and formulating vocabulary for searching, using LCSH, printed indexes, and thesauri. A difficulty I have found with using the small cooperative groups is that a significant amount of time is involved in presenting the same information that can be relayed more quickly through lecture. Often, too, the total class size is too large to enable small group interaction.

Teaching Effectiveness

I believe that my teaching effectiveness is an important measure of my success. To be an effective coordinator of an instruction program my methods, instructional materials, and philosophy of instruction should be models and motivate other instruction librarians. In order to reflect upon and to improve my teaching, I have prepared this teaching portfolio. I also keep a *teaching journal,* where, after teaching a session, I record the successes and problems encountered. Before teaching the session the next term, I reread the journal entry and revise my materials and instruction plan if needed.

Summaries of *student evaluations* of my teaching [C] reveal that over ninety percent of the students strongly agree or agree with the statement "The librarian was knowledgeable and well-prepared," reflecting from their perspective that I have command of the subject. Over ninety percent report that they can do a keyword search using the online catalog, and over eighty percent say that they can do a journal title search. Just over seventy percent agree with the statement "As a result of the instruction I now feel more comfortable using the library." Most of the students I teach are freshmen, who are typically overwhelmed by the size and complexity of the library; over seventy percent agreement with that statement seems to me encouraging. Helping freshmen become comfortable in the library is a significant goal for ENGL 105 and BIS 142.

Selected comments from the evaluations, taken from the responses to what was "most helpful" and "most confusing" reflect that the hands-on practice during the session was most useful. A frequent response to "What was most confusing?" is "Nothing was confusing." An occasional student will comment "The presentation before we worked was very long and boring." Some of the most positive responses to "What was most helpful?" have been: "Judith making the library seem more down to earth." "Before the instruction I was scared to use the library. Now I do feel more comfortable finding information." "I already knew how to use DataQ I a little, and the session really strengthened what I already knew." "Everything was well-explained."

Comments from faculty members on the "Faculty Evaluation of Library Instruction" forms [E] are very positive. They like the hands-on approach for their students. Nearly all of them wrote that the instruction was quite effective for their students. In addition to forms, I have *letters of support/thanks* from a BIS 142 instructor with whom I continue to collaborate each semester, and the Director of Women's Studies, [E] reflecting my teaching strengths. I have also included two *peer evaluations* of my teaching [E].

My effectiveness as a reference librarian is reflected in *support letters* from my colleagues [E], in their comments about my competence. I have scant evidence of student perceptions of my reference service except for the numerous but undocumented verbal "thank yous" and an occasional comment on student evaluations: "The next week when I was at the library she was more than helpful when I couldn't work the InfoTrac" or a *thank you note* such as the one in Appendix D. One BIS 142 instructor wrote, "This helpful attitude of yours obviously continued as many students commented that when they returned to the library, they would seek your help and always receive it."

Conference presentations and publication projects related to teaching
During 1994–95 I presented at two conferences, one at the state level and the other at the national level. These presentations relate to my research interest(s): the research/writing processes of undergraduates, evaluation of instruction, and the teaching portfolio as a means of self-improvement for instruction librarians.

The reception of this program was highly positive. It represents another phase of ongoing collaborative work that began with a team-teaching project in 1991 and progressed to a national presentation at CCCC (Conference on College Composition and Communication) in 1993. My co-authors are English professors, and our collaboration involves an instruction model (for freshmen) that integrates the research and writing processes. [See Appendix F.] We have just signed a book contract for a freshmen-level research and writing textbook based upon this work. [F] Our proposal for a workshop demonstrating this model has been accepted for presentation at the NCTE conference "Global Conversations in Language and Literacy" in Heidelberg, Germany, August 12–14, 1996. [F]

This presentation resulted from my professional reading. Having been inspired by an article from *RQ* by Carole Larson and Laura Dickson (1994), I decided to apply their technique to developing standards for instruction librarians. This breakout session received favorable response as is reflected in the *letter* summarizing the evaluations. [F] I used the results from the trial run with the reference department to devise a *form for peer evaluation* [E], which I used to evaluate my teaching. I continue to work with the information that I received through this breakout session at ALA in an article.

In May 1994 I co-presented a session on the teaching portfolio at the 1994 LOEX Conference. This presentation will be published as part of the proceedings, which are expected to be published within the next year.

Workshops and consultancies
As a result of our 1994 LOEX presentation, a librarian colleague and I received an invitation to serve as paid consultants and co-presenters of a workshop on the teaching portfolio for academic librarians at Miami University in Oxford, Ohio in November 1994. An intensive two-day program included presenting the concept of the portfolio, interactive sessions that enabled participants to begin work on a portfolio, and individual consulting sessions with librarians, guiding and critiquing their portfolios. [E] A *summary of evaluations* for the introductory session reflects the positive reception of the workshop. [E]

The LOEX session also resulted in an invitation to present a workshop on the teaching portfolio for the MLA BI Roundtable on March 29, 1996 at Olivet College. [E]

Teaching Improvement

To develop my professional competence, I have attended several *workshops to increase my skills* (with the WWW and software programs) as well as faculty development programs to get ideas for new teaching strategies. [See list in Appendix E.] Other professional development activities included attending programs related to instruction and reference at the Annual and Midwinter ALA conferences. I also participated in a program sponsored by the Michigan Library Association's BI Roundtable, featuring Carol Kuhlthau, well-known for her study of the research process. [E] Attendance at this workshop specifically supported my teaching approaches and work on the textbook project.

Goals

1. Continue discussion and writing of a document outlining the instruction program for the University Libraries, incorporating the work of the University Libraries' Task Force on Information Literacy.

2. Encourage more widespread evaluation of instruction sessions.

3. Discuss and plan how to provide effective instructional support for the World Wide Web.

4. Provide more opportunities (such as brown bag lunches) for instruction librarians to exchange ideas about teaching.

5. Design a web-based tutorial to provide basic instruction for on and off campus students.

6. Continue to redesign ENGL 105 and BIS 142 instruction to make it more effective and interactive. Incorporate an introduction to the World Wide Web.

Appendices

Appendix A: Teaching and Reference Responsibilities: Job Description, Statistics
Appendix B: Instructional Materials: Handouts, Instruction Plans
Appendix C: Student Evaluations
Appendix D: Student Products
Appendix E: Peer Evaluation
Appendix F: Teaching Improvement Activities

TEACHING PORTFOLIO
Indira Chatterjee
Department of Electrical Engineering
University of Nevada, Reno
Spring 1996

Table of Contents

1) Teaching Responsibilities, Methods, and Philosophy
2) Course Projects and Assignments
3) Student Evaluations
4) Teaching Awards
5) Teaching Workshops Attended
6) Research on My Teaching
7) Letters of Recommendation for Students
8) Goals
9) Appendices

Teaching Responsibilities, Methods, and Philosophy

I teach two classes per semester. I have taught classes at the sophomore level (EE201, Introduction to Network Analysis, a class taken by all engineering majors), junior level (EE351, Electric and Magnetic Fields, a required class for all EE majors), senior/graduate level (EE451/651, Distributed Systems and Antenna Design and EE452/652, Microwave Engineering, both of which are senior technical electives, which can also be taken by graduate students) and graduate level (EE79lj (new number EE751), Antenna Theory and Design, a class which I introduced into the graduate curriculum). I also have supervised two laboratory classes, one at the sophomore level (EE200, which is a co-requisite to EE201) and the other at the senior/graduate level (EE450/650, which is a co-requisite to EE452/652). I supervise the teaching assistants who teach the labs, and as often as possible make sure I go to the lab while the class is in session to see how the students are performing. I helped design and set up the experiments and projects for these labs. I also taught two weeks of a Biomedical Instrumentation course (EE426/626), one week of Materials (EE202) as a guest lecturer, and gave a guest lecture in the Introduction to Electrical Engineering (EE101) course. I taught during the Spring 1992 semester a class which was transmitted by television link to one of the local industries (EE351). Course syllabi for all the courses are included as Appendix A.

Every semester I volunteer to teach the EIT (Engineer-in-training) review class in Electric Circuits. Letters acknowledging my effort and some student comments are included in Appendix B.

Several M.S. and Ph.D. students have been and are presently under my supervision. In addition, I serve on the thesis and dissertation committees of several EE, Chemical/Metallurgical Engineering, Physics, Computer Science, and College of Education students. Reprints of five published papers are included as Appendix C. These papers resulted from work that two graduate students and three undergraduates did under my supervision on separate projects. All three undergraduates went on to do graduate work, one at the University of California, Davis, the second at the University of Utah, Salt Lake City, and the third here at the University of Nevada, Reno. I believe that my involving these undergraduates in research was a crucial factor in making them go on to graduate work. The past two summers (1994, 1995) I was research mentor to two undergraduate students under the EPSCoR Women in Science Undergraduate Summer Fellowship program. I believe I am one of the few faculty in the College of Engineering to involve undergraduates in research projects.

Every semester, students register for independent study courses under my supervision. In the past I have also served as undergraduate advisor to over 20 students and supervised several honors projects. At present I am undergraduate advisor to all Freshmen, Sophomore, and Transfer Electrical Engineering students.

As a teacher I believe that I should never intimidate a student or talk down to him or her. I feel that a teacher never stops learning and that by teaching a course one learns more and more. I would like my students to say that they have learned a lot in my classes, that I care about the students, that I know the subject well, and that I am one of the best teachers they have had. It is important to me because I work hard at being a good teacher, and I do my best to get across the subject matter in a way that the student is not intimidated, but rather finds it fun to learn.

I always make sure that my lectures are very well-prepared and organized. I firmly believe that a disorganized lecture is very distracting to the students. I encourage questions during the lecture and never put down a student for a silly question. Patience is my motto. I encourage interaction both in the classroom and outside. I ask students a lot of questions as I lecture and encourage answers and discussion. I believe this makes them think and keeps up their attention; otherwise a lot of students get completely lost. Since most engineering courses are design and problem oriented, I place as much emphasis on working problems as on the theory. Many practical examples are incorporated into the lectures at appropriate places.

I try to use simple language to explain difficult concepts and emphasize the basics. My philosophy in the required classes is not to overload the students with complex information, but rather to reiterate over and over that the basics are important. They can then go out and read to find other information they may need. All concepts are illustrated by problems and wherever possible by examples from the real world.

I also use video and laboratory demonstrations to illustrate key concepts, since the courses I teach have concepts which are sometimes very abstract and hard for the students to comprehend. I have collected a lot of software packages, which are made accessible to the students. Homework assignments are given involving these software packages and the students have found them very useful in illustrating abstract concepts. I bring into the classroom devices, materials, etc., which we are going to discuss on that day so that they actually can see them instead of just resorting to textbook pictures. I sometimes use transparencies in addition to the blackboard to supplement complicated equations, diagrams, etc. I try to always be available to the students for discussion, help with class material, etc.

In addition to the above, I have for the past three years conducted a half-day session on antennas with groups of high school students for Science and Technology Day. In this session, graduate students and I have lectured to them on antennas and then guided them through some interesting antenna measurements and graphics. The program for Science and Technology Day is included as Appendix D.

I have also lectured to freshman honors students at a retreat. A letter from the Dean of the College of Engineering acknowledging this is included as Appendix E. I have taken part in several early outreach programs on campus, and letters describing my involvement are in Appendix E.

I stay current in my discipline by reading the appropriate journals, attending conferences, and presenting papers on my research at these conferences. Every now and then something I have heard at a conference will seem appropriate to introduce into my classes. Reading journals also helps me introduce new topics into my classes.

Course Projects and Assignments
In the course EE351, the students use a software package called CSP (Charge Simulation Program) to model various problems and to get a better insight into the subject. They work independently and write a short paragraph in each problem trying to explain the results. It makes them think about how the subject matter that they have learned in class and from the textbook applies to real problems.

In the course EE451/651, the students use three different software packages, EMWAVES, MININEC, and PC ANTENNA DESIGN. Once again these software packages are used to give them a better feel for a difficult and abstract subject. They also use them to design and test various antennas. I also show them video demonstrations of experiments which help illustrate important concepts and present some experiments in our laboratory. In the course EE452/652, several software packages are used by the students (PUFF, WGVMAP, LIBRA, HFSS) to aid in testing their designs, and to illustrate difficult concepts. The students also each research a particular topic and write a paper, as well as make a presentation on the topic in front of their classmates. They are graded on the presentation, visual aids, etc. The idea here is to improve their communication skills, which is a very important skill required by employers. Guest lecturers are brought in from local industry to talk about real-world practical subjects they are involved in from their industry. I also arrange field trips to local industry so that students can see some of the material they learn about in the classroom actually being used.

In the course EE791j (new number EE751), a lot of emphasis is placed on design, using software to design, analyze, and test the design. A series of computational exercises have been designed (as part of an Instructional Enhancement Grant) which are assigned to the students throughout the semester. Students also have the opportunity to make antenna pattern measurements in the state-of-the-art anechoic chamber facility in the Engineering Lab Center. All this is geared towards giving the students a practical experience in the classroom, so that they are prepared to work in industry.

Examples of term papers, computer assignments, and special assignments are included as Appendix F.

Student Evaluations

Some of the comments made by students in my classes are as follows:

- Dr. Chatterjee's mastery of the subject matter is outstanding. To take a course like this from an instructor of her caliber is an honor and a privilege.

- Dr. Chatterjee is extremely well organized; her lectures are excellent.

- Provides a lot of examples and videos explaining the course's problems and methods.

- Took the time out of the lecture to answer all the "dumb questions" we always have.

- Dr. Chatterjee has done a lot of things well. She was always helpful and encouraging inside and outside of class. For an engineering student, myself in particular, this extra help is very important. Also, Dr. Chatterjee never intimidated students. There was no such thing as a stupid question as far as she was concerned.

- Dr. Chatterjee is a very good teacher. She explains the material as clearly as possible considering the complexity of the material. Her tests are fair and complete.

Student evaluation summaries for all the courses I have taught since 1988 are included in Appendix G.

Overall instructor ratings for all courses I have taught
(highest rating being 5)

Course Number	Semester	Overall rating	Avg. rating of all similar level classes in the department
EE751	Fall 1995	4.83	4.17
EE451/651	Fall 1995	4.58	4.17
EE452/652	Spring 1995	4.50	4.29
EE351	Spring 1995	4.47	4.01
EE451/651	Fall 1994	4.81	4.20
EE351	Spring 1994	4.37	4.32
EE452/652	Spring 1994	4.75	4.32
EE351	Spring 1993	4.68	3.83
EE452/652	Spring 1993	5.00	4.26
EE452/652	Spring 1992	4.33	4.28
EE201	Spring 1992	4.32	3.72
EE451/651	Fall 1991	4.43	4.25
EE791j	Fall 1991	4.50	4.25
EE201	Spring 1991	4.26	**
EE351	Spring 1991	4.45	**
EE452/652	Fall 1990	4.83	**
EE201	Fall 1990	3.97	**
EE451/651	Spring 1990	4.06	**
EE351	Spring 1990	3.89	**
EE351	Fall 1989	4.52	**
EE791j	Fall 1989	4.50	**
EE212	Spring 1989	4.25	**
EE355	Spring 1989	4.58	**
EE212	Fall 1988	3.69	**
EE355	Fall 1988	4.50	**

**Not available

I have also received unsolicited letters from some of my students about my teaching. One student made this statement: "Your teaching was easy to follow, made me want to learn, and want to get the answers right. Hence I did well, had a good time, and now still remember almost everything out of your class."

Teaching Awards

In 1992 I was chosen as one of the five finalists for the Distinguished Teaching Award of the University of Nevada, Reno. In 1993 and 1994 I was chosen as runner-up for this same award. In 1995 I was awarded the F. Donald Tibbitts Memorial Distinguished Teacher Award of the University of Nevada, Reno. Letters of support from the chair of the Awards Committee and the Dean of the College of Engineering are included as Appendix H. A quote from the letter written by the Dean of Engineering: "To be recognized by your peers is a high honor indeed. We are very fortunate to have a teacher of your caliber in the college, and I want you to know how much your abilities and talent are appreciated." I am also in the 1994 Who's Who Among America's Teachers. Letters informing me of this are included in Appendix H.

Teaching Workshops Attended

I attended the CAEME (Center for Computer Applications in Electromagnetics Education) workshop on Effective Integration of Computers and Software Tools in Education at the University of Utah, Salt Lake City in August 1992. The program is included in Appendix I. It was conducted by the CAEME NSF Center. Several lectures were held on the implementation of EM software into the classroom as well as multimedia techniques. As a result of this workshop I have implemented a lot of software in my classes, video demonstrations, etc. I receive all updated software and information from the center, and these give me new ideas of what to do to make my lectures more interesting. Examples of student assignments using these software packages are included as Appendix I.

Research on My Teaching

I obtained an Instructional Enhancement Grant from the University of Nevada, Reno during the Spring 1993 semester. This involved designing computational exercises in antenna design and analysis for use in two courses (EE451/651 and EE751). Since neither of these courses have labs associated with them, I thought it would be a good experience to incorporate computational projects involving the subject matter at various appropriate places in the courses. As a result of this grant, a senior EE undergraduate student was assigned the designed exercises as an independent study to see how he would carry them out and to get his feedback on them. He completed it during the summer of 1993 and said it was a really good experience and that he learned a lot from the exercises. These exercises have since been incorporated into my courses. The report submitted to the Office of Academic Affairs on this grant activity is included as Appendix J. I will be presenting a paper on the results of incorporating these exercises into the two courses at the Frontiers in Education conference to be held at Salt Lake City, Utah in November 1996. The abstract is attached as Appendix K. I have applied for an extension of the above grant. This extension would involve updating the exercises to incorporate the latest version of the software and to include new exercises pertaining to the personal communications industry.

Letters of Recommendation for Students
I have written many letters for students to help them obtain scholarships, jobs, internships, etc. I believe these letters show my commitment to helping these students. Such letters helped one student go to Oxford University, England for graduate study on a full stipend, another to participate in a summer internship at Oakridge National Labs, and several students have received admission and stipends for graduate study at well-known universities, etc. A sampling of such letters is included in Appendix L.

Goals
My immediate goal is to work on updating the exercises devised using the Instructional Enhancement Grant so that a new version of the software can be used. New exercises will also be designed.

My long-term goal is to apply in a couple of years to the National Science Foundation for a grant to involve undergraduates in research.

Appendices
Appendix A: Course syllabi
Appendix B: EIT letters and student comments
Appendix C: Reprints
Appendix D: Science and Technology Day Program
Appendix E: Freshman Honors lecture and Early Outreach letters of support
Appendix F: Examples of term papers, special and computer assignments
Appendix G: Student evaluations
Appendix H: Letters of support from the Dean of Engineering and chair of the Teaching Awards Committee, Who's Who Among America's Teachers letters
Appendix I: CAEME Workshop Program and examples of student assignments using software
Appendix J: Report on Instructional Enhancement Grant
Appendix K: Abstract of the paper to be presented at the Frontiers in Education
Appendix L: Letters of recommendation for students

TEACHING PORTFOLIO
Diane M. Clark
Department of Music
Rhodes College
Spring 1995

Table of Contents
1) Statement of Teaching Responsibilities
2) Statement of Teaching Philosophy and Goals
3) Description of Methods Used in Specific Courses
4) Description of Curricular Revisions and Steps Taken to Improve My Teaching
5) Peer Evaluation of My Teaching
6) Student Evaluation of My Teaching
7) Audio and Video Tapes of My Instruction and of Student Performances
8) Samples of Student Work
9) Successful Students
10) Other Evidence of Good Teaching
11) Future Teaching Goals
12) Appendices

Statement of Teaching Responsibilities
My primary teaching responsibility is in the area of applied voice, and this is the one subject I have taught in every semester of my twenty years at Rhodes College. Applied voice involves giving voice lessons to individual students, one on one. My students include music majors, music minors, and general students. Students may be in my voice studio from one to eight semesters. In addition to their individual 45-minute or one-hour lessons, I meet my students weekly in a one-hour class session entitled "Voice Performance Laboratory." This is a voluntary time commitment on my part, and I receive no additional teaching credit or pay for it. However, I consider it an extremely valuable part of the teaching of applied voice. Students in applied voice earn one or two credit hours a semester. Approximately one-third of my teaching load (eight students) each semester is devoted to applied voice, and I usually carry a one- or two-student overload (compensated on a per-student basis).

My additional teaching responsibilities in 1994–1995 included courses in Music and Wellness, The Language of Music, Effective Public Speaking, the Silk Stockings women's barbershop ensemble, and the multi-course Senior Experience. In 1995–96 my responsibilities included courses entitled Learning to Read Music, Developing the Speaking Voice, Beginning Voice Class, men's and women's barbershop ensembles, and the Senior Experience. (See Appendix A for more complete information about the courses I teach.)

Statement of Teaching Philosophy and Goals

I consider myself more fortunate than most college professors for two reasons. My first career was as a church educator, and my main job was to teach others to teach. I spent six years full-time and many years part-time in that work, and I feel that I gained a firm foundation in the principles and techniques of good teaching. Secondly, both my master's and doctoral degrees are in the field of vocal pedagogy. That has certainly given me an advantage in that I specifically studied the process of teaching my principal subject area.

My lifelong study of vocal performing has led me to the pursuit of several personal goals, and I try to model for and share with my students the importance of these five challenges:

1) developing one's creative capacity and particular talents

2) nurturing aesthetic sensitivity

3) acquiring skills for effective communication of ideas and feelings

4) achieving a sense of wholeness or balance in one's life

5) taking risks in order to grow and stretch one's boundaries

I believe that these five themes run throughout all my teaching, regardless of the subject area. For example, my course on Music and Wellness emphasizes the importance of music as a tool in promoting physical, emotional, mental, and spiritual balance or harmony in one's life. This same balance is important in developing the ability to sing well or to speak well. Likewise, one must nurture one's creative capacity, whether one is learning to interpret an art song sensitively, persuade an audience through a rousing speech, compose a piece of music, or discover ways that music can help people suffering from chronic pain or daily stress.

Description of Methods Used in Specific Courses
Applied voice
The purpose of applied vocal study is for the student to improve his/her skill in singing and to gain knowledge and appreciation of a selected portion of vocal music literature (art song, opera, music theatre, sacred music, etc.). As I assist the student in working on these tasks, I also have the important goal of helping him to become his own voice teacher; i.e., to become his own best critic and guide in vocal development. I encourage students to stretch their knowledge by exploring literature that is new to them, and I encourage risk taking by having them perform in public as frequently as possible. I stress that singing is both a musical and a dramatic art, and we work to develop creative abilities and communication skills in both these areas.

The language of music

This course exposes students to the basic rudiments of music theory, covering vocabulary and concepts in rhythm, melody, and harmony at the beginning level. Students learn via lecture, discussion, music writing assignments, and computerized instruction.

Music and wellness

This topics course focuses on the use of music as a tool in achieving health and wellness. It covers three main areas: music therapy, music medicine, and music in general wellness. Instructional methods used are lecture, discussion, readings, written assignments, exercises with music, and an individual special project.

Effective public speaking

This course focuses on helping students develop skills in oral communication. Students make weekly speeches in a variety of formats and receive constructive criticism on each presentation.

Silk Stockings

This ensemble, established in 1994–95, provides an opportunity for women students to perform music in the barbershop style. Performances are given on campus and in the Memphis community.

(See Appendix B for a more complete description of courses; selected course syllabi, which include general information, course objectives, course requirements, and an explanation of the grading system used; and additional course materials.)

Description of Curricular Revisions and Steps Taken to Improve My Teaching

Applied voice

For the first time this year I was able to use the video camera in the voice performance lab to allow students to learn by seeing and hearing their own performances.

Music and wellness

This course was taught for the first time, and I learned from student evaluations (complaints!) that I was a bit overzealous in what I expected of students in this course. I asked for a biweekly report summarizing all assignments read and all activities conducted in class. This proved to be a tremendous amount of writing (and a lot to grade!). I certainly hope to offer the course again in future years, and I will make numerous revisions based on the very helpful evaluative comments that students wrote as a part of their final examination. (See Appendix D.) I will ask for shorter summary reports that give the students a chance to choose the topics that intrigue them the most.

The language of music

Having conferred at length with the Dean of Academic Affairs in the spring of 1994 about ways to improve my teaching, I followed his advice in this course by redesigning the course syllabus to make the course objectives more detailed and clear. (See Appendix B, Syllabi, Music 103-1, S94 and S95.) For example, instead of this objective, "You will be able to demonstrate an elementary aural, visual, and kinesthetic facility with the fundamental elements of music," there are now nine specific objectives which specify work with scales, intervals, triads, seventh chords, etc. I also made a concerted attempt to make tests and home-work assignments more reasonable by assigning fewer worksheets, allowing students to pledge a minimum time spent if they were unable to complete a section on the Practica Musica computerized instruction program, and asking fewer questions on tests.

Silk Stockings

There were eighteen women in this brand new group in the fall semester of 1994. At the end of the first semester, after receiving the students' comments and suggestions, I discussed these ideas with the eight women who made up the ensemble for the spring 1995 term. I allowed this smaller group to establish their own rules and policies and to have input into the selection of repertory, as they had requested. This seemed to keep things running more smoothly during the spring term. (See Appendix B, Syllabi, Music 197-3, F94 & S95.)

Effective public speaking

Again, attempting to follow the dean's suggestion about not expecting too much from students, I redesigned the course syllabus to allow for fewer new speeches, and I made one assignment optional. (See Appendix B, Syllabi, ID100-1, S93 & S95.) I also took lessons from Lemuel Russell in the Media Center to learn how to operate the video equipment, so that I could more easily use that equipment in this class, as well as in other performance situations.

General

For several years I have participated enthusiastically in campus opportunities to improve my teaching. Two years ago I attended two workshops on Writing Across the Curriculum and incorporated a great many ideas from that experience into my various courses; e.g., the theory class assignment to explain a concept to a young child, the one-minute paper administered at the end of a class to check students' mastery of the concepts covered that day, and free-writing exercises to stimulate thinking on a particular subject. (See Appendix F for samples.) I have attended numerous sessions in our Rhodes Topics in Teaching Forum and several workshops sponsored by our Computer Center. I attended the Portfolio Work-shop at Rhodes in May of 1995. (See Appendix H for documentation.)

Since September 1994, I have participated in the *Vocalist*, an Internet discussion list for persons interested in singing and related topics. I have learned a great deal from the 600 professional and amateur singers, speech therapists, medical doctors, and other knowledgeable vocalists who participate in this forum, and I have shared much of this information with my voice students. I participate regularly in the activities of the National Association of Teachers of Singing, including reading the *NATS Journal* and adjudicating in local and regional student auditions. In June 1995, I attended a seminar on music technology in Indianapolis, IN, sponsored by the College Music Society, and participated in workshops at the Institute for Music, Health, and Education in Boulder, CO, where I am a faculty member.

Peer Evaluation of My Teaching

In the Music Department, faculty members are constantly treated to the results of one another's teaching, as we listen to students perform regularly in recitals and in applied music examinations. (See Appendix C for applied examination adjudication forms of my students.) I was particularly gratified by recent comments from faculty following the senior presentation of one of my students who had struggled quite a bit during her four years of study. One professor wrote, "It was really an amazing performance in every way. She deserves an A+ ... You, my dear, are to be congratulated for shining up a diamond in the rough." Another wrote, "Congratulations to you for being so patient and supporting of her; in fact, we all had something to do with the progress, but the applied teacher is in a more critical role down the stretch." (See Appendix C for complete copies of these e-mail messages.)

Each spring I send singers to the student vocal auditions sponsored by the National Association of Teachers of Singing, where they are adjudicated by other voice teachers. My students generally receive high grades and comments such as "Thank you for a very well-prepared audition!" "Very musical singing," "You seem to have a good understanding of your text and are showing that— good," "Nice work and feeling for the music," "Voice clear and supported, beautiful, focused," "I heard you last year—much improved! Bravo!" (See Appendix C for NATS adjudication sheets.)

Several years ago I presented a session in the Rhodes Topics in Teaching Forum on "Vocal Tips for Effective Lecturing." About two dozen faculty attended that session, and several expressed interest in learning more about good voice usage. The following year I offered a free one-hour coaching session to any interested faculty member, and had seventeen takers representing all four divisions in the college. They had the following responses following their sessions with me: "I have been particularly aware in class of the need to be animated, to surprise the students, to do something to get their attention, and I believe I have made some progress in that direction" (English); "What a wonderful, encouraging teacher you are. I had a splendid time and gained so much useful knowledge (and know-how) during our session" (French); "Diane, many thanks for the best hour I've spent in at least three years here. I am certainly putting my best voice forward—or at least will keep trying" (Japanese); "Thanks, I notice a difference already. I had sunk to a low point in many ways before our meeting, and now I do feel rejuvenated, confident, and enthusiastic" (Biology). (See Appendix C for additional peer evaluations.)

Student Evaluation of My Teaching

I have always asked students for their comments on my courses, because I am interested in learning how to do a better job as a teacher. When I have erred as a teacher, it has always been on the side of expecting too much of students rather than too little, and this has occurred because I personally have most appreciated those teachers who have demanded. Recently I received a letter from a former student telling me how glad he was that I had treated him that way in college and how he wished someone was holding his feet to the fire in the same way now!

Students in my Music and Wellness class made these statements about their experiences in the course: a) "Music has always made me feel good, but now I know specific ways I can utilize it for my benefit. Through toning, guided imagery, chant, musical biofeedback, entrainment, and many others, I can relax, focus, express emotions, heal myself, and move towards a higher level of wellness. I can also recommend and defend music intelligently as an important addition to any activity or profession"; b) "The exercises with music as well as the freewriting activities have helped me to journey inwardly and return having made consequential discoveries about my mental, physical, and spiritual being, my relations with others, and my connection with the world around me"; c) "In five years, I believe I will notice music being incorporated into the medical field. Its healing qualities lead me to believe that it will become a main aspect in my life. I will sing to my children, and I will tell people about the effects of music on patients with diseases."

I am making a sincere effort to learn from those students who take the time to write thoughtful and candid remarks. Appendix D contains a variety of kinds of student evaluations of the various courses that I teach.

Audio and Video Tapes of My Instruction
and of Student Performances

Appendix E contains a videotape of my instruction in The Language of Music class in the spring of 1994. Also included are videotapes of students in Effective Public Speaking for several semesters and the Silk Stockings concert in November of 1994. Audio tapes include my faculty recital of 1990 featuring the compositions of eight of my vocal students, the Voice Division's November 1994 presentation of Mozart's *The Marriage of Figaro* with my students singing the leading roles of Figaro and Susannah, and a junior voice recital (spring 1995) by bass-baritone James Harr, music major.

Samples of Student Work

Appendix F includes graded tests and homework papers from The Language of Music course as well as samples of original art songs written by voice students.

Successful Students

One of the joys of teaching applied music is watching the later successes of one's students in their various fields of endeavor. I am particularly proud of my former Texas Tech student, soprano Mary Jane Johnson, who won the first Luciano Pavarotti competition and has for the past several years enjoyed an international career in opera, singing in such great houses as La Scala, the Paris Opera, and the Santa Fe Opera. She appeared in the Rhodes McCoy Visiting Artist Series in 1991. One of my former Rhodes students, Mario Ramos, heads the Honolulu Opera and formerly managed the Fort Worth Opera. Several of my students have gone on to earn degrees at prestigious graduate schools such as Indiana University, Northwestern University, and Cincinnati Conservatory. Others are successful in theatre, teaching, and church music. (See Appendix G for additional information about student accomplishments.)

Other Evidence of Good Teaching

I am often invited to teach in the Memphis community, particularly in the area of developing public speaking skills. I have presented seminars for Nationwide Insurance, Piggly Wiggly, and the Executive Women of Memphis, and have done extended courses for the Junior League of Memphis and Nationwide Insurance. (See Appendix H for additional information.)

Currently I am education chair for the Greater Memphis Chorus of Sweet Adelines International, where I instruct the ensemble in vocal techniques and music theory. (See Appendix H for sample materials.)

Future Teaching Goals

In the recent past I have been concerned about the perceptions that some students have had about my attitudes toward them and about my teaching approaches. I believe that students feel best about a learning experience when they believe that they have some control over how things go. Thus I am making a concerted effort, through such means as the periodic one-minute papers and both mid-course and end-of-term evaluations, to seek ways to solicit student input into course design and execution. I am trying to discover ways to give students more options or choices within the framework of my courses. I am attempting to view things more from their perspective and to adjust my expectations to a more reasonable level.

I am very concerned about learning more about the use of technology in teaching and am spending a great deal of time this summer in attending workshops to help with this. I hope to develop ways to use technology in all my courses, and this will be quite a challenge in certain areas.

I hope to increase the use of video equipment with my voice students so that they can have more frequent opportunities to learn by seeing themselves in action. I plan to implement the idea of having each voice student maintain his own videotape whereon he can record his progress throughout the various semesters of his vocal study. I want to offer video opportunities to students in my performing ensembles as well.

I am in the process of designing a new course entitled "Developing the Speaking Voice" to be offered in the spring of 1996. This course will be a 3-hour course designed to incorporate content from my previous 1-hour course in "Effective Public Speaking" and also from the Theatre Department's 3-hour course entitled "Voice and Diction for the Actor." The course will be designed to meet the needs of theatre students, voice students, and general students as they seek to develop their oral communication skills.

Whenever possible I read books on human behavior in an attempt to learn better people skills. I will continue to strive to find more positive ways of interacting with my students, for I know that people learn more effectively when they feel affirmed. One of my recent readings stated that the way to get people to do what you want them to is to find out what *they* want and help them get it. Then they are more than happy to do what you want. I believe this wisdom can be applied very well to the teacher-student relationship, and I plan to explore this concept as fully as possible.

Appendices

Appendix A: List of my teaching responsibilities in 1994–95 and 1995–96

Appendix B: Course descriptions, syllabi, handouts, tests, and other related materials

Appendix C: Peer evaluations of my teaching

Appendix D: Student evaluations of my teaching

Appendix E: Audio and video tapes of my instruction and of student performances

Appendix F: Samples of student work

Appendix G: Information about successful students

Appendix H: Other evidence of good teaching

TEACHING PORTFOLIO
Daria T. Cronic
Department of Foundations and Special Education
Clemson University
Spring 1996

Table of Contents
1) Statement of Pedagogical Philosophy
2) Statement of Teaching Responsibilities and Objectives
3) Record of Supervision of Student Teachers
4) Description of Teaching Methodologies
5) Syllabi, Exams, Handouts, and Workbooks From Courses Taught
6) Methods to Motivate Students
7) Descriptions of Efforts to Improve My Teaching
8) Student Evaluation Data From Previous Courses Taught
9) Measures of Student Achievement
10) Future Teaching Goals
11) Appendices

Statement of Pedagogical Philosophy
Learning is the empowering process of adapting to our environment in such a way that through personal growth and exploration, the learner develops necessary skills for independent living at a level of his or her own choosing. It is individual and personal and should be available to all prospective learners. The process and outcome of learning are freedom to choose to succeed, to choose one's own pace and mode of learning, and to accept the consequences.

My role as an educator is to develop the self-confidence of the learner and to motivate and challenge him to access learning, to develop problem solving skills and self-advocacy skills, to practice and master these skills in a safe environment, and to productively employ his skills. In other words, education enables the learner to take responsibility for his own learning and living through the guidance of a mentor and a facilitator.

I am passionate about setting goals for oneself. I often ask students how they perceive themselves. I am interested in their relationship to their environments, to themselves, and to their performance or outcomes. One of my favorite lessons is enlightening a student to the power of his thoughts and his self-determination. Once the learner realizes that he is in control of his future, I encourage him to set forth the necessary effort to achieve his goals.

With learning comes growth and change. With growth and change come risk-taking. Many learners lack the confidence to step outside their comfort zone. It is my responsibility to encourage them to take necessary risks in a controlled environment and to be available to share their successes and failures. Part of the beauty of failure is learning to monitor and adjust to develop another innovative way to gain the desired result. When learners see failures as opportunities for innovation, they are more likely to take calculated heuristic risks in their growth processes.

Statement of Teaching Responsibilities and Objectives

In addition to the rigorous responsibility of supervising student teachers (described below with details in Appendix A), I teach undergraduate and graduate education majors from all disciplines in ED 471/671: Introduction to the Exceptional Learner. Sometimes there are students from the Calhoun Honors College in the class, and I will individualize special projects for them as their course of study is more rigorous than that of the average college student. I have taught three semesters of this class while I was a full-time doctoral student carrying at least 12–16 hours each semester. The classes ranged in size from 36 to 52 students.

In teaching the Introduction to the Exceptional Learner class, required of all education majors at Clemson, my objective is to give my college students a broad overview of the variety of characteristics of students with special needs and how to include them in a variety of academic settings. My personal goal is to plant a seed of compassion and collaboration for students who have special needs within my college students. A tertiary goal is to offer the opportunity to become more familiar with the needs of students with special needs through dual certification.

This class is designed to develop tolerance for learners whose needs are different from those of the average learner. This tolerance is modeled by me, and an informal, hands-on, professional development throughout my teaching acquaints the learners with characteristics of students they will encounter in their own classroom situations. Evidence of the effectiveness of my methodology is suggested by student evaluation and written comments collated in Appendix D. This course will provide a survey of topics related to the nature, cause, and remediation of exceptional children's disabilities. Students will become aware of the history and definitions of each major disability. Students will become familiar with current approaches to identification, assessment, and intervention used to maximize the exceptional learner's abilities. Upon meeting all the course requirements, students will have acquired a knowledge of:

1) History of special education

2) Legislation and litigation surrounding special education

3) Main provisions of P.L. 94-142 and its amendments

4) Placement and service options for exceptional children

5) Strategies and approaches, including technological adaptations, for serving special needs students

6) Family dynamics and exceptionality

7) Early childhood special education

8) Definitions, causes, characteristics, and interventions in the following categories of exceptionality:
   a. Mental retardation
   b. Learning disabilities
   c. Behavior disorders
   d. Communication disorders
   e. Sensory impairments
   f. Physical and other health impairments
   g. Severe handicaps

More specific information about the course is included in the syllabus and other material evidence in Appendix B.

Another course which I have been privileged to teach is the ED 301: Principles of American Education. This course is a foundations requirement for all students. In this course, students are reminded that the seeds of their professional demeanor and reputation begin at this time. High expectations are communicated in terms of attendance, class participation, research projects, group enrichment projects, and a variety of testing situations. Students are expected to keep abreast of current trends in education by discussing educational topics found in periodicals and on local news. Outcomes for these students are varied. They must work within a variety of groupings to produce lessons and presentations. Some of these presentations are planned while others are extemporaneous. It is important that these students develop skills in planning lessons and delivering presentations. It is equally important that they develop opinions about education based on research from their presentations and readings so that they will be informed educators of the future. The final outcome for the course is the submission of a two-page philosophy of education based on the issues and trends we have discussed throughout the course. More specific information about the course is included in the syllabus and other material evidence in Appendix B.

A third course which I have taught is ED 701: Theories of Educational Psychology. This master's level course is designed to create reflective classroom technicians. Upon completion of this course, teachers use the technologies of classical, operant, and cognitive theories to better design a motivational learning environment for their classrooms.

Record of Supervision of Student Teachers

In the Spring of 1994, I supervised six student teachers while taking 13 hours of my doctoral program. This experience was so successful that I continued to supervise student teachers through my three years at Clemson University. In the Fall of 1994, I supervised 13 student teachers while taking 16 doctoral hours, and in the Spring of 1995, I supervised 14 student teachers while carrying 16 doctoral course hours. In the Fall of 1995, I supervised 12 student teachers and 12 student teachers in the Spring. During this period of supervision, I was a visiting lecturer carrying three and four course loads. Note Appendix A for teaching assignments. My duties included collaborating with team members of the Center of Excellence for Rural Special Education, eight on-site visitations, working closely with each student with his teaching and with his various projects (see examples of projects in Appendix A), building rapport with principals and cooperating teachers, collaborating and communicating weekly with cooperating teachers, and administering the APT. I also assessed their performance through a portfolio process (for example of portfolio expectations see Appendix A).

Description of Teaching Methodologies
In my teaching, I use many personal experiences and case studies to make the material practical and relevant. For the same reasons, I invite professionals who specialize in various areas of disability to address the class (see sample syllabus in Appendix B for how I allocate time to guest speakers, an effective tool in expanding students' learning and keeping the pace of the course lively and engaging for the students).

In all classes I teach, the time is spent partly in lecture, partly in answering students' questions, and partly in modeling instructional strategies. Cooperative and collaborative learning are a vital ingredient to the class. Each class is divided into groups of four to six students who are given course topics to research in more depth. The presentation topics coincide with the topics I address and are used for collaboration, problem solving, research to find auxiliary materials (much like situations they will find themselves in as regular educators), and as a review for the tests. Since these students are future teachers, the presentations help them practice their oral communication, organizational, and research skills.

I incorporate personal growth and development in my teaching because I believe that every educator has the responsibility to foster the learner's personal development. Many of the outside assignments incorporate personal and professional growth. See Appendix C for matrix and for service learning project.

I give many handouts, many of which I developed in my own pedagogical practice to help communication and collaboration between regular and special educators. My students will find this helpful when referring students with disabilities and discussing their characteristics with other professionals.

I encourage my students to call me by putting my telephone number on the syllabus. I like a personal connection with them. I want to know if they are not coming to class. Once again, I am modeling a relationship I would like for them to develop with their own students.

Syllabi, Exams, Handouts, and Workbooks From Courses Taught

The syllabi of the courses are contained in Appendix B. They change each time I teach each of the courses. Each time I teach a course, I learn a great deal from my students. Sometimes their gift to me is a new strategy, or topic, or point of view on an issue. Other times their gift to me is to heighten my creativity or awareness, in which case I create a new challenge or project for them. Typically, the syllabus states the objectives, information regarding grading and examinations, outside personal and professional growth assignments and due dates, and weekly section coverage. The syllabus sets the tone for the course and is the first impression the students have of me. I want that impression to be that I am approachable, but my expectations of the professional quality and quantity of their work is high and I expect them to behave as though this is their avocation.

Along with oral explanations of the outside assignments, I give detailed handouts of the outside assignments for the students to refer to later. For examples of my handouts, see Appendix B.

Methods to Motivate Students

I try to motivate my students by exposing them to professionals who are continuing to develop their skills through lifelong learning. See Appendix C for approval to video classroom speaker. With the various reform movements on the horizon, modeling professional development and a commitment to cutting-edge technology are of quantum importance.

I further motivate my students through peer performance with the group presentations. An example of the group presentation grading scale and student performance can be found in Appendix C. They are accountable to their group as well as to the entire class.

I like to give my students a chance to experience new schemas and to challenge their old ones. This will entail taking risks and developing new tolerances for learners who may be foreign to them.

Descriptions of Efforts to Improve My Teaching

I continue to improve my teaching through attendance at conventions, seminars, and workshops as well as making presentations at similar events. Recently, I attended a forum "Showcasing Exemplary Practices" which highlighted many programs across the state of South Carolina addressing the mandates of Act 135. I attended the workshops that pertained to inclusion and transition. Another workshop described the middle school initiative. Sessions addressed collaboration, planning, scheduling, and curriculum and instructional methods that facilitate success in the middle school. Barbara Nielson has held town meetings to enlighten the inhabitants of South Carolina in the area of Goals 2000. I attended a four-day workshop in preparing portfolios. This was not only helpful for my career and evaluation, but it will be useful as I guide my practice teachers through their portfolio development process.

In an effort to improve my teaching, I have made numerous presentations and have submitted my research for publication:

Cronic, D. T. *You Can Do This! Transition Curriculum.* South Carolina Council for Exceptional Children Convention. Greenville, SC, February 1996.

Cronic, D. T. *Portfolio Uses for Professionals.* South Carolina Council for Exceptional Children Regional Behavior Disorders Convention. Myrtle Beach, SC, November 1995.

Cronic, D. T. *Service Learning for Exceptional Populations.* Clemson Service Learning Summer Project. Clemson, SC, August 1995.

Cronic, D. T. *Recontextualizing Teacher Education to Meet Rural Special Education Needs.* National Council for Exceptional Children. Indianapolis, IN, April 1995.

Cronic, D. T. *Procedures for Children with Learning Disabilities: Secondary Strategies for Success.* Presented for teleconference class, ED 475/675. Clemson, SC, April 1995.

Cronic, D. T. *Successful Strategies for Adults with Learning Disabilities.* South Carolina Inter-Agency Adults with Disabilities Conference. Hilton Head Island, SC, March 1995.

Cronic, D. T. *Self-Advocacy: Skills for Successful College Students with Learning Disabilities.* South Carolina State Council for Exceptional Children Convention. Charleston, SC, February 1995.

Cronic, D. T. *You Can Make A Difference: Be a Special Educator.* Teacher Cadet Spring Workshop. Fairfax, SC, March 1994.

Cronic, D. T. *The Rewards of a Career in Special Education.* Teacher Cadet Delegation. Columbia, SC, February 1994.

Cronic, D. T. *The Center of Excellence for the Recruitment, Training, and Retention of Special Educators.* South Carolina State Council for Exceptional Children Convention. Myrtle Beach, SC, February 1994.

Cronic, D. T. *Communicating and Cooperating with Co-workers and Supervisors.* Laurens County Disabilities and Special Needs Board. Laurens, SC, September 1992.

Cronic, D. T., *Helping Students with Disabilities in a College Setting.* Piedmont Technical College, Greenwood, SC, September 1991.

Publications

Cronic, D. T. (1995). The Americans with Disabilities Act: Testing the learning disabled. *Illinois Law School Quarterly, 15* (4), 216–223.

Cronic, D. T. (1995). *Inclusion: Beauty and the Beast.* Clemson Kappan. In press.

I have also written a grant to research and develop inclusion practices. See Appendices E, K, and G for evidence of my teaching development through professional presentations, grants, and publications.

Student Evaluation Data From Previous Courses Taught
My teaching evaluations have consistently been above college and department averages in most areas. See Appendix D for student teachers', students', and classroom teachers' comments and evaluations. The first spring (1994) that I supervised student teachers, I was not in the information loop and frequently, I did not know due dates or evaluation procedures until the last moment. The evaluations for that semester are lower than the other semesters. I have learned to ask many questions, and I have collaborated in developing grading rubrics as well as developing a written syllabus that encompassed the expectations for the entire student teacher block and field experience.

Measures of Student Achievement
There are numerous projects in each class. In the Introduction to the Exceptional Learner, I stress projects which are schema altering and useful in their future classrooms. The service learning project of their choice with individuals who have disabilities allows those students who have never encountered people with disabilities to learn about them as people rather than merely as theoretical entities.

The next project is a matrix (see Appendix C) of differing types of disabilities and various categories that may be helpful in identification and referral in future professional placements.

There are three exams during the semester. The first is a factual recall of the information of the first five chapters. The second has some recall and some practical application. The third exam asks the students to select one question out of six and give characteristics of the learner they selected given the parameter of the question, develop a learning environment that would be conducive for the student given the situation, and justify their treatment of their response. For examples of exams and for selective evidence of student learning in representative copies of student performance on exams, see Appendix D.

Collaborative projects for group presentations bring together students from varying content and learner backgrounds and require them to go beyond the information found in the book. Often more characteristics, current research, and teaching methods are addressed in this presentation. These presentations are useful as a review before the tests and allow the students to demonstrate their organizational and teaching skills.

The workbook selected for the class is to act as a study guide for each chapter. Some students complain that it is redundant and excessive. I am taking this concern under advisement and am collecting data as to the actual efficacy of the assignment. However, grades of students with learning disabilities are greatly enhanced through study skill techniques. Those students in the class who feel they do not need this structure are provided a model that will help learners different from themselves. I collect these workbooks on three different occasions and grade them. The grade adds to their total, and I am once again modeling sound instructional practices for organizational and study skills. This course will help students pass the NTE questions in special education. See Appendix C for representative samples of projects, videos of presentations, workbooks, and other products of student learning.

In accordance with the Principles of American Education, my goal is to help students become contemporary educators through keeping current with issues that are developing as we sit in class. We discuss those issues and study their origins and implications for future educators. This class works collaboratively on several assignments. At the beginning of the semester, the students are asked to fill out an interest inventory and I select students for various group research topics based on their interests or areas in need of development. This research is enrichment for the class. Students are given due dates throughout the semester and are expected to present their topics in innovative and motivational ways. The students are then asked to rate themselves and their group in relation to their collaborative process. The students in the audience are asked to evaluate the content and presentation of the topic. Other collaborative opportunities arise extemporaneously as students develop their skills in organizing and presenting information in a coherent, multimodal fashion.

Students are also expected to be researchers. Each student is required to research a topic of his choice. Once the student has become an expert in his topic area and I have graded his paper, another collaborative opportunity occurs for students to share their research via panel discussions.

A final and pervasive goal of this class is for each student to develop his philosophy of education. This is an ongoing process which culminates in each student writing his philosophy (within two pages) for his final exam.

In the Theories of Educational Psychology, the expected outcomes are for students to teach a concept using motivational methods, to anchor the concept to past experiences, to help the class organize the information, and to make the information meaningful to facilitate recall. Students are videotaped while they are presenting their concept and asked to evaluate their performance in an in-depth evaluation/concept paper. The evaluation consists of reflective teaching in which the students describe techniques that were successful as well as not successful.

They are then required to determine the factors contributing to the success or failure of the lesson and give alternative suggestions for improvement or enrichment.

Future Teaching Goals

The goal foremost in my mind is to teach at the postsecondary level full-time and to supervise student teachers. I prefer working in a collaborative model in which courses have been evaluated and revised based on contemporary professional needs. Too often we compartmentalize the professional skills, and we do not allow the skills to be developed in natural settings as a part of natural consequences. Or in the other extreme, teacher preparation programs often do not model and teach directly the important skills needed by all beginning teachers as they enter the pedagogical world. Within this constraint, I would like to make the Introduction to Exceptional Learners a showcase class that includes a field trip and present it in a more multimedia format with inclusionary outcomes. It is very important to expose all students to the exceptional learner. This exposure should be a positive and informative experience which will be helpful to students as they enter their own classrooms. I will still maintain the personal and hands-on approach to discussing and discovering individuals with disabilities.

As a full-time instructor, I will be developing my classes in other areas. An example of my ability in instructional design can be located in Appendix I. My scope and knowledge in the area of special education is broad, and I could comfortably teach a variety of courses which prepare students to become teachers in this area. As I have accrued 30 hours above the master's level in educational administration, I would be interested in and qualified to teach college courses in educational administration for certification as a public school principal.

As for the student teacher supervision, I would like to refine the model currently in practice at the Center of Excellence in Rural Special Education. For more information about the Center of Excellence, see Appendix F. I feel this model meets the professional needs of the students.

Appendices

Appendix A: Student Teacher Assignments and Evaluation Forms
Appendix B: Course Syllabus and Assignment Instructions
Appendix C: Course Exams and Student Outcomes
Appendix D: Performance Evaluations
Appendix E: Presentations and Workshops Attended
Appendix F: Center of Excellence for Rural Special Education
Appendix G: Publication Letter
Appendix H: Résumé
Appendix I: Instructional Design
Appendix J: Letters of Acknowledgement
Appendix K: Grant

TEACHING PORTFOLIO
Anthony P. Ferzola
Department of Mathematics
University of Scranton
Spring 1996

Table of Contents
1) Teaching Philosophy
2) Teaching Responsibilities and Strategies
3) Evaluation of Teaching
4) Representative Course Syllabi
5) Teaching Improvement
6) Teaching Awards and Honors
7) Teaching Goals
8) Appendices

Teaching Philosophy
My philosophy of teaching is something which has evolved over time. Many components have been consistently a part of this pragmatic philosophy. The parts are not mutually exclusive.

To be a good teacher, one should:

1. *Have a thorough knowledge of the subject area.* You cannot teach something well unless you know it well. A thorough knowledge and experience of the subject of mathematics allows me to see and make connections between seemingly diverse concepts and show these connections to the students.

2. *Make the subject interesting for others so that they are more likely to learn it.* You must be able to communicate your love of your area, and you must strive to engage your students. Genuine enthusiasm for your subject can be infectious. To keep my students interested, I use various teaching strategies (explained in the next section) so the class remains fresh and involved.

3. *Be well-prepared.* A conscientious teacher should be well-prepared. Course syllabi and lectures should be created with clear objectives in mind. At the same time, a good teacher needs to be flexible enough to change the pace of a course and be willing to entertain, in detail, ideas or questions which arise spontaneously in the classroom.

4. *Make the classroom a friendly, nonthreatening learning environment.* I believe that a friendly, nonthreatening classroom maximizes the possibility for real learning to take place. I am sensitive to the fact that students view mathematics as a "hard" subject. I make it clear from the first day that asking questions is a welcome and imperative part of the learning process. I

encourage them to visit my office as often as necessary. I ask students for a mathematics autobiography so as to best tailor my instruction to my audience. All this adds up to the type of supportive environment I believe is needed for students to succeed.

5. *Understand that learning is an active experience.* Students need to be active, not passive, participants in the adventure of learning. I use discovery type problems, as will be elaborated in the next section, to assist students in finding results on their own. I encourage my students *to conjecture* as well as *to prove*.

Teaching Responsibilities and Strategies

My teaching responsibilities are focused on the traditional undergraduate mathematics courses. I have taught fifteen different mathematics courses at the University of Scranton. The courses taught with the greatest frequency are Pre-Calculus (Math 103), Calculus I, II, and III (Math 114, 221, and 222, required of math majors), Business Calculus I and II (Math 107 and Math 108, required of School of Management students), Discrete Structures (Math 142, required of math and computer science majors), and Differential Equations (Math 341, an elective for natural science majors). Another important responsibility of mine is the supervision of mathematics student teachers. By visiting their classes and constructively critiquing the mathematics content of their presentation, I see benefits for myself, my students, and the community-at-large.

I use predominantly a traditional lecture approach in my university classes. I strive to be as prepared as possible so that the goal of the class and the course is always as clear as possible. This is accomplished by knowing your subject area and thinking long and hard on how best to present each topic.

I have successfully employed three different teaching strategies: weekly journal writing, cooperative learning, and computer projects. These techniques are blended; I pick and choose my approach based on my audience and/or the mathematical topic being discussed.

Weekly journals

I find these extremely useful for various reasons. I often ask students to tell me how they are feeling about the course, their performance, or a specific topic. This is an excellent sounding board, especially for those prone to mild mathematics anxiety (e.g., business students). Students are more open with you on paper than in face-to-face conversation.

I often ask students to write about the mathematics they have learned (e.g., "Explain how to find the local extrema of a function to an intelligent high school student."). This forces them to really think about the processes involved ("if you can't explain it, you don't truly understand it"). Such assignments are challenging yet appropriate for all students, especially so for mathematics and mathematics education majors.

Cooperative learning

I believe peer teaching and learning is often more comfortable for students and can give those with particularly short attention spans a much needed alternative. Students have different learning styles; some learn better in a group environment, and the better students can learn by teaching.

I use group learning periodically with topics that lend themselves to this format. For example, when teaching a topic such as integration by simple u-substitution, I assign each of four or five groups a different problem, each one containing a variation on the theme. Then each group designates someone to put the solution on the board. By the end of class, everyone has seen all the variations involved. See the positive comments of colleagues and students below with regard to the success of this activity.

Computer projects

I use the computer algebra system *Maple* in courses with natural science and education students. This is done for three reasons. First, the computer is an important tool for their present and future. Second, with the computer, unwieldy problems can be assigned which would be ridiculous to do by hand. Third, the computer gives me the opportunity to assign nontrivial discovery-type projects. Students discover mathematical results by themselves (the computer is just a tool) which depend on what was done in class but are one step beyond what was done in class. A "lab report" is required where students have to report their results, their conjectures, and their conclusions. The computer projects often involve applications from other disciplines (physics, biology, economics, etc.). Applications and analogies help make the mathematics real and understandable. See the positive student comments below on the usefulness of computer applications.

I believe these strategies enhance my ability to accomplish two goals related to my teaching philosophy. The journals and the group learning help create the friendly learning environment I seek; all three strategies make students active learners. The benefits are found in an often paraphrased Chinese proverb: You tell me, I forget. You show me, I remember. You involve me, I understand.

Evaluation of Teaching

Both orally and in writing, my peers have expressed great satisfaction with my classroom work. Here are some representative comments from my *colleagues:*

"His lecture was carefully aimed at his audience . . . [It] was clear and understandable to the students . . . He was relaxed and his students responded in kind." (Dr. Grainger)

"Your work is no doubt the work of a teacher! Very well-prepared and knowledgeable. I enjoyed the class." (Dr. Otarod)

"Dr. Ferzola is using group study in this class . . . It is a nice and direct way to involve the students. The students also enjoy it!" (Dr. Xiong)

"...the students formed themselves into groups. They were markedly lively now; and as Anthony went round guiding them, responsive to their questions, I noticed every evidence of the students having both understood and enjoyed the work." (Dr. Lakschmanan)

All teaching evaluations by departmental members appear in Appendix A.

The results of the IDEA form (a widely used student rating form) together with the written comments by my students appear in Appendix B. Their observations are overwhelmingly favorable. I have had great rapport with all my classes.

The following table gives a summary of the numerical instructor rating. The columns headed 1 through 5 indicate the number of responses to the item "I rate this instructor an excellent teacher" with 1 = Definitely False, 2 = More False than True, 3 = In Between, 4 = More True than False, and 5 = Definitely True.

Course	1	2	3	4	5	Average
Pre-Calculus Fall 1991	0	0	0	2	8	4.80
Business Calculus II Fall 1992	0	0	2	7	15	4.54
Calculus I Fall 1996	0	0	0	5	14	4.74
Discrete Structures Fall 1992	0	0	1	4	12	4.65

Here are some sample *student* comments:

"Dr. Ferzola is an excellent teacher who thoroughly explains the material and then fairly tests students on it. I have never understood anything mathematical so well." (Calculus I)

"...In addition, he told a bit of 'math history,' which was very interesting. The computer assignments were a great aid to understanding the topics, and the extra knowledge helped on the regular assignments." (Differential Equations)

"Understands that students come from different courses and have different skill backgrounds." (Business Calculus I)

"I like the way he applied the information to science today through the use of computers." (Calculus I)

"Personally, I liked the idea of journals as communication between teacher and student." (Discrete Structures)

"I felt the journal writing helped because you actually took them seriously." (Business Calculus II)

"I like the group work because it enabled me to practice the problems before I went home and did the homework alone." (Pre-Calculus)

Appendix D contains unsolicited letters from former students who say they have benefited from my teaching. Christina Samilo, who had me for *Vector Calculus* and whom I supervised as a student teacher, said, "I just wanted to thank you. I learned so much from you as a mathematician and as a mathematics teacher." Christina is teaching high school mathematics in the Minersville High School.

Laura Negvesky is another alumnus of the University. She was my student in *Vector Calculus,* and I supervised her senior honors project on *Exterior Differential Forms.* She wrote, "I want to thank you for your great teaching and for all your help, especially on my senior project. The mathematics and the research skills you taught me are coming in handy right now." Laura is a graduate teaching assistant at the University of Dayton.

Representative Course Syllabi

Appendix C contains sample syllabi, exams, and projects. The samples are taken from the main courses listed above. The projects reflect my work with journals and the computer. The sample exams contain examples of test questions that involve student writing (e.g., "Explain, in words, the *process* of proof by mathematical induction"). Students receive the wrong message if they have to do writing assignments for the course but there is no writing on the exams.

Teaching Improvement Activities

I work hard at being current both mathematically and pedagogically. The latter is done by efforts such as:

- Supervising student teachers. This allows me to stay current with instructional strategies. I also learn from these "apprenticed" teachers. I see great ideas I try in my own classes, and I see mistakes best not repeated.

- Attended the NSF Workshop: A Computer on Every Desk: Implications for Mathematics Courses, Ithaca College, June 1992. Here I learned valuable ideas about the computer in the mathematics classroom. I took these ideas, revised them, and implemented computer projects in my courses.

- Attended the Summer Academies for the Advancement of College Teaching, Boiling Springs, PA, August 1992. Here I was exposed to techniques in cooperative learning. I was made more sensitive to different learning styles and incorporated some of the ideas into my own classes. My courses are enriched by using group work.

- Attended Dr. Peter Seldin's Workshop on the Teaching Portfolio, University of Scranton, October 1995. This workshop, which helped produce the present document, was most helpful. The creation of the portfolio is basically a reflective exercise; it forces you to think about how you teach and why you teach as you do. This kind of professional self-analysis is healthy; it helps you to focus on what you are doing right and to consider perhaps rethinking some teaching strategies.

In addition to attending the talks of others, I give presentations and write about how I use the computer in mathematics courses. I enjoy talking about my teaching with others.

- *Calculus with a Computer Algebra System,* 42nd Annual Conference of the Pennsylvania Council of Teachers of Mathematics (PCTM), March 1993.

- *Teaching Mathematics with DERIVE,* University of Scranton, Department of Mathematics Seminar, March 1993.

- *Ordinary Differential Equations,* First International *DERIVE* Conference, University of Plymouth, Plymouth UK. July 1994.

- Published *Using a Computer Algebra System to Enhance a Traditional Undergraduate Course in Ordinary Differential Equations,* PRIMUS, 4(4), 383–395. December 1994.

Honors Relating to Teaching

Though it is not strictly an award for teaching, one recognition deserves special mention. I received the 1994 Polya Award, a national prize given by the Mathematics Association of America (MAA), for outstanding expository writing in the *College Mathematics Journal (CMJ).* The honor was for my paper *Euler and Differentials,* which discussed the work of the great eighteenth-century mathematician Leonhard Euler in calculus. The editorial policy of the *CMJ* states: "The *CMJ* seeks lively, well-motivated articles that can enrich undergraduate instruction and enhance classroom learning." Thus, I consider this award a recognition of my teaching. See Appendix D for letters from colleagues speaking to the prestige of this award. Dr. Alexanderson, secretary of the MAA, wrote: "I would like to take this opportunity to congratulate you on this well-deserved recognition." Dr. Robert Powell, a mathematician and Dean of the Graduate School at the University of Scranton wrote: "Having read [the article], I can certainly concur with those who supported your nomination for the George Polya Award." A reviewer said: "The author reminds us 'how much fun it is to read Euler,' and in the process the reader learns how much fun it is to read Ferzola as well."

Teaching Goals

I would like to state two goals, the attainment of which will begin immediately. These goals should enhance my teaching performance and my future teaching portfolio.

1. Collect graded exams and projects to allow me, my colleagues, and my stu-

dents to see and review what I consider "A" work versus "D" work. This will give all involved a clear idea of my standards and expectations.

2. Periodically have my course material reviewed by colleagues. My fellow department members are a great resource; I will seek their professional views on my syllabi, exams, and projects. My course materials should improve with the extra input of my peers.

Appendices
Appendix A: Peer Evaluations
Appendix B: Student Evaluations
Appendix C: Sample Syllabi, Exams, and Projects
Appendix D: Letters from Peers and Alumni

TEACHING PORTFOLIO
Daniel M. Gropper
Department of Economics
College of Business
Auburn University
Fall 1995

Table of Contents
1) Teaching Responsibilities
2) Statement of Teaching Philosophy
3) Description of Instructional Practices
       Undergraduate Teaching
       Graduate Teaching
4) Evidence of Teaching Effectiveness
       Evaluations
       Awards
       Invited Presentations to Business Community
       Student Achievements
5) Efforts to Improve Teaching
6) Goals
7) Appendices

Teaching Responsibilities
My teaching responsibilities cover a wide range of courses, including auditorium sections of introductory classes, smaller classes for juniors and seniors, MBA classes both on campus and on videotape, and small advanced graduate seminars. My guiding theme in each of these classes is the broad applicability of economic principles, and how those principles can help us understand the world around us. Over the last few years, I have been involved in teaching the following courses:

Level	Course Title
Undergraduate	U102-Political Economy (team taught) (required)
	EC200-Introduction to the National Economy (required)
	EC360-Money and the Financial System (elective)
Graduate	MBA Program-EC656-Managerial Economics (required)
	Ph.D Program-EC668-Special Topics in Econometrics (team taught) (elective)

I am also pleased to have had the opportunity to be involved with several theses and dissertations with students here at Auburn University. I have directed the undergraduate honors thesis of Scott Lloyd, the master's thesis of Janice Jackson, co-chaired the doctoral dissertation of Ter-Chao Peng, and I have also served on about a half dozen other thesis and dissertation committees.

In the summer of 1995 I taught an independent study course for four senior economics majors which was designed to provide them with an unusual learning experience. They developed a cost-of-living index for Auburn and several other cities in Alabama, and investigated how the consumption patterns of students differ from the average consumer in the official government statistics. The purposes served were several. The students got an interesting and unusual out-of-the-classroom learning experience which allowed them to apply economic theory in the real world. Finally, the College of Business and the university further developed ties with local government and businesses.

Statement of Teaching Philosophy
It is my belief that teaching, in all its forms, is the central purpose of the university. Preparing our students to be thinking individuals and community members is absolutely vital if our society is to continue to flourish. The ways in which we best prepare our students is to not only teach them the most current facts and figures, but also to encourage them to learn to think critically on their own; only if they learn to be clear thinkers themselves will they be prepared for the challenges they will face. We best prepare our students when we prepare ourselves; that is done not only by keeping abreast of our own particular fields but also of important developments which advance the knowledge in other disciplines. When our research is published or presented at meetings, we in essence teach our colleagues in our respective disciplines, both within and outside the university. When those findings are extended and disseminated by university extension efforts, we teach an even broader audience. As we advise and direct our graduate students, we teach not only them but also the many students whom they will teach. In this sense, undergraduate education, graduate education, research, and extension all work toward the same ultimate goal: to contribute to a more broadly educated society.

In my teaching efforts, I strive to take actions consistent with this goal. I have worked with my students not only in the classroom but outside as well. This has sometimes been done formally, such as when I have spoken with the students in the economics club or with business professionals in various organizations. More often, it has been done informally with students in office hours, or between or after classes. I also integrate my research into my classroom lectures, particularly in graduate courses. This helps bring home to our students that not only are we trying to learn what is already known, but also that we are striving to extend the boundaries of present knowledge. While I believe I do a good job with my students, as my evaluations and letters indicate, I continually strive to do better. To become complacent about our teaching is to assure that we will fall behind, shortchanging our students and ourselves.

As professors, we face both enormous responsibilities and enormous potential. We owe it to ourselves and our students to do the best we possibly can.

Descriptions of Instructional Practices
Undergraduate teaching

In designing and delivering my classroom lectures, I have made it a particular point to solicit and pay attention to student feedback regarding effective (and ineffective) teaching techniques. I also make it a point, when feasible, to solicit student feedback after mid-term exams so that I can adjust my presentations, if necessary. The responses to my mid-term evaluations have generally been very positive, and have helped me improve my teaching methods, particularly in large classes. I tell my students that if things can be improved, I would prefer to know before the course is over, so that I can make adjustments. I have also found that I get the best, most candid responses from my big classes; my smaller classes tend to be unwilling to say anything critical.

In the large introductory lecture classes (which average between 150 and 240 students), I use different methods than in the smaller upper-level classes. The large classes are mostly straight lectures, with notes in outline form on transparencies. I switched from writing on the board to using prepared transparencies as a result of student feedback. Even though I find the transparencies a bit more confining, the students show a marked preference for them. I also put out a supplemental package of old exams so that all students can get them—not just those with good connections. We have some excellent facilities for supplemental classroom materials, and I use those to show videotapes once or twice a quarter.

In the upper-level classes, I encourage more discussion and student involvement in lectures. I also give more homework and writing assignments. I make it a point to know all my students and call on them by name, and offer positive reinforcement for good participation. Knowing all of my students by name has positive effects in more ways than I previously had realized, and I always thought it was a good idea. The effects on attendance, interest, and motivation are all positive, and while I will occasionally forget a name, I always use that as an opportunity to make a joke about my own shortcomings.

Graduate teaching

The graduate teaching I have been involved in encompasses two very different programs: the Masters in Business Administration (MBA) program and the Ph.D. program in Economics. The approaches to each are different, but in both I have made efforts to adjust my teaching methods to improve the overall results. In my MBA class, I have changed from requiring more homework assignments to substituting a statistical demand estimation project that more closely approximates real world economic analysis. The open-ended part of that project requires the students to gather data from outside sources in an effort to better estimate the demand for some particular commodity (so far I have done demand for chicken and for gasoline). In response to comments from students and alumni, this quarter I have modified the assignment to be a team project rather than an individual one. I also bring a lot of examples from my previous work experience, my current research, and my consulting activities. Employing the practical applications rather than just the theoretical models seems to work best for the MBA students.

Effective teaching at the Ph.D. level, in my view, is best accomplished by getting the students actively involved in research projects. By including them, they develop a better understanding of the nature of economic analysis, and the wide range of applicability of economic principles. They are better economists as a result. To implement this idea, I have worked with a number of our graduate students on several different projects. Including students on these projects not only helps them learn; it improves their credentials and helps them get launched in the profession.

Evidence of Teaching Effectiveness
Evaluations
Evaluations of my teaching effectiveness are available for a wide variety of classes, and from my students, peers, and department heads. The most recent evaluations for the classes I teach on my own are summarized in the chart that follows with departmental averages when they were available. Other copies of my student evaluations are included in Appendix A. As the chart shows, my scores on the Auburn University standard evaluation questionnaire are both consistently good and also above the departmental (and College of Business) averages.

Questions	Winter 1995 EC 200 (n=117)	Dept. Avg.	Spring 1995 EC 360 (n=29)	Dept. Avg.	Summer 1994 EC 656 Campus	Video
Explained material clearly	4.5	4.3	4.5	4.3	4.1	4.9
Instructor was actively helpful	4.6	4.3	4.7	4.4	4.4	4.8
Instructor was well prepared	4.9	4.6	4.7	4.6	4.5	4.9
Instructor spoke clearly	4.8	4.6	4.9	4.6	4.8	4.9
Instructor stimulated my thinking	4.3	4.2	4.4	4.1	3.8	4.8
Course objectives were clear	4.6	4.5	4.6	4.5	4.5	4.8
Instructor motivated me	4.2	4.0	4.2	4.0	3.9	4.5
Class was well organized	4.8	4.4	4.5	4.3	4.1	4.9

These scores are on a 1–5 scale, with 5 as the best score. There was no departmental average for Summer 1994; the evaluations were administered separately for the regular on-campus and video students. In addition, the written comments from the students support what I try to accomplish in the classroom, as illustrated by some excerpts reprinted here:

"I enjoyed this class and learned a lot from it. It was well-organized and thought-provoking."

"He asked for our feedback and listened, using some of the ideas we mentioned. I think overall he was a great professor."

"He presents well-prepared, interesting lectures in a practical format so that students may relate/apply information to daily life/work. The class has been challenging and stimulated my thinking. I was extremely impressed, especially in light of the fact that it is such a large class . . ."

My evaluations from my department heads have also been supportive, as the excerpts from the material in Appendix B demonstrate.

"Professor Gropper's obvious dedication to excellence in the classroom and his meritorious performance therein are truly valuable assets to the department." (From the 1995 evaluation by David Laband.)

". . . his students describe Gropper as an enthusiastic, motivating, and knowledgeable leader in the classroom. His teacher effectiveness ranking is doubly impressive considering the fact that he often labors in a classroom setting (the large auditorium, for example) that is not conducive to impressing students." (From the 1994 evaluation by James Long.)

Such official recognition from department heads is gratifying.

Awards
I was very pleased to receive recognition from the Auburn Panhellenic Council as an Outstanding Faculty member in 1995. This annual recognition was given to twenty-two of the more than one thousand faculty members across the entire university. I feel quite honored; nothing beats getting an award from your students. Appendix B includes the listing of all faculty so honored for 1995.

Invited presentations to the business community
Periodically I have been asked to speak about the economy to business groups in the area. This has included talks to the Chattahoochee Valley chapter of the Purchasing Managers Association, and to several local banks and their customer groups. These talks have been generally well received, and have often given me useful examples to bring back to my classroom. I also try to bring one or two guest lecturers from the banking industry into my Money and Banking course

each quarter. I expect that strengthening our ties to the local business community will have several positive effects on our students, both in terms of their learning experiences and in job placement.

Student achievements

Professor Steve Caudill and I co-chaired one dissertation, that of T. C. Peng, who is now a professor at Feng Chia University in Taiwan. Prior to Dr. Peng finishing his dissertation, we presented a jointly authored paper on estimation of lottery revenues at a major regional professional meeting, and subsequently have published that research in a refereed journal. We have also involved several of our graduate students in research projects, which have resulted in several more publications in refereed journals. One of these publications is on student cheating behavior, another is on statistical measures of operating efficiency in private firms, and another examines the cost of savings and loan failures.

Several of my former students have gone on to law school or other graduate programs, others are employed at a variety of colleges and universities, government agencies, and private firms.

Efforts to Improve Teaching

Since coming to Auburn, I have employed several specific methods in an effort to evaluate and improve my teaching. I have taken suggestions from my formal student evaluations seriously, and have modified my methods to take into account those suggestions I thought had the most merit. Two specific examples illustrate this process. In the first MBA class I taught, several students suggested that there were too many chapter homework assignments without enough practical relevance to the real world, so I replaced half of those assignments with an applied demand estimation project using real world data. This project requires that the students combine statistical skills with economic theory to conduct the estimation; they also write up and present their findings to the class. If Auburn University changes to semesters, I will add a second applied project for the MBA students which the time constraints of a nine-week quarter system simply do not allow. A second specific example is that some of my large lecture classes complained that it was too hard to see my writing on the board, so I subsequently switched to transparencies in those classes. My sense is that the students end up with a better structured set of notes when I use transparencies.

One of the things many students seem to appreciate is my informal midterm evaluation, where they can give me suggestions to correct any problems then, before that class is over. As an example, in Winter 1995 this review helped me make some adjustments in the pace of my lectures and led me to offer two review sessions which were apparently appreciated, as shown in the comments in Appendix A.

In addition, I also periodically watch the videotapes of some of my lectures to review my presentations. Finally, several of my colleagues and I discuss what supplemental materials we are using that seem to be particularly helpful, and or less than helpful. Exchanging ideas with others helps keep all of us from slipping into a rut.

Goals

I have certain goals for my students, my institution, and myself. I want my students to be thoughtful, deliberative, and open-minded. I want my students to have both good professional job opportunities and the knowledge, skills, and abilities to take advantage of those opportunities. I am interested in making this institution as good as it can be; with the many good things Auburn University already has done, many opportunities remain for improvement. As for myself, I want to be the best educator possible, through my classroom teaching, research, and outreach activities. Through continued efforts with our students in and out of the classroom, through continued efforts in policy-oriented research, and outreach activities to the business community and the state and local governments, I will strive to do my best to take the specific actions necessary to achieve these goals.

Appendices
Appendix A: Student Evaluations
Appendix B: Faculty Evaluations, Letters, and Awards
Appendix C: Publications with Former Graduate Students
Appendix D: Course Materials

TEACHING PORTFOLIO
Ellen Hendrix
Department of English and Philosophy
Georgia Southern University
Spring 1996

Table of Contents
1) Philosophy
2) Teaching Responsibilities & Syllabi
3) Teaching Strategies
4) Assignments & Graded Essays
5) Evaluation and Assessment
6) Student Evaluations
7) Success Rates
8) Continued Improvement
9) Contributions to the University & the Students
10) Professional & Personal
11) Future Goals
12) Appendices

Philosophy
Working with students is both challenging and rewarding, and I look forward to the opportunities that await me in my classrooms each day. I feel that college students need to know how to assimilate and interpret information effectively; in short, they need to know how to think for themselves. I consider it my responsibility to help students learn how to think critically.

I consider each student to be an individual with special needs as well as definite strengths. In helping my students to reach their personal goals and my course goals, I must first help my students meet their needs and realize their strengths. I best help my students by getting to know them and caring about them as individuals. This caring translates into understanding, so when we read about the experiences of others as a class and we relate personal experiences, we learn about and better understand each other and our world. When my students have achieved a better understanding, they can then begin thinking about the world around them, thinking about the things that are right and the things that are wrong. Then my students can begin considering ways in which to change themselves and their world.

Students learn better when courses are experiential in nature and in structure, so by incorporating understanding and thinking into my classes, I am able to make my classes more meaningful for my students because they become active participants in events and activities. Their participation leads to the development of knowledge as well as skill.

Teaching Responsibilities & Syllabi

My teaching responsibilities include ENG 151, ENG 152, and ENG 090. I occasionally have the opportunity to teach other courses as well (ESL 151, ENG 290, ENG 120, GSU 120, EP 121A), but my primary courses are composition. Composition I (ENG 151) is an intensive writing course wherein students are required to write six essays and a research paper during the quarter. The students learn the various modes of essay development by reading and examining professional and student essays. The students then use the various modes as they write their own essays. Composition II (ENG 152) is a writing course which continues and advances the skills developed in ENG 151, but in ENG 152 the students read literary works. In well-developed essays, students respond to the works they have read, using the modes of essay development they learned in ENG 151. ENG 090 is an intensive writing course designed to help students master the skills necessary to pass the writing portion of the Georgia Regents' Exam. The class meets for two hours a day for 16 days prior to the Regents' Exam each quarter. The students conclude each class period by writing an essay on a Regents' topic. I read these essays and respond to the students using the same criteria I use when grading the Regents' Exam itself.

My course syllabi (Appendix A) outline my expectations for each course. Each syllabus includes a Course Objective so that students are aware of the course goals on the first day. Each syllabus also includes an overview of assignments as well as an explanation of how course grades will be determined so that students can begin to assume responsibility for their performance from the first day of the course. The "Evaluation Criteria for Composition and Rhetoric Program" (Appendix B), the criteria outlined by my department for freshman composition, explains the differences between A, B, C, D, and F essays. The "Grading Criteria: Freshman Composition I & II" (Appendix C) is my more detailed explanation of the criteria that I use for grading and the three main areas I consider in determining essay grades. I give these criteria, along with the syllabus, to my students on the first day of class because I want the students to know from the beginning of my courses that the work is intense and that my expectations are high.

Finally, each syllabus encourages students to schedule conferences with me and to use the department tutors so that they can get help with individual problems throughout the quarter. Because college composition courses are often more difficult than the traditional English classes that students have taken in high school, I find that students are often overwhelmed by the courses but do not know that they can get the help that they need outside of class. By including these statements in my syllabi, I let my students know that I am there for them and that tutors are available for them as well. I also schedule a mandatory conference with every student prior to mid-quarter so that I not only tell students that I want to help; I show them as well. I truly want to help those who want to learn.

Teaching Strategies

Since my courses are primarily composition/writing courses, my most challenging objective is to convince students that they can learn to write effectively. The best way that I have found to teach students to write is by having them write and then asking them to respond to what they have written. Class time is often devoted to generalities—techniques, modes, strategies, patterns, etc. However, each student has individual needs and strengths that may not be met in a general or abstract lecture, so I like to work with students individually as much as possible. I usually do this by meeting with students outside of class in one-on-one conferences. These conferences enable me to focus on each student's writing. In these conferences I am better able to praise a student's strengths and meet his/her needs. Ideally I like to work with students through one or two drafts of essays before they turn in a final draft, the one I will grade. I have found that this extra effort results in a more solid final effort.

I offer my students the opportunity to have conferences throughout the quarter. However, my role changes as the quarter progresses. At the beginning of the quarter, I am instructor, both showing and telling. I point out errors, explaining the problems and showing the students how to correct them. As the quarter progresses, I become more of a facilitator, helping students find problems and errors but encouraging the students to offer their own solutions and/or corrections. Toward the end of the quarter, I like to consider myself an advisor, responding to specifics as students find their own problems and offer their own solutions. By doing so, my students become not only good writers; they become knowledgeable writers as well.

Assignments & Graded Essays

Both ENG 151 & ENG 152 concentrate on developing students' skills in thinking, reading, and writing. The general guidelines for each course are outlined by my department (Appendix D). However, my department gives me a great deal of flexibility in how I teach my students to think, read, and write. For the most part, I have found that my students come to me unprepared for the level of work that I expect, so I begin each quarter with some basic instruction in what I feel makes a well-organized and developed composition. In ENG 151 I frequently use a handout (Appendix E) to give my students a better understanding of the many components of an essay and the different areas that they need to consider as they write and rewrite their essays. In ENG 152 I use two handouts (Appendix F) to help students make the transition from the personal essay to the literary essay. Through the handouts, students see that the basic structure of the essay remains consistent: They need a clear thesis statement; they need to begin their body paragraphs with topic sentences that support their thesis statement; they need to support their topic sentences with details and examples; and they need introductions and conclusions. But the handouts also show students how to discover meaning in the works that they read so that their essays can be analytical, not simply reports on what they have read.

Graded student essays (Appendix G) provide a clearer picture of what I expect out of my students and how I evaluate my students. The appendix includes a sample A, C, and F essay. These essays demonstrate the fact that I adhere to departmental standards for grading and that I also provide extensive written feedback to my students as I strive to meet their individual needs and encourage them to reach their potential. The time and effort that I put into my students' essays show the students that I am interested in them and their writing. The fact that I am as willing to praise as I am to criticize also shows them that I want them to improve and to realize their ability. The result of all of my work is the ultimate success of most of my students.

Evaluation & Assessment
Student evaluations
My student evaluations (Appendix H) from all of my classes at Georgia Southern University are overwhelmingly positive, and students most often comment on my enthusiasm and compassion. The Department of English and Philosophy does not currently use a numerical system of evaluation, but it does ask that students comment openly on a teacher's effectiveness.

When asked if they would recommend me to another student, responses are consistently "Yes," followed by comments such as "even though she is tough, she is very helpful and will go to any measure to make sure [students] understand." When asked if she thought she had learned anything, one student wrote, "Yes, I feel that I am a terrible writer. After taking Mrs. Hendrix, I know so much about English. I feel confident about my writing." Perhaps the most positive responses result when students are asked to comment on any significant strengths and weaknesses of the instructor. They rarely note weaknesses and invariably comment on strengths. One student wrote, "Mrs. Hendrix is an excellent motivator. She encourages students to do well and would help with anything a student needed. [She] goes out of her way to help."

I feel that numerical ratings would be as generous as the students' personal comments, but I value the comments far more than I would value a number because the comments prove that I have taught my students how to write and how to feel good about themselves as writers—I have made a difference in their lives.

Peer evaluations
In my department, the Composition Committee is charged with evaluating all new faculty during their first year of employment in an effort to document effective teaching and to offer advice when necessary. A Classroom Evaluation (Appendix I) conducted by two colleagues as representatives of the Composition Committee attests to my effectiveness in the classroom. My peers were most

impressed with my ability to "engage the students' interest" and to "negotiate the students toward an understanding of [literature]." My peers' final comments were perhaps the most positive:

Ellen Hendrix is an excellent teacher. She causes her students to think seriously and deeply about the subject at hand. Ms. Hendrix teaches in such a way as to connect the literature to the issues that the students are dealing with in their everyday lives.

These comments confirm for me that I am, in fact, living up to my own teaching philosophy.

Success rates

The departmental evaluation instrument does not provide quantitative data to support teaching effectiveness, but the percentage of students passing the Regents' Exam after taking my ENG 090 course does. Since joining the faculty in September 1993, I have taught ENG 090 four times. My students have had a considerably higher passing percentage than the university every time. More importantly, when I consider that the majority of my students (50 out of 52) have been repeaters, the passing rate becomes even more impressive. The following graph tracks my students' success:

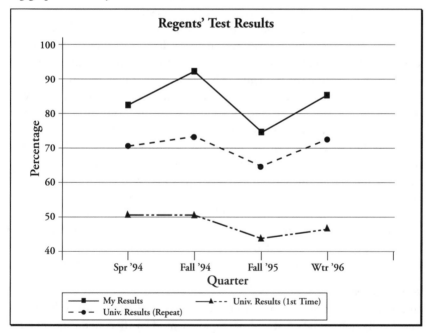

Continued Improvement
Contributions to the university & the students

My own improvement is best demonstrated through the success of my students.

For this reason, I co-edit and contribute to a department publication, *Outstanding Student Essays* (Appendix J). Each year, my co-editors and I invite colleagues to submit student essays which they feel reflect the primary objective of freshman composition: to communicate ideas and experiences clearly and effectively in a variety of writing situations. When essays that my students have written are selected for the publication, I feel honored because my peers have confirmed that my students have achieved the goals of my courses.

Professional & personal

I strive to continue to improve as a teacher in many different ways. One way is that I attend conferences and workshops in an effort to find more effective and innovative ways to help my students. For example, last year I attended a workshop on "African American Language Variation." Since so many of my students are African American and come to me with dialectical problems that interfere with their ability to communicate effectively, I felt that I needed to be more knowledgeable about why these students speak and write as they do. I can help them improve only if I understand their needs.

From this workshop and other conferences that I attend, I am able to glean information which I use to improve my own performance. Occasionally, I make discoveries of my own that I feel will help others. For this reason, I often present at conferences myself (Appendix K) in an effort to help others better understand and meet the needs of their students. By attending conferences and making presentations, my first goal for the future is continued self-improvement so that I, like my students, might one day realize my full potential.

Future Goals

My ambition is to be the best possible teacher that I can be so that I might truly make a difference in the lives of my students. The best way to achieve this goal is to evaluate and improve my effectiveness continuously. For this reason, I have established the following goals:

1. Attend at least one national conference and submit to attend at least one major conference each year.

2. Request an annual peer evaluation by two peers and/or my department chair so that I might continue to improve.

3. Track students' improvement more carefully from their first essay to their last essay or from first to last draft of one essay so that I can document my effectiveness and explore possible weaknesses in an effort to improve myself.

4. Evaluate my course syllabi annually in an effort to insure that I am integrating new strategies and discoveries into my courses.

Appendices

Appendix A: Course Syllabi
Appendix B: Evaluation Criteria for Composition & Rhetoric
Appendix C: Grading Criteria: Freshman Composition I & II
Appendix D: Departmental Syllabi for ENG 151 & ENG 152
Appendix E: Handout: A Checklist for Writers
Appendix F: Handouts: Writing About Literature & Writing About Fiction
Appendix G: Graded Student Essays
Appendix H: Student Evaluations
Appendix I: Peer Evaluation
Appendix J: Outstanding Student Essays
Appendix K: Conference Presentations (List) & Publications

TEACHING PORTFOLIO
Colleen Kennedy
Department of English and
Assistant to the President
College of William and Mary
Spring 1996

Table of Contents

1) Statement of Teaching Responsibilities
2) Curriculum and Course Development
3) Teaching Methods, Goals, and Strategies
4) Representative Course Syllabi and Assignments
5) Participation in Faculty Development Seminars
6) Presentations to Groups About Teaching
7) Evaluations of My Teaching
8) Measures of Student Performance
9) Other Recognition of Good Teaching
10) Goals for the Next Five Years
11) Appendices

Statement of Teaching Responsibilities

I am in the second of a three-year position as Assistant to the President of the College of William and Mary, a position I assumed in August 1994; until that time, I taught two courses a semester and directed the College's Writing Resources Center. I usually teach

- two reading-, writing-, and discussion-intensive freshman seminars a year (15 students), one in English and one (an Introduction to Film) in Interdisciplinary Studies

- an upper-division course in Contemporary Literature or Modern Fiction (35 students)

- one course of my choice (usually a special topics course)

- a 1-credit course for student writing consultants in the pedagogy of tutoring writing

I also try to lead or participate in at least one faculty development seminar each year, and I give one-time presentations on writing to groups of new faculty and graduate students. Although these are not responsibilities dictated by the college or the department, they are personal ones, and I consider them a major part of my teaching.

Since 1988, about one-half of my teaching has been in interdisciplinary, team-taught courses. In addition to the introductory film course, I have taught an interdisciplinary honors course called "Self and Other" and a cross-disciplinary course in philosophy, literary theory, and linguistics. I have also taught two graduate English courses, one in postmodernism and one in literary theory. And I direct, on average, one M.A. and one honors thesis each year, and serve on two or three honors, M.A., or Ph.D. examining committees. I list all of my teaching assignments since 1991 in Appendix 1.

During my term as Assistant to the President, I will teach one course a semester of my choice (probably two writing-intensive seminars—one freshman, one senior—each year); at the end of my term, I anticipate resuming the responsibilities I describe above.

Curriculum and Course Development

I am fortunate to have been involved in several broad-scale curricular development programs at the college, and to have been encouraged to develop individual courses on my own. As Writing Director, I worked closely with the Director of the Charles Center for Interdisciplinary Studies to develop and implement a program of freshman seminars, offered in departments and programs across the curriculum, that satisfy the College's freshman writing requirement. More than 75% of our required freshman seminars now satisfy that requirement; they are offered not only across disciplines in the School of Arts and Sciences, but also in the Schools of Law and Business. I also worked for three years on the Curriculum Review Steering Committee, which successfully proposed new General Education Requirements, and I served for two years on the Educational Policy Committee responsible for implementing these.

I have also designed or helped to design several courses: With a faculty member in Modern Languages, I led a faculty development seminar that developed the team-taught freshman seminar in "Introduction to Film Studies"; I designed two courses now offered regularly in the English Department, "Contemporary Literature" and "The Theory and Practice of Tutoring Writing"; and I designed or co-designed special topics courses in postmodernism, linguistics and literary theory, the self-reflexive novel, and two different courses in representations of women in literature and the media. Finally, I have conducted four graduate-level or upper-division independent studies in literature, one graduate independent study in film, and one Wilson Summer Interdisciplinary course in representations of women.

Teaching Methods, Goals, and Strategies
Methods
I teach primarily by discussion. In the film class I give two lectures a semester to a group of about 100; and occasionally, when I assign difficult articles on literary theory or when I want to provide a model for what I expect in oral presentations, I will give brief (10–20 minute) lectures in which I provide background

and/or take the students through the major premises of the argument. But probably 90% of my teaching is discussion based, meaning that I direct students' reading (through informal writing assignments or study questions) to particular issues that we then work through and debate in class. Most days, I try to make sure that at least two-thirds of the time is devoted to the students' presenting their ideas; my role is to pose the questions, clarify student comments, encourage debate, explain misunderstandings or challenge risky interpretations, and keep the discussion generally on track. To stress the importance of oral communication, I require at least two formal oral presentations (and usually more) in seminar-sized classes, and quasi-formal group presentations in the larger, 35-student classes.

I assign frequent writing—particularly informal writing—as well: My students write on the average one short paper every two weeks in addition to at least two longer assignments (due midterm and end-of-term) which require multiple drafts; they write a series of short assignments, primarily microthemes and response papers; and they write very informally in class almost every day. Detailed assignments for the formal papers, microthemes, and response papers are attached to the syllabi I include in Appendix 2. I also assign some kind of group work—sometimes problem solving (e.g., reading difficult stanzas of a poem), sometimes reading and revising each other's work—every fourth or fifth class in seminar, and more frequently in larger classes. I have also begun to incorporate regular research exercises into my seminar classes, exercises that require students to use a database; and I require students to participate in listserves on e-mail.

Goals

I have two related goals. One is obvious and, unfortunately, almost a cliché in pedagogical research these days: I want the students to learn as much as they possibly can in my class. My second goal is the flip side of the first: I want to remember, always, that saying all I have to say is less important than making sure the students hear and learn. What I most want my students to learn is not so much a body of material (although that is an important first step), but to be able to think independently. I want to give them the tools to be able to analyze the many "texts" of their cultures, whether they be literary, filmic, visual, or whether they be "high" (like canonical literary texts) or "low" (like advertisements). I feel I have been most successful as a teacher when a student comes back to me years later—as one did recently at a presentation I made to parents—and says, "I can't watch anything anymore—films, TV, MTV—without analyzing it to death!"

I emphasize discussion and writing as heavily as I do for several reasons:

- These activities force students to think on their own: They cannot rely on my interpretations because I give those only after students have come up with their own

- Students learn better generally when they are forced to verbalize ideas, whether theirs or someone else's

- Writing and talking through ideas is the way of teaching most conducive to my discipline (literary interpretation)

While I sometimes feel the need to lecture—to present material more quickly and more concisely than students can get on their own, or to explain material that is unfamiliar, or to provide a model for their own presentations of their research—I am persuaded by the research that shows that students might remember about 20 minutes of a 60-minute lecture. Also, since my discipline requires less in the way of background knowledge than, say, the hard sciences, and more in students' ability to read literary texts and produce and support interpretations for a community of learned readers, it is important that students begin almost immediately to produce interpretations on their own.

Strategies

I have appended some of my most successful writing assignments (see Appendix 2); what I describe here are the more amorphous strategies I use to prepare and encourage students to develop and articulate their ideas.

Prior to a given class, I might assign response papers or microthemes to help students prepare for discussion. One common assignment I use in the film seminar, for example, is a very short essay in which I ask students to define an unfamiliar term, like "deep focus," in one sentence; to describe an example of its use in the film we are studying in a second; and to explain, in a third, how that instance of its use contributes to the film as a whole. Sometimes the topics for response papers are open, in order to allow students to determine for themselves what is important about a text; sometimes they are quite pointed questions about a text or even one part of a text. I frequently begin a class by asking students to summarize their response papers or to expand on their microthemes (since the latter are short, usually 100 words or so). Alternatively, I will open a class with a question to which I ask students to write an informal response (for example, "what was the thesis of this article?" or "how does this stanza fit into the rest of the poem?"); students' answers will then become the basis for the following discussion (I do not collect these—my purpose is to stimulate careful thought and to show the students the value of writing as way of developing ideas). I also encourage students to develop work they've done in informal assignments in their formal papers.

My chief strategy, then, is to integrate as thoroughly as possible students' written and oral expression. Although many people believe the reverse, students are—in my experience—more comfortable expressing academic ideas in written form than in oral presentations. Therefore, I use both formal and informal written responses as ways to open up discussion, to ascertain whether or not students understand the text or the assignment, to keep students focused on issues (where that's the goal) or to discover how students see a text when left to their own, and to encourage participation of shyer students by giving them a written text to rely on.

Representative Course Syllabi and Assignments
In Appendix 2, I include representative syllabi for four different courses: a freshman seminar course on "Major American Writers," a freshman seminar in "Introduction to Film Studies" (both the team-generated reading list and my individual course calendar and list of assignments), an advanced course in "Contemporary Literature," and a senior seminar called "Dead Women: The Aesthetics of Contemporary Literature and Feminist Literary Criticism." My syllabi always include

- a course description

- a statement of my goals in the course and my expectations of my students

- an overview of the assignments, due dates, and the percentage of the final grade I assign to each

- a reading list and course calendar

- detailed assignments with my grading criteria appended

I have chosen these four courses because they represent, horizontally, the breadth of my current teaching in the undergraduate curriculum and, vertically, my goals (in their most recent incarnations) for students ranging from generic freshman (the film course) to highly specialized senior English majors.

Participation in Teaching Development Seminars
As Director of the Writing Center, I designed, with various other faculty members over the years, several workshops on Teaching with Writing. Although I was the nominal "expert" in the groups, I learned as much if not more than the other participants—many of the assignments I give (like microthemes) and many of the techniques I use (like frequent group work) I've developed from the ideas of other instructors. I have become very conscious of practicing what I preach—ironically, I found I sometimes lectured my colleagues about the value of discussion and participation. The workshops have made me very self-conscious, in a way that had helped me constantly improve. I have participated in at least one faculty development seminar every summer since I arrived at the college in 1988; in addition to those on writing, I have worked in seminars designed to develop the team-taught courses I describe above. Although these seminars were partly content driven, we spent a considerable portion of the time writing syllabi, discussing pedagogy (particularly the role of lecture vs. discussion), and developing assignments. In every case, I have taken away a new strategy or an idea for an assignment or a way to clarify my criteria or goals for my course. All of the courses developed were team-taught, and teaching with faculty members from a range of

disciplines has been the most rewarding and educational experience I have had at the college, because I have learned so much from my colleagues.

Presentations on Teaching

I have written one article on teaching with writing in K–12, aimed primarily but not exclusively at teachers of gifted students; with Dean of Undergraduate Studies and Geology Professor Heather Macdonald, I gave a presentation to faculty members at the University of Wisconsin on the development of writing-intensive freshman seminars; I co-authored an article with Heather Macdonald and Susan Conrad on using writing in geology courses; and I helped train Professor Macdonald's undergraduate geology TAs to tutor writing. I have trained our writing consultants at the College to tutor writing across disciplines; and I have made presentations to both groups of new faculty and to graduate students on designing, commenting on, and grading writing assignments. I include my chapter on teaching writing to gifted students, the article I co-authored with Macdonald and Conrad, and unsolicited letters I have received about individual presentations and the Teaching with Writing seminars as Appendix 3. I am pleased that my co-participants in these seminars generally noted the same qualities that my students note about my teaching. As one colleague put it, "While Colleen was not dogmatic about the interpretation of any of the assigned reading, she had definite views herself and required sensible support for our views. Yet she was always open to another view. I realize how much respect she showed for us in her approach. And her sense of humor keeps the clock moving."

Evaluations of My Teaching

I include in Appendix 4 representative student evaluations of my teaching done at the end of the term on standard English Department or Interdisciplinary Studies forms. I have chosen student evaluations from the same courses for which I have provided syllabi and assignments. I include student responses to open questions and, for the English courses, quantitative responses. In determining merit ratings, the English Department considers instructors' scores in relation to a departmental average in two categories. Instructors are scored on a 5-point scale, with 5 being excellent, 4 very good, etc. I list below my own and the departmental average for each category:

	My Average	*Departmental Average*
"Quality of Instruction"	4.5	4.1
"Overall Evaluation of Course"	4.4	3.9

I have scored consistently above the mean since 1991 (and with only one exception since 1988); I have received scores substantially above the mean in other categories as well, including "Instructor Receptive to Differing Opinions," "Instructor's Availability and Helpfulness," "How Stimulating Was Course?"

"Grading Pattern Clearly Defined," and especially "Instructor's Comments Helpful." Interdisciplinary Studies courses are not evaluated quantitatively, but I have included students' written evaluations of the film course.

In Appendix 5, I include peer evaluations of my teaching done by colleagues with whom I have team-taught or for whom I have provided guest lectures. The letters included are letters written for my tenure decision; hence they sometimes touch on issues of governance or scholarship. Over the next few years, I will compile letters directed specifically toward my teaching and toward the goals outlined in this portfolio.

My teaching evaluations have been consistent—I include one letter written by the chair of the department at UC Irvine, where I did my graduate work, as evidence of this both comforting and disturbing consistency. To summarize, according to both my student and peer evaluators, my strengths are my energy, my love of my work, and my concern for my students; I am very proud of the fact that my students consistently describe my classes as challenging and rigorous, and yet generally praise my openness and the relaxed atmosphere of my discussions. When students mention a weakness, it is usually the same one—that I am not clear enough in articulating what I want. This is a problem I think I will always struggle with. I strive to clarify my criteria, to define as sharply as possible my assignment questions, and to keep my comments coherent and limited to what students can process from one given assignment to the next; I hope I can say, without seeming defensive, that I work continuously to clarify my expectations and that I am fairly happy with what I provide. My interpretation of this comment is that students don't "give me what I want" precisely because they are thinking about the assignment in terms of what I want instead of what they have to say—and that means they are not sufficiently compelled by the material, or—worse, in some ways—that they are not ready for it. I can usually help these students to some degree in individual sessions or through the Writing Center, but they are a challenge in that they often need more courses—or in some cases, just more time in the world—before they are ready for what the majority of the students are doing quite competently.

Student Performance
I will include in Appendix 6 representative portfolios of student writing from all four of the courses I include in Appendix 2: These will include all response papers, microthemes, draft, and formal essays with my comments and evaluations. With each portfolio, I will include a brief description of the student's improvement (or lack thereof). I will also include in this appendix unsolicited letters from alumni about my teaching, a brief bibliography of articles published by my former students and developed from papers they wrote for my courses, and a list of students who have successfully pursued careers directly related to work they did with me at William and Mary: for example, former

writing consultants who have gone on to direct/create Writing Centers or to receive competitive teaching assistantships at prominent universities.

Other Recognition of Good Teaching

In 1994, I received an Alumni Teaching Fellowship from the college's Society of the Alumni. This award recognizes five younger members of the faculty each year who are particularly outstanding as teachers. The letter of award is included as Appendix 7.

Goals for the Next Five Years

To improve my lectures

While I am fairly confident in my abilities to lead discussion, I am not comfortable lecturing. I lecture twice a semester in the film course, and occasionally as a guest in colleagues' classes; more to the point, I plan to develop a new course on film adaptations of literary texts that would be at least half lecture. I want to work specifically on better organizing lectures (I often run out of time), on better integrating visual materials (primarily film clips), and on better anticipating audience needs (in guest lectures, I sometimes pitch the lecture too high, given the students' limited knowledge of background material). I don't really have a time-frame in mind—in some ways, the need is immediate; at the same time, I would expect to improve over years.

To design a course in Film Adaptation of Literary Texts

Ideally it would be team-taught. I have already done some of the research; over the next year, I plan to view about 20 more adaptations, to negotiate the team-teaching with two other colleagues in American literature and the chair of our department, and to plan the syllabus and structure of the course.

To educate myself about newer technologies

I want to incorporate them into my courses as resources become available on campus. I already encourage students to submit their work on disk or via e-mail; and I establish e-mail listserves for all of my seminars. I want to investigate particularly the use of hypertext technology for my literature courses and CD-ROM technology for the film courses. Some training is available on campus; I also plan to attend at least one conference devoted to such technologies. I would like to know enough to write grants and make recommendations to our development office by next fall; if we can find funding, I would like to propose a faculty development seminar for summer '97 and begin using the technology the following fall.

To implement teaching seminars

During my term in the President's Office, I want to help the director of the Charles Center for Interdisciplinary Study, the Dean of Undergraduate Study, and the provost implement broad-based teaching enhancement seminars. I am particularly interested in significantly increasing the use of teaching portfolios in my own department (English).

To accumulate evidence of student progress
Specifically, I plan to do the following:

- With students' permission, I will collect representative portfolios of student work in the four classes I describe in section IV, containing commented and graded response papers, drafts, and formal papers to show students' progress

- With the assistance of audio-visual services, I will have videos made of a seminar class, a larger literature class, and one lecture

- With the assistance of colleagues from the School of Education, I will experiment with pre- and post-testing

- I will continue to collect unsolicited letters from alumni regarding my teaching, as well as articles that former students develop from papers they have written for me. (I have included some of these in Appendix 6)

Appendices
Appendix 1: Classes Taught
Appendix 2: Representative Syllabi and Assignments
                 English 207W: Major American Writers
                 Interdisciplinary Studies 150W: Introduction to Film Studies
                 English 370: Contemporary American Literature
                 English 475: Dead Women: The Aesthetics of Contemporary Fiction and Feminist Literary Criticism
Appendix 3: Articles on Teaching and Responses to My Oral Presentations on Teaching
Appendix 4: Student Evaluations of My Teaching
                 English 207W: Major American Writers
                 Interdisciplinary Studies 150W: Introduction to Film Studies
                 English 370: Contemporary American Literature
                 English 475: Dead Women: The Aesthetics of Contemporary Fiction and Feminist Literary Criticism
Appendix 5: Peer Evaluations of My Teaching
Appendix 6: Evidence of Student Performance (including portfolios from)
                 English 207W: Major American Writers
                 Interdisciplinary Studies 150W: Introduction to Film Studies
                 English 370: Contemporary American Literature
                 English 475: Dead Women: The Aesthetics of Contemporary Fiction and Feminist Literary Criticism
Appendix 7: Other Recognition of Good Teaching

TEACHING PORTFOLIO
Stephanie L. Kenney
Exceptional Child Program
Georgia Southern University
Fall 1996

Table of Contents
1) Teaching Philosophy
2) Teaching Responsibilities and Strategies
3) Representative Course Syllabi
4) Evaluation of Teaching
5) Honors Relating to Teaching
6) Teaching Improvement Activities
        Conferences/Workshops Attended
        Presentations/Research Influencing My Teaching
        Publications Influencing My Teaching
7) Formative Self-Evaluation and Goals
8) Appendices

Teaching Philosophy
My teaching philosophy directly reflects what I believe learning is and how/under what conditions successful and maximum learning can take place. The following statements embody my beliefs.

- Learning is achieved when a student can be observed applying that learning or skill.

- Learning is developmental and must be built upon previously firmly mastered understandings.

- The most effective learning requires time for critical and reflective thinking.

- The process (timeline and style) of learning is idiosyncratic to each individual, and this must be reflected in the learning opportunities provided to a group of students.

- Students will achieve in direct proportion to the amount of communicated expectation and concomitant support provided.

- Learning opportunities must utilize students' strengths in an effort to enhance their areas of need.

- There is often a vast difference between adolescent learners and adult learners which must be addressed across graduate and undergraduate courses via use of qualitatively different teaching techniques and learning opportunities.

- The most effective teacher is the one who is constantly evaluating and learning, thus modeling the process for students.

- The most effective learning environment provides a diversity and divergence of ideas and opportunities.

Teaching Responsibilities and Strategies

My teaching responsibilities have included Identification and Education of Exceptional Students in the Regular Classroom (EXC 450), Classroom Behavior Management (EXC 468), Nature of Intellectual Disabilities (EXC 453), and Approaches and Methods for Teaching the Mild Intellectually Disabled (EXC 452), and graduate courses including Identification and Education of Exceptional Students in the Regular Classroom (EXC 650) and Characteristics of Students with Behavior Disorders (EXC 673). In addition to classroom responsibilities I am also responsible for the program advisement of over 100 graduate students. I provide daytime and evening office hours to accommodate both undergraduate and graduate students who need advisement regarding my courses or programmatic issues. Additionally I am privileged to be the advisor of our students' major preprofessional organization, Student Council for Exceptional Children. (A list of courses taught and enrollment by quarters is offered in Appendix A, along with a departmental record of advisee load.)

My teaching methods and strategies vary somewhat across the courses I teach. For example, for courses that cover characteristics, I require field visits in which my students can observe firsthand students who demonstrate those characteristics we are discussing. To supplement the real-life visits I use videotapes. These videotapes are stored in my office file cabinet; however, an annotated bibliography of these videotapes can be found in Appendix B. Lecture, discussion, and small-group activities are a part of each class. I use lecture/discussion format to check for understanding of their ongoing reading assignments. I use small-group activities to assess their abilities to apply information they have read and discussed during lecture. Further, in connection with journal-reading assignments, I use class time to discuss the articles students have read to help them make the connection that research can and should inform their teaching practices. (See Appendix C for EXC 452 Syllabus, including sample lesson plan demonstrating the methodology used to help students make connections between research and teaching practices.)

In the EXC 468 course, I teach from a reflective management focus, using case studies, self-evaluation, and application activities. I take this approach because I believe, based on my own public school teaching experience, that students must first understand themselves and be able to articulate their emerging philosophy of instructional and behavioral management before they can become effective classroom managers. I also use a lecture/discussion format to check for understanding of weekly reading assignments. (See Appendix D for EXC 468 course syllabus, including application activity and case study samples.)

Similarly, in the graduate class, EXC 673, taken by students who are currently teaching in special education classrooms, I use a question/discussion format in which we deal with issues related to their text and journal readings. They are required to visit other classrooms and respond to what they saw happening. My lesson plans reflect that we address how they are currently dealing with BD children, why they do so as they do, and how, based on their current observations, reading, and reflection, they might improve their style/methods. This format allows me to a) clarify and expand on information presented in assigned readings and in their journal readings, and b) check on the progress of their reflection on their own teaching. (See EXC 673 syllabus including in-class activity and sample lesson plan in Appendix E.)

Because I believe learning is idiosyncratic to each student, my goal at the first session of every course I teach is to facilitate the student in finding out where he/she is experientially and belief-wise with the course content. Therefore, I begin every course I teach by requiring students to write a brief paper in which they must relate their personal response to issues which will be central to the course content. For example, in EXC 468, I require them to write about their belief regarding the cause and control of behavior, what is "good" and "bad" behavior, and so on. This gives me a sample of their written expression skills as well as a baseline on how students are currently thinking about the topic. (See Appendix F for student writing sample pre and post.) This is followed by a discussion in which students are encouraged to orally express to the class what they believe and why they believe as they do, thus bringing their previous experiences forward for their conscious deliberation. Additionally, small group activities provide students with opportunities to present their personal view of the discussion topic. Why questions are asked in order to get students to think about their thinking and feelings. Finally, most tests/exams require application of knowledge and are given as take-home assignments to allow students to think/reflect and generate a qualitatively better product.

I believe that if students believe they have the tools and support to master a skill or develop a concept, they will happily do so. In order to motivate my students to achieve better performance I a) give them clear and thorough guidelines for all activities and assignments in the form of criterion checklists, and b) promise and provide ongoing support to complete the assignments successfully, including opportunities to improve their work after feedback is given. I want my students to teach masterfully rather than at 80 or 90 percent proficiency. Therefore, I allow them to practice until they master each task. Examples of these practices can be seen in my syllabi presented in Appendices C through E.

I also teach developmentally, building skill/concept upon skill/concept. For example, during EXC 452, an introductory methods course, we learn first the foundation for our lesson plan, how to write the behavioral objective; next we learn to develop the foundation for our instruction, the lesson plan; finally, we begin to talk about appropriate materials and methods. Each step is practiced and mastered before we move on to the next. This builds success and fosters in them a confident, positive approach to their learning. This developmental progression can be seen in the EXC Syllabi (Appendix C) as well as in the sample Unit Plan activity in Appendix G.

Representative Course Syllabi
Learning is a challenging process for students and teachers. I believe that it is my responsibility to remove as much ambiguity from my courses as possible. Therefore, my course syllabus is designed to be the guiding document for the course; it charts the course for me and gives my students direction for their study, thinking, and learning activities. Included in my syllabi are course descriptions and objectives, grading guidelines, attendance expectations, tentative course schedules (including specific due dates of all readings, assignments, and examinations), and guideline/criterion checklists for every assignment. Students are taught how to use the syllabus as their course guide in order to make them responsible for the progress of their learning while also eliminating much of the unproductive ambiguity that so frustrates students. (See Appendices C–E for sample course syllabi.)

Evaluation of Teaching
Student evaluations are the major formal vehicle I use to improve my instruction to meet the perceived needs of my students; it provides me with the learners' perspective which is so essential to maintain as I prepare and improve courses. The evaluations discussed in this section and provided in Appendix H represent the evaluations I have been given to date at Georgia Southern. Because of the many differences between the institution at which I previously taught and Georgia Southern (e.g., institutional and departmental goals), I have chosen to include in my portfolio only those data and documents that pertain to my tenure here at Georgia Southern University. Documentation of my previous record of exemplary teaching and research will be made available upon request. Because I am concerned about the quality and accuracy of student feedback via formal instruments, I consented to participate in a field test and comparative study of two student evaluation instruments at Georgia Southern University. The Fall 1995 student evaluation data on the "School of Education Student Evaluation of Teaching" instrument of my two courses (54 students) indicates the following mean student ratings from 1 (Deficient) to 5 (Excellent) ranged from 4.2 to 4.6 (see Appendix H). Example ratings/items follow:

- 4.4 The instructor demonstrated skill in planning and organizing for instruction.
- 4.4 The instructor demonstrated a range of teaching strategies.
- 4.5 The instructor communicated effectively.
- 4.6 The instructor demonstrated interpersonal skills.
- 4.6 The instructor demonstrated skill in evaluating student performance.
- 4.6 The instructor demonstrated knowledge of the subject.

Anonymous student evaluation narratives reflect the strengths of my instruction (see Appendix I). Examples from my two Fall 1995 courses are as follows:

"Dr. Kenney was very thorough, fair, and helpful. I learned a lot."

"Dr. Kenney has been a great teacher; I have learned a lot from her. She really has a passion for what she teaches. She is very good at interpersonal skills; she makes you feel comfortable and is always willing to help. I also felt she was interested in me personally..."

"Dr. Kenney was an excellent teacher: A person who truly seems to care about her work, exceptional children, and her students..."

In addition to formal student feedback through quarterly evaluations, I practice an informal method of asking students at the end of each class to please see me privately if any personal questions, needs, or expectations relative to that particular session have not been met. I feel this strategy works. However, because the informality does not provide hard data for ongoing self-assessment of my session-by-session effectiveness, I have addressed a procedure to improve upon this strategy in my goals.

Honors Related to Teaching
Over the past several years, in previous public school and university teaching positions, I have received awards addressing my teaching and research scholarship. A list of these as well as letters of commendation can be found in Appendix J.

Teaching Improvement Activities
I believe that if I am to continue to be a learner and thus an effective teacher, I must continue to gain new information and skills via conference and workshop attendance as well as affirm myself and inform others of my work by presenting to local faculty and at regional, state, and national conferences. The following is a description of the activities I have recently done to continue this process of learning. Complete documentation of my participation in these and other activities can be found in Appendix K.

Conferences/workshops attended

- Teaching Portfolio Workshop (1996). This workshop, sponsored by Georgia Southern University, provided me with a mentor who over three days helped me to begin the ongoing process of teaching portfolio development. This process was invaluable for my personal professional purposes as well as for giving me ideas to help me better prepare to introduce the portfolio process to my students.

- Georgia Special Education Administrators' Conference (1996). This conference gave me an opportunity to sit in on and review classroom management theory and practice from a fresh perspective. I gained several new ideas from many old tried and true theories. I plan to fit them into my EXC 468 course this summer.

- Summer Conference of South Carolina Council for Children with Behavior Disorders (1995). This conference gave me the opportunity to meet and interact with many of the leading researcher/practitioners in the field of behavior disorders. I was able to ask them questions about their theories and methodologies which I have been practicing and espousing to my university students. Because I was able to get clarification on the application and effectiveness of one methodology about which I have been reading for years, Developmental Therapy/Developmental Teaching, I plan to use it as a central focus of my EXC 676 course this summer quarter.

- 14th Annual Lilly Conference on College Teaching (1994). This conference provided a variety of sessions. The one that was most useful to me focused on the development of student portfolios. This was extremely helpful because our undergraduate program will be moving in this direction within the next year.

- Michigan Association of Teachers of Emotionally Disturbed Children (attended numerous years). This conference focused on methods/materials used in the management and instruction of students who have behavior/emotional disorders. At this conference I accomplished two things year after year, and they were the improvement of my skills/understanding, and the self-affirmation of my choice of a profession. Probably of all the years I attended this conference, the session that has most impacted my public school and university teaching is the session in which I learned about how the cognitive developmental theory can be applied to the behavior of children through a "levels of behavioral development" instructional and behavior management process. I teach the theory and practice of this process in both my methods and classroom management courses. (See syllabi for these courses in Appendices C and D.)

- Annual Conference of Michigan State Council for Exceptional Children (attended numerous years). This conference focused on methods and issues related to the teaching of children who had any handicapping condition. It was at this conference that I had my first exposure to things that really shaped my public school teaching of special needs learners, such as the theory and practice of Gardner's Multiple Intelligences, and Feuerstein's theory of Mediated Learning Experiences. These theories and my practice of them continue to contribute to my students' learning today. (See syllabi for these courses in Appendices C and D.)

- National Council for Exceptional Children Conferences (attended numerous years). This conference offered a broad range of strands related to teaching students with special needs. My most memorable event, however, was the year that I attended the Council on Children with Behavior Disorders' annual meeting and met many of the leaders in the field of BD whose work and research I had read as an undergraduate and graduate student. This experience brought my field of work and my day-to-day activities with my students alive. That experience continues to impact on my teaching of what is now the history of special education/BD. (See syllabi for these courses in Appendix E.)

Presentations and research influencing my teaching
Presenting at and attending conferences continue to bring me to a qualitatively different level of understanding of my role as a special educator: that I have a responsibility to learn from others' research/practice and, reciprocally, to do research of a very practical nature and disseminate it to in-service teachers, preservice teachers, and higher education colleagues both at conferences and in the university classroom. I have given numerous presentations related to my practice and research in the area of classroom teaching and teacher preparation. These are included in Appendix L. My goal now is to extend my activity to the southern region of the country. I have been invited to present a piece of my research at the Summer 1996 Conference of the Georgia Council for Exceptional Children. This particular research centers on methods of managing instructional computer integration in elementary and middle school classrooms. Most importantly I am currently presenting this research in my methods and classroom management classes here at Georgia Southern University. I believe that when it is presented and practiced at the preservice teaching level it has its greatest influence on my students' ultimate teaching practices.

Publications influencing my teaching
My publications to date also reflect my concern regarding improving and enhancing special education instructional management and methodology.

These have been disseminated at conferences as well as shared in my methods and classroom management courses. I have also developed course packets to address specific needs of the course for which I could not find adequate commercially published material. A list of these publications can be seen in Appendix M.

Formative Self-Evaluation and Related Goals

It is easy for me to be fully committed to my profession, to love to profess what I firmly believe, and to thoroughly enjoy the process of learning but not engage myself in the essential component of teaching, systematic evaluation of the processes and products of my instruction, and related tasks. This initial development of my teaching portfolio has enabled me to reflect, for the first time since I began teaching at Georgia Southern University, on the total picture of my teaching. In doing so I have been able to clearly identify areas that need either immediate or long-range attention. They are as follows:

1) I need to develop a portfolio of products that document the results of my teaching. Therefore, during the spring quarter I will systematically track the progress of three of my EXC 673 students (low, medium, and high achieving) in order to determine whether or not I am meeting their diversity of needs.

2) I need to address formal formative evaluation of my instructional effectiveness. Therefore, during the spring quarter I will systematically request biweekly written feedback from my EXC 673 students regarding their satisfaction with their growth in the course and my instruction/methods.

3) I need to elicit feedback from colleagues for peer evaluation purposes. Therefore, during the summer quarter I will videotape myself during instruction of the EXC 468 course and ask a colleague to critique it with me. I will then include the videotape and my colleague's critique in my portfolio. If this seems to be a useful process, I will continue to do a videotaping each quarter thereafter.

Appendices

Appendix A: Courses Taught/Enrollment by Quarter, and Advisee Load
Appendix B: Annotated Bibliography of Videotapes used for EXC 450, EXC 453, and EXC 673 Syllabus
Appendix C: EXC 452 Syllabus including Sample Lesson Plan
Appendix D: EXC 468 Syllabus, Sample In-Class Activity and Case Study
Appendix E: EXC 673 Syllabus and In-Class Activity
Appendix F: Pre- and Postcourse Student Conceptual Writing Samples
Appendix G: EXC 452 Unit Plan Development Sample

Appendix H: Sample Quantitative Portion of GSU College of Education
             Student Evaluation
Appendix I: Sample Narrative Portion of GSU College of Education Student
             Evaluations
Appendix J: Teaching Awards and Letters of Commendation
Appendix K: Conference and Workshop Documentation
Appendix L: Presentations/Research Documentation
Appendix M: Publications Documentation

TEACHING PORTFOLIO
Robert R. Llewellyn
Department of Philosophy
Rhodes College
Fall 1996

Table of Contents
1) Personal statement of purpose and objectives in teaching
Teaching responsibilities and objectives
Teaching philosophy and recent changes in teaching strategies
Representative course syllabi—two current examples
2) Statements from others reflecting experiences with my teaching
Course evaluations
Student evaluations
Colleague evaluations
Professional accomplishments directly relating to
teaching performance
3) Representative examples of outcomes of my teaching
Student work under my supervision
Special academic projects that have been reviewed by faculty
colleagues
4) Future teaching goals and course changes under consideration
5) Appendices

Personal Statement About Purpose and Objectives in Teaching
Teaching responsibilities and objectives
I am an instructor in two areas of the college's curriculum. Approximately two-thirds of my teaching is in the basic humanities program of the college called The Search for Values in the Light of Western History and Religion. I teach both the first year (Humanities 101 and 102) and the second year of the program (Humanities 201 and 202, the philosophy track). This totals 12 credit hours per academic year. The remaining one-third of my teaching is in the discipline of philosophy. I teach a variety of standard philosophy courses: Logic, The Philosophy of Natural Science, The Philosophy of Plato, Early Modern Philosophy, Medical Ethics, Special Topics in Philosophy consisting of topics in contemporary ethics and theories of rationality. With the exception of Logic, these courses are usually taught on an alternate year basis. Logic is taught every year, but this responsibility is shared on an alternate year basis with another colleague. I team-teach the Senior Seminar in Philosophy (Contemporary Developments in Philosophy) with my two colleagues.

I focus attention on two examples in this portfolio, one course each in the above two areas of teaching responsibility: Humanities 201-202 and Philosophy

310: The Philosophy of Natural Science. I choose these two courses because in them I am presented with some of the greatest challenges to my teaching ability, and in their current form they represent some strategies that I have recently adopted to respond to those challenges.

Teaching philosophy and changes in teaching strategies

Philosophy is a second-order discipline; that is, it reflects upon some area of human interest or experience in a reasoned way. So for example, one of my courses is titled The Philosophy of Natural Science. Because philosophy has this character, I affirm the following principles in my teaching of philosophy.

Teaching must begin where the students are in their understanding of the subject. I must find common ground with my students from which we can begin. (In this portfolio I refer back to this principle as *Principle I.*) In addition to some limited pre-evaluation of where students are in respect to a subject, I have from time-to-time administered a midterm evaluation to determine whether I am correctly understanding where students are in the course.

Teaching must give my students the information necessary to arrive at a reasoned stance in regard to that subject. I must establish a basis for communication using a language that my students and I can appreciate and use. (In this portfolio I refer back to this principle as *Principle II.*) Here is where the design and structure of a syllabus, especially in the choice of the required texts, are most important decisions.

Teaching must establish that though final answers may not be discovered in the context of the course, nevertheless, the discussion of issues is not only essential but fruitful in our understanding of the subject. I must ensure that alternative points of view are freely and reasonably presented and/or expressed; however, I must exercise caution to ensure that neither my students nor I become distrustful of the discipline of reasoning. (In this portfolio I refer back to this principle as *Principle III.*) The greatest challenge to the discipline of philosophy comes from many post-modern writers who question precisely this principle.

Because of these three principles, my teaching strategies have changed since earlier periods in my teaching career. Class discussion rather than formal lecture is the predominant mode of my current teaching. Shorter and more frequent writing assignments are assigned in lieu of the classical end-of-term, and longer, research paper. A student project is assigned that allows a student to work on a subject that he or she is personally interested in pursuing. I work to ensure that students are engaged with the material in an ongoing fashion, and not just at critical times in the semester such as tests or exams.

Changes in my teaching strategy have been influenced by two teaching seminars in which I have participated in the past four years. The first was a two-part writing across the curriculum seminar with Toby Fulwiler (a memorandum in the Appendices, section 10, records the fact of my invitation); the second, a workshop on critical thinking with Richard W. Paul (the cover page and table of contents from this in-service seminar is included in the Appendices, section 10). In addition, I have participated in several on-campus computer technology workshops that introduced a variety of ways of facilitating communication with students using electronic mail, distribution lists, and discussion groups.

The writing across the curriculum seminar was designed to help those of us who are not English teachers to better structure writing assignments in our courses; for example, to insist on first drafts which are evaluated prior to a rewrite as a final version. What I learned in addition are ways to use writing as a means for students to show a continuing engagement with the materials in my courses; for example the use of journals to record initial responses to assigned reading (see Principle I).

The critical thinking seminar was designed to convince us that if we truly want students who are capable of reasoned, independent, judgment then we must structure our courses in ways that actively put students in situations where this type of judgment is exercised and evaluated. What I learned in addition are ways to incorporate different teaching methodologies into my classroom; for example, small group discussions with reports sanctioned by the group to the larger class (see Principle III).

The computer workshops have pointed to ways in which I might extend classroom engagements beyond the typical class periods and provide a means whereby those students who are more reluctant to speak up in class can express their ideas to me and others. I have yet to incorporate this computer-assisted technology into my course structures, but plans are under development for courses in the next academic year.

Representative course syllabi: Two examples

Two complete course syllabi are included in the appendices (see section 4). In the paragraphs below I call attention to some features of these two courses that reflect my approach to teaching. Principle II in my approach to teaching is most clearly illustrated by the materials selected for the courses; these materials give the students and me a basis for communication. If these materials are too difficult, obviously the course flounders.

Humanities 201-202 begins with a conscious effort to establish links with the previous year's work in 101-102 (the previous course ends with Augustine, and 201 begins with Augustine; see day 3 in the syllabus) (see Principle I). In addition, the course incorporates contemporary discussion in philosophy by using a current secondary source (Stephen Toulmin, *Cosmopolis: The Hidden Agenda of Modernity;* see day 2 in the syllabus). Students maintain a daily journal in which they record a response to each day's assigned reading. (The appendices, section 6, contain a copy of one of the best student journals.) The journal is then edited and either an "Introduction" (Humanities 201) or a "Prospective"

(Humanities 202) is written (see Principle III). The five papers assigned over the course of the academic year (both semesters) are means to develop different approaches to writing in philosophy: expository, analytical, critical, compare and contrast, and reflective (see Principle III). (The Appendices, section 6, contain copies of these assignments.)

Humanities 201-202 (along with 101-102) is evaluated at the end of each academic year in a faculty development seminar (the Douglass Seminars) sponsored by the College for the Humanities Division. This is an opportunity to have the course assessed based on our immediate experience, to have new course materials introduced for consideration, and to have colleagues competent in various areas bring others of us "up to speed" with unfamiliar materials. (The appendices, section 8, list the seminars and their topics for the past five years.)

Philosophy 310 is in the college's curriculum because the college attracts and educates a significant number of natural science majors, especially students who anticipate a career in health care (hence, my interest in and teaching of medical ethics). The course begins with a brief essay prepared by each student on "What is science?" (See Principle I.) This essay is part of a final examination which asks the student to evaluate critically the statement made at the beginning of the course. (The appendices, section 5, contain an example of this assignment.) In addition each student is asked to interview a member of the science faculty at the college and prepare a report. (See Principle III.) Students are to read and to prepare a book report on a contemporary book of their own choosing about science, its history, or some aspect of its development. Tests are pre-announced essay assignments on the three books that comprise the core reading for the course. (The appendices, section 5, contain copies of these assignments.)

Statements From Others Reflecting Experiences With My Teaching
Course evaluations
Student course evaluations. The Student Instructional Report (SIR) is used by the College as the primary instrument for student evaluation of teaching. The SIR scores for the two representative courses included in this portfolio are summarized in a spreadsheet that is included in the appendices. (The SIR reports and the narrative evaluations are included in the appendices, sections 1 and 2. A self-maintained spreadsheet of SIR results over the past four years is contained in the appendices, section 3.)

The uninterpreted scores seem to reflect good teaching; however, when compared with college-wide scores, and the division of these scores into quintiles, they are considered at best "average" and at worst "well below average." It is this perception, in the context of teaching and learning that occurs at Rhodes, that leads me to be especially concerned about the way in which my teaching is viewed by students, not only in terms of style but also in terms of accomplishment.

Narrative evaluations point to aspects of my teaching that may be cause for student dissatisfaction: lengthy reading assignments ("I have a problem doing the entire assignment") and the steady, and even rapid, pace at which the course moves ("Had trouble keeping up with the readings"), formality of classroom environment ("You seem a bit formal"), abstractness of the materials presented ("No background whatsoever").

On the other hand, there is indication from the narrative evaluations that some things are working well. In reference to Humanities 202: "He makes difficult philosophical ideas easier to grasp." "Particularly good: organization, preparation, sense of purpose/goals for the material." In reference to Philosophy 310: "Made me think about my own view of science." "Liked the fact that we had class discussions rather than straight lecturing for one and one-half hours."

I have supplemented the SIR evaluation form with questions of my own, designed to obtain more specific formative information about aspects of the course that may cause special difficulty for students (see the appendices, section 1, for copies of these questions). I have learned, for example, that students do not want to prepare journals; my objectives and their tolerance of them are obviously not consistent (53% reported that the journal was the least successful element in the course). On the other hand I have learned that my strategy of requiring more frequent papers may be successful; at least they are preferred to more frequent formal testing (71% reported that the writing assignments in lieu of formal testing and a term paper was the most successful component in the course).

Colleague course evaluations. I do not have written course evaluations written by colleagues. Since a good portion of my teaching is interdisciplinary teaching I do in fact get feedback especially on those things that I do for the entire course, e.g., common lectures. This feedback is oral, and for the most part casual commentary. I have been pleased with responses from my colleagues. However, it is clear that all of us at the college could benefit from some means of recording such feedback so that as we assess our teaching and ask others to do so there is a record of good achievement, as well as work that needs improvement, in the eyes of our colleagues.

Professional accomplishments directly relating to teaching performance
Within the past three years I have done several things directly related to my philosophy of teaching. I have presented a paper, on two occasions (at Hendrix College and at Vanderbilt University to the Tennessee Philosophical Association meeting), on teaching an essential argument in the *Republic* of Plato. It is currently being revised for possible publication in the *Teaching Philosophy* journal. (A copy as submitted for review is in the appendices, section 9.) At the formal Phi Beta Kappa initiation and luncheon for 1994, I gave a brief address titled "The Risks of Learning" in which I sketched the dangers of being educated—as Plato

saw them through his allegory of the Cave—and suggested that those dangers are ours as well. The remedy, sanctioned by Plato as well, is a view of the self that knows through dialogue with others. (A copy as delivered is in the appendices, section 9.) Both of these pieces reflect my commitment to Principle I stated above.

In February 1995 I gave the first of three lectures in the Seidman Town Hall Lecture Program at the college. The title of my contribution to the series was "Moral Conflict, Moral Confusion, and Moral Challenge." In this presentation I respond to some of the directions of thought reflected in post-modern philosophy, especially the critique of Enlightenment rationality. In part, I agree that this critique makes a sound argument against a particular model of rationality, but I suggest that the wholesale questioning of the concept of rationality itself is misplaced. This presentation is very much a reflection of teaching that I do in my philosophy of natural science course and in courses that address contemporary ethical issues.

Representative Examples of Outcomes of My Teaching
Student work under my supervision

In the appendices, section 6, I have included the following items that represent work under my supervision that I consider to be reflective of what a typical student will do:

a. A sequence of papers from Humanities 201-202 from one student, showing the five types of writing that are required. These papers are marked, showing the manner in which I respond to student writing. In general, comments about style appear in the left margin; general comments about content, in the right margin.

b. This same sequence but showing the highest quality of accomplishment on each of the five assignments. These are papers that I may use as models with my students as they receive the assignments.

c. A student journal from Humanities 202 that is especially well done. The format for the entries is followed carefully. The content of the entries is substantive. The "Prospective" reflects a sound means of organization. The entire effort by the student reflects creativity that is serious about the task assigned.

d. The record of an interview with a science faculty member by a student in Philosophy 310. Copies of these records are also given to each science faculty member who is interviewed.

e. The initial essay on "What is science?" and the critique of that essay at the end of the course. The difference between the two is some measure of student progress from the start of the course.

Special academic projects that have been reviewed by faculty colleagues

Since 1992 I have directed one honors project that was accepted by the faculty as a basis for a degree with honors (Wilbur "Trey" Harrison, "Justification of Belief Within a Specific Tradition" 1993). As the honors project supervisor, I assisted the student in defining the topic, in conducting the research in support of the project, in meeting with the student to discuss common readings, and in reviewing progress in writing about the project.

I served as second reader on two other projects accepted by the faculty as a basis for a degree with honors (Robyn Thiemann, "The Mind-Body Problem: An Examination of Three Current Theories" 1994; and Chris Williams, "Towards an Ecological Theology: Integrating Process and Ecofeminist Theologies" 1995). For both of these projects, my involvement was late in the academic semester, and it consisted primarily in reading a first draft of the honors paper, in making comments about changes that would likely result in improvement of the project, and in reading the final version of the paper as a part of the final certification of the project as honors quality work.

Future Teaching Goals and Course Changes Under Consideration

1) It is my immediate objective to have my teaching at Rhodes viewed as consistently above average. In order to do this I need to address at least two dimensions of my current teaching style. First, I need to reserve time, probably at the beginning of the class and lasting for no more than 10–15 minutes, in which I summarize or outline the main points from the reading assignment for the day. I should not expect students to be willing to initiate discussion immediately upon having read the assignment (see Principle I). Second, I need to encourage more engagement with the subject from my students by increased use of small group discussions as opposed to open discussions from the class members with me and by more constant references to contemporary situations in which the points being discussed are relevant (see Principle III).

2) I am uncomfortable using audio-visual materials in my classes, though I have incorporated such materials in very limited ways in two other classes that I teach, and my initial response is that they were viewed by students as effective parts of their education at Rhodes (see Principle I). Part of my reluctance is a simple ignorance of the materials available and the quality of them. In part I am unsure how to follow up effective audio-visual presentations. Within the next three years I want to be better acquainted with audio-visual and computer-based resources. When I next teach Logic I want to make extensive use of computer-based logic technologies. It is reasonable to expect that such materials can assist me in better accomplishing Principle II since the contemporary student is much more receptive to this means of gaining information.

3) It is clear that group projects, including oral and written presentations, are more effective than individual projects (see Principle III). These projects also benefit from the extensive resources available on-line from computer bulletin boards and archival resources. This material is best approached with assistance from many hands on the project. I need to incorporate such projects in my classes in lieu of projects assigned to individuals. Not only would this increase the possibilities of collaborative learning; it would also teach forms of research that are computer-based. I will do more to incorporate this strategy in my courses this next academic year.

4) I am not at this time making the most effective use of journals maintained by my students. This resource can be a means of checking on current levels of understanding and accomplishment in a course. It can also be the basis for initiating class discussions if appropriately introduced (see Principle I). I will give greater attention to journal preparation by monitoring student entries in my courses this next academic year.

5) In general, I want to work towards a greater variety of experiences in the classroom with more student presentations, audio-visual support, and computer-assisted learning.

6) The example cited of asking students to write on their understanding of science before we begin the formal reading for the course and then asking students to critique that essay at the end of the course reflects something that I need to do more of: pre- and post-course evaluation. I designed an instrument to use in a special topics course in "Moral Confusion." At the time I was not fully aware of the potential for such an instrument in actually assisting me in accomplishing my course objectives. I plan to write similar instruments or use standardized instruments in other courses.

Appendices

Appendix 1:   Student Instructional Reports (including copies of Supplemental Questions) from previous four years

Appendix 2:   Narrative evaluation sheets from college-wide teaching evaluations from previous four years

Appendix 3:   Spreadsheet summarizing SIR data on five basic questions

Appendix 4:   Course syllabi for past two years (updated every two years since my teaching schedule includes some alternate year courses)

Appendix 5:   Basic course assignments, such as paper assignments, tests, and examinations

Appendix 6   Representative student projects (as graded), including both exemplary and not-so-good work

Appendix 7:   Miscellaneous communication and correspondence in regard to my teaching

Appendix 8: Faculty development seminars for the staff of Humanities 101-102 and 201-202 (the Douglass Seminars) for the past five years

Appendix 9: Publications/presentations relating to teaching performance over the past four years

Appendix 10: Conferences/workshops relating to teaching performance over the past four years

TEACHING PORTFOLIO
R. Heather Macdonald
Department of Geology
College of William and Mary
Spring 1996

Table of Contents
 1) Teaching Responsibilities
 2) Teaching Goals and Methods
 3) Course Syllabi and Assignments
 4) Student Career Development Activities
 5) Evaluation of Teaching Effectiveness
 6) Student Accomplishments
 7) Honors Related to Teaching
 8) Teaching Development Activities
 9) Dissemination of Teaching Experiences
10) Future Plans
11) Appendices

Teaching Responsibilities
My teaching responsibilities in the Department of Geology include teaching undergraduate courses, advising students, and encouraging their professional development. I teach the sequence of introductory courses *Physical Geology* and *Historical Geology*. *Physical Geology* is a large lecture-based course (~100 students); some students in the course are planning to major in geology or environmental science, some are taking the course to satisfy their natural science requirement, and some are terrified of taking a science course. *Historical Geology*, in which I teach the lecture and all the laboratory sections, is taken by students choosing to take a second geology course (~50–70 students). I also regularly teach *Sedimentology and Stratigraphy*, a junior-level course (lecture and lab) required for geology majors but also taken by other students including anthropology majors and geology minors. In the past few years this has enrolled ~20–30 students. In alternate years I teach *Marine Geology*, a large lecture course (~60–100 students) that includes senior geology majors as well as first-year students who have taken *Physical Geology* the previous semester. I have taught *Introduction to Geologic Research*, a required junior-level course that prepares geology majors for their independent senior research project. I also supervise students working on these required projects and advise geology majors on course selection, summer opportunities, post-baccalaureate plans, and overall professional development. During the three years I have been Dean of Undergraduate Studies, Arts and Sciences, my involvement in teaching in the Department of Geology has been limited. In this portfolio, I

focus on introductory courses, student career development, and teaching development activities.

Teaching Goals and Methods
In my classes, I want students to be actively involved and to develop as independent learners. In general, they should have the experience of "doing" geology—at whatever the level of the course. I want them to learn the material covered in the course to better understand the Earth—its materials and the internal and external processes that are acting on it—and, more importantly, to understand the approach geologists take to asking and answering questions about the Earth. One of my goals is that students, especially those who are intimidated by natural science, will learn a different way to study the natural world and gain confidence in their ability to understand one of the natural sciences. I also want to develop students' oral and written communication skills. In my contacts with students, both in and out of courses, I want to help them develop professionally by providing them with information, opportunities, and encouragement. Finally, the atmosphere in which teaching and learning takes place is important to me, and being enthusiastic about what I do and teach, having an interest in the students, and trying to be open and fair helps to establish an environment in which all students are encouraged and challenged.

In my introductory classes, I still teach primarily by lecturing, although I use a variety of other approaches to encourage student learning. I show slides almost every class, and videos on occasion, because it helps students to see examples of geologic features and processes. I commonly use various informal cooperative learning activities and classroom assessment techniques (CATs) to engage the students in processing the material. In one cooperative learning activity (Think-Pair-Share), I pose a question or problem, ask each student to write out a response, and then have the students discuss their response with another student. I then call on a few students to answer, ensuring some accountability, getting different perspectives, and bringing the short discussion to closure. This gives each student time to compose an answer and to discuss the answer with another student. In one CAT (the one-minute paper), students write about the most important point of a lecture or ask a question left unanswered by the lecture at the end of the class period. Reading the ungraded papers takes relatively little time, but provides valuable feedback on student understanding.

I have increasingly supplemented lectures with a variety of writing assignments, oral presentations, and group assignments to increase the active involvement of students in learning. Writing assignments are important because, through the process of writing, students can both develop their writing skills and learn geology. Although I hated talking in class when I was a student, I think my students should be talking about geoscience—to me, to each other, and to the class. As teachers, we should promote conversations among students about the subjects we teach. Giving group assignments and structuring those assignments to promote effective group work provides an opportunity for students to learn from each other. It is also good experience because many positions today, including those in the sciences, involve people working together. Collectively, these types of assignments promote students working together as colleagues.

A National Science Foundation grant has supported my efforts to incorporate small group learning experiences in large lecture classes. Faculty from across campus (Writing Program and School of Education) have helped me develop a series of cooperative learning assignments involving a final written or oral product. Small groups of ten to fourteen students meet together nine to ten times a semester during the lecture period. An undergraduate teaching assistant who has been through a training program monitors each group and provides feedback on writing assignments and group activities.

In many respects, what I am trying to do in large lecture courses happens more naturally in the laboratory and field. *Historical Geology* labs may start with a short lecture, but most of the period consists of students working together on an assignment as I move around the room asking questions, then discussing the results as a group at various points during the lab period. I encourage students to work with each other, and some of the assignments involve peer teaching. In the field, students are confronted with a problem that is not artificially constructed. I ask questions—What do you see? What does it mean? What is an alternative explanation? How could you determine which is a better explanation? Students are working together as peers as they discuss the geology.

I try to establish a supportive atmosphere in which students work comfortably with each other and me and have both fun and serious discussion. I encourage students to get to know each other, commonly using icebreaker activities. To help students achieve, I set clear expectations, comment on student papers, and note improvements and/or make suggestions on papers and exams. In addition to office hours, I offer study groups and encourage all students, especially those who receive D's or F's on exams, to participate.

Career development of geology majors is an important component of my teaching. I give students information about careers in the geosciences and about how a background in geology can be used in other careers. Students can learn more about what geoscientists do when guest lecturers talk about their job/career as well as their area of expertise. I also encourage students to participate in activities outside the classroom, such as volunteer programs in local schools, externships, and summer research internships at other institutions.

Course Syllabi and Assignments
Copies of the most recent syllabi from my introductory courses are in Appendix A. The syllabi list the day-by-day topics and reading assignments, give the

objectives of the course, and describe the various ways students participate in the course and how they will be evaluated. Writing assignments and formal group work are two components unusual in a large introductory geology course. Students in each course write two or three short (one or two page) papers; they also participate in peer review groups or other group work that results in some type of oral presentation.

Copies of writing assignments are included in Appendix B. Many of these involve reading outside the textbook, either from the primary geological litera-ture or the popular science literature (e.g., essays in John McPhee's *Control of Nature*). In one assignment for *Physical Geology*, students describe one (of sever-al) rocks, then read another student's rock description and see if they can identi-fy the rock described by the student. In another assignment, students write about garbage and the waste disposal problem, water supply issues, or a geosci-entist's job and career. For each choice, students get information from a source other than the textbook. For the first two choices, they read articles on reserve in the library, then write a letter to an elected official or an editorial. For the third, they contact a geologist from a list I provide, conduct an informational inter-view, and write a career profile of the geoscientist.

Assignments from *Historical Geology*, also included in Appendix B, demon-strate the ways I have incorporated formal group work involving individual writing assignments and group oral presentations. One assignment involves the students in an ongoing geological controversy: The cause of the mass extinctions (including dinosaurs) at the end of the Mesozoic Era. After reading a summary article of vari-ous explanations of the extinctions, each student reads an article from the primary literature. After the students work in groups to build an argument for or against a particular explanation, the class debates the cause of the extinctions.

The response paper assignment in *Historical Geology* is an unusual approach to talks given by visiting speakers. Rather than requiring students to write a summary of the talk, I have them write about what they found most interesting and submit one question they had about the talk. This promotes careful and critical listening and encourages a questioning approach.

An example of a lab exercise that involves peer teaching is an introduction to the major groups of fossils. I want the students to learn the characteristics of several groups, and provide materials (handouts, books, fossils and modern examples, and a set of questions) for each group. I arrange the students into small groups where they learn about their assigned group of fossils, answer the questions given, and then teach the rest of the class about the characteristic fea-tures of that group.

Student Career Development Activities

I provide students with information on careers through a variety of mechanisms such as discussing careers in class, requiring attendance at visiting speaker programs, and encouraging students to read the departmental newsletter, which gives information on alumni and their jobs. Through assignments in my courses, students develop writing skills, oral communication skills, and critical thinking skills as well as a good geological background; such skills are considered important by both employers and graduate schools. Students can participate in a variety of experiences that develop skills and expertise, such as being a teaching assistant in geology courses, attending professional meetings, participating in summer internship programs, doing a senior research project, and working with local elementary school classes. I encourage students in their career development by suggesting that they take advantage of such opportunities, offering graduate school advising sessions, reviewing resumes, and nominating them for various awards.

Evaluation of Teaching Effectiveness

The summarized numerical components of my student evaluations are given in Appendix C. The quality of teaching in the geology department is consistently and uniformly high. On a scale of 1 to 5 (where 5 is excellent), the departmental average has been between 4.4 and 4.5 in a recent two-year period. The overall averages for several of my courses are given below.

Course	Term	Overall Average
GEO 102	spring 1993	4.60
GEO 101	fall 1993	4.57
GEO 101	fall 1992	4.55
GEO 101	fall 1991	4.69

One of the evaluation items that is directly related to my teaching goals and is important to me is "The instructor shows enthusiasm for the subject matter." My score on this item is consistently high, and in the Fall 1992 semester was 4.90. I would like to have a similar score for questions related to the level of the course (i.e., more or less challenging). I have attempted to evaluate my teaching methods through student evaluations of specific assignments—both an overall rating and a rating of various components of each assignment. These are discussed in more detail in the section on *Teaching Development Activities*.

I have selected three quotes from student evaluations that describe what happens in my classes from their perspective. I am pleased that they recognize my enthusiasm and appreciate the value of the various teaching methods I employ, and more importantly, that they think that have learned in the process of taking my course.

- "Enthusiasm. That's what defines the shape of this course: even those who don't care much for geology can't seem to help enjoying themselves and learning in the process."

- "Dr. Macdonald is an excellent instructor who really seems to care; e.g., we discussed *strategies* for studying after I did poorly on my first exam instead of her telling me to put in more time."

- "I felt the group projects were valuable—for our knowledge of geology, a new way to learn, and for our interactions in a group setting."

Letters from students and former students included in Appendix D give their view of my teaching. The first African American geology major at the college wrote to thank me for my support and encouragement over the years. One former student commented that I am "one of those unusual teachers who manages to combine a comprehensive and challenging class with one that is both interesting and fun. Her students are easily involved through her hands-on teaching style and genuine concern and interest for their needs." And that is what I try to do—both encourage and challenge students.

I have collected a variety of information about changes that take place in my courses. For example, in *Historical Geology*, students completed a questionnaire to measure their confidence in discussing various scientific topics. On a four-point scale, their confidence in discussing topics covered in the course increased from 1 to 1 1/2 points by the end of the course, and their confidence in topics covered in *Physical Geology* increased somewhat. Students also completed a survey at the beginning and end of the course in which they rated their ability to write and to work effectively in groups. These ratings increased slightly over the semester. Appendix E includes successive drafts of papers written for both introductory courses and short essays students wrote on similar topics at the beginning and end of the semester in the courses that involved formal group assignments.

Student Accomplishments

Many geology majors, with my support, have received summer research internships. In a recent year these included internships at the University of Tennessee, the University of Delaware, Woods Hole Oceanographic Institution, the School of Marine Science at the College of William and Mary, and a Keck Geology Consortium project for minority students. Three students who assumed leadership roles in a partnering program with local elementary schools have presented a poster session at the Southeastern Section Geological Society of America meeting.

I am pleased with the recognition my students have received. For example, in a recent five-year period, three of my students received the Penelope Hanshaw Award given to an outstanding woman geoscience student by the Association for Women Geoscientists (Potomac Chapter) on the basis of academic excellence and their contributions to the goals of AWG. I am also pleased that one student received the Bill Greenwood Award (outstanding minority geoscience student), also given by AWG-Potomac Chapter.

Honors Related to Teaching

I am one of several geoscientists in the 1995/96 National Association of Geoscience Teachers (NAGT) Distinguished Speaker Program and am also President of the NAGT. I am fortunate to have received several teaching awards. At the College of William and Mary, I received the Thomas Jefferson Teaching Award in 1990, given annually to a faculty member early in his/her career. In 1992, I received the first Biggs Earth Science Teaching Award. This award is given by the Geological Society of America (GSA) to a faculty member in his/her first ten years of teaching in recognition of his/her contributions to geoscience education. Bruce Goodwin, my department chair, submitted a nomination packet including letters from students, former students, and colleagues. A committee of the Education Division of GSA made the selection.

Teaching Development Activities

Feedback from students is an important source of information that I use to evaluate and improve my courses. For example, I have data from the four major group assignments in *Historical Geology*. Students rated each assignment overall and also rated various components of the assignments. The extinction assignments described earlier received the highest rating, consistent with my evaluation. I will modify the organic evolution assignment, which received the lowest rating, the next time I teach the class. A summary of the ratings is given in Appendix F. Whenever I try something different in class, I have students complete a questionnaire. I then use the results to modify the assignment. I try to determine what components of the assignments work, then try to repeat those in other assignments.

I also try to improve my teaching by reading, attending conferences, and participating in workshops. I get ideas about specific approaches and assignments from the *Journal of Geoscience Education*, the *Journal of College Science Teaching,* and various educational publications. I try to incorporate topics from material I read in the geologic literature into my courses. For example, I am continually adding articles on the extinction controversy to my collection, which I make available to students preparing for that assignment. One of the most important workshops in terms of its effect on my teaching was the workshop on *Teaching with Writing* that I co-directed with Colleen Kennedy, Director of the Writing Program at William and Mary. I learned about other teaching approaches and techniques as well as how to better incorporate writing assignments and peer review sessions into my own courses. I developed critique sheets to focus student attention on certain aspects of each paper they were reviewing. Another influential experience was the *What Works* Conference on Building Effective Collaborative Learning Experiences held in 1994. The workshop by Barbara Millis provided me with an excellent overview of collaborative learning and specific cooperative-learning structures. I was first introduced to teaching portfolios and their value in a workshop given by Peter Seldin (Pace University) and Linda Annis (Ball State University).

In my position as Dean of Undergraduate Studies, I have worked to promote discussions about teaching at the College of William and Mary. I have invited guest speakers to give talks and workshops and have arranged for faculty members at the College of William and Mary to give workshops to their colleagues on campus. With other colleagues, I have organized teaching enhancement projects in which faculty in a variety of disciplines examine successful teaching techniques, explore ways to enhance their teaching, and develop a course portfolio (a teaching portfolio for a specific course).

Dissemination of Teaching Experiences

I have given talks and workshops on various aspects of teaching at several institutions including the University of Kansas, Emporia State University, Murray State University, the University of Wisconsin–Eau Claire, the University of Maryland, and the United Arab Emirates University. I was invited to speak at the symposium "Innovative Approaches to Teaching Introductory Geology" at the annual Geological Society of America (GSA) meeting in 1990. I was also invited to give a talk in the session "Great Ideas from Great Teachers" at the 1995 southeastern section GSA meeting. With other colleagues, I have organized workshops on effective and innovative geoscience teaching at GSA meetings.

I have also written articles about various geoscience education topics (Appendix G). Examples of three of my recent presentations include *More Than Lectures: Alternative Teaching Strategies in Introductory Geology Courses; Developing Student Career Choices;* and *Teaching Portfolios to Document and Improve Teaching in the Geosciences.* I have also organized two theme sessions at Geological Society of America meetings—one on using writing assignments to teach geology and another on using group work in geoscience courses—and one symposium on assessing teaching and learning. The papers from the writing and group work sessions have been published in the *Journal of Geoscience Education.*

I value collaboration and have benefitted greatly by working with several geoscience colleagues. In particular, I worked with Susan Conrad (Duchess Community College) and Ann Bykerk-Kauffman (California State University–Chico) in organizing the writing and groups sessions, respectively, and in editing with me the resulting papers. Barbara Tewksbury (Hamilton College) and I have worked together on various projects designed to promote geoscience education, including the NAGT Distinguished Speaker Program and workshops on effective and innovative teaching given at professional geoscience meetings.

Future Plans

I am choosing to return to the teaching faculty and have several goals for the future. In all of the courses I teach, I want to move away from lectures and will design activities that are more challenging and involve the students more in doing what geologists actually do (rather than listening to me lecture). I also want to participate in peer evaluations of teaching. Although I have received recognition for the quality of my teaching, none of my colleagues has seen me teach in the classroom. I think this will be a challenging experience, but one that will be very beneficial to me. I also plan to continue to work with colleagues to promote innovative and effective teaching in the geosciences.

Appendices
Appendix A: Course Syllabi
Appendix B: Sample Assignments
Appendix C: Student Evaluations
Appendix D: Letters From Students and Former Students
Appendix E: Successive Drafts and Graded Student Papers
Appendix F: Student Ratings of Assignments
Appendix G: Publications on Geoscience Education

TEACHING PORTFOLIO
R. M. MacQueen
Department of Physics
Rhodes College
Spring 1996

Table of Contents
1) Teaching Responsibilities
2) Teaching Philosophies and Methods
3) Student Evaluations
4) Curricular Revisions
5) Professional Teaching Involvement
6) The Teaching/Research Role
7) Goals
8) Appendices
    A. Course Syllabi
    B. "Sporting Quiz" Description

Teaching Responsibilities

In the last several years, I have been responsible for instruction in three under-graduate courses in the physics department:

a) Physics 101: Introductory Astronomy (alternate semesters): A survey course directed toward nonscience major students. The course may be taken to fulfill the college natural science distribution requirement, or as an elective course. Enrollment per section has been limited to 40;

b) Physics 111-112: Introductory Physics: A two-semester, calculus-based introductory course required for physics and mathematics majors, premedical and other (few) interested students, with the total numbering 20–30; and

c) Physics 305-306: Dynamics: A third-year required course for physics majors, typical class size three to six, comprising a survey of advanced mechanics, including nonlinear systems.

In addition, I have been responsible for Physics 101L, Introductory Astronomy Laboratory; and have shared responsibility and serve as coordinator for the Physics 415L-416L Advanced Laboratory sequence required of physics majors, and bridging their third and fourth years. Syllabi for the lecture courses are given in Appendix A.

Finally, I serve as advisor to 14 students, of whom seven are second-year. Of the remaining, five are physics majors who have requested that I advise them.

Teaching Philosophies and Methods

I believe that learning is hard work; those who are willing to expend the necessary effort will understand and hence, learn. My reward system (grades) reflect this belief by placing considerable weight on daily/weekly assignments, which require substantial effort on the part of the students. To be successful in courses in science requires that students think critically and analytically, and that they have an adequate factual background to assimilate the current topic. The common language of science is mathematics; students must translate (even at a simple level) the topic under study into this common language. My teaching methods vary according to my perception of the differing needs of students but each course is essentially a lecture course.

In Astronomy, Physics 101, I attempt to interest and excite the nonscience major students in the subject, with the hope that they will carry that interest into later life. Most of the students have had little exposure to science, so they need to understand how science is "done," and how scientific methods differ from those of the humanities. Thus, the class is a balance between appealing to the students' experience (simple examples of distance, speed, and time relations in terms of highway travel, for example, to cosmological scales) and the completely unintuitive (e.g., general relativity). I hope to impart both a sense of unity (the physical principles) with a sense of awe over the scope of the subject. I stress the latter, for I think that is what the students will carry away from the course.

Students are required to complete a term paper in the Astronomy course; I expect the paper will explore facets of the course which are appealing to the students at a depth beyond that offered in the textbook.

In this class, I employ several specific techniques to encourage students. First, I employ "redemption points" on the final examination to encourage those students who have had difficulty with the initial, basic material—mainly of fundamental concepts of gravity, light, and atoms. (Redemption points are extra credit that a student may earn as a reward for learning material which was missed on earlier tests.) Second, the students' term paper grade is weighted equally with the average of all hour tests, permitting those students who are good verbally and less so mathematically to have an opportunity to "shine" (the paper is graded according to style and grammar, in addition to content). Another motivational method in Physics 101 involves "sporting" oral quizzes (see Appendix B). My idea of "sporting quizzes" will be included in a new book by Sheila Tobias and Jacqueline Raphael: *In-Class Examinations in College Science: New Theory, New Practice*, in press. Finally, students in 101 turn in a biweekly brief summary paragraph of an article in the current popular astronomical literature. My goal is that they comprehend any such popular writing on astronomy when they complete the class. Several students have expressed their pleasure as they become increasingly aware of their ability to do just this.

In the Physics 111-112 course, there are dual needs to be met: For the physics and mathematics majors, the course must stress the unity of the subject and elucidate the principles and practices of physics. For premedical students, broad coverage and applications are crucial (for the MCATs). These differences sometimes conflict. For example, premedical students may chafe at an extended discussion of the derivation of an expression, in which principles common to other topics in physics are discussed, or mathematical issues are paramount. On the other hand, physics majors tend to be more interested in topics such as cosmology, quantum effects, etc. At present, my goal is to spread the unhappiness equally!

I place heavy emphasis upon homework assignments in the 111-112 course: they account for 40% of the grade. I assign homework—both for individual and group effort—regularly and expect the students to expend a significant amount of effort on it. For the group assignment, I appoint students to small (usually four person) groups, ensuring that in each group there is a wide range of mathematical ability, no minority of females, etc. Group problems typically require more complicated analysis, or new principles, or a different approach—in short, they are problems amenable to discussion and debate, and thus promote student interaction and discussion. They are assigned at a rate of about two per week. On request, I offer a great deal of office hour assistance to 111-112 students. For example, I will work through a problem (or have them do it with coaching) completely.

In Physics 305-306, the third-year physics students (sometimes a math major) have all committed to career directions. So this course is intended to expand their understanding of physical phenomena and their application to more sophisticated mathematical techniques. I hope that students in this course will be motivated principally by the subject. A central theme of this course is the common mathematical and theoretical thread which links seemingly disparate elements and subjects. I attempt to stress this unity. This course provides a significant and demanding checkpoint for students intending a career in physics.

This course involves the most class interaction and discussion because it is small, and the students have a common interest and similar mathematical background. In this course, term papers are required, and I expect that students will make some individual, original contribution to the subject: For example, they might pull together two differing approaches to a subject, carry out a numerical calculation of a result for which an analytic approximation has been offered, etc. Finally, homework assignments play a major role (40%) in the students' grade. Unlike the Introductory Physics class, I purposely offer little assistance on homework.

Student Evaluations
Student Instructional Reports (SIRs) have been a principal measure of teaching results at Rhodes; and certain summary questions (Q35 and Q39) are deemed

central to the evaluation of a faculty member with regards teaching. SIRs are not administered to small classes; thus, no data is available for Physics 305-306. The following tables present a time history of the most recent four SIR national percentile rankings for Physics 101 (Astronomy) and 111-112 (Introductory). In addition to Q35 and Q39, I include Q34, because it is one of my weakest ratings, and an area of uncertainty to me, and Q15 and Q18, which relate, respectively, to stimulation of student interest, and student self-assessment of effort expended.

Table 1: Physics 101 (Astronomy)
Percentile Ratings

Year/Term	90F	91F	92S	94F
Q35 Overall Quality of Lectures	80%	90	90	60
Q34 Overall Quality of Exams	40	70	60	10
Q39 Overall Quality of Instruction	90	90	90	40
Q15 Has Your Interest Been Stimulated?	70	90	90	50
Q18 Great Degree of Effort in Course?	10	70	80	90

Table 2: Physics 111- 112 (Introductory Physics)
Percentile Ratings

Year/Term	92F	93S	93F	94S	95S	95F
Q35 Overall Quality of Lectures	60%	60	70	80	80	80
Q34 Overall Quality of Exams	40	20	20	10	60	40
Q39 Overall Quality of Instruction	70	60	80	50	90	70
Q15 Has Your Interest Been Stimulated?	70	50	30	50	40	40
Q18 Great Degree of Effort in Course?	60	80	90	90	90	90

What is to be learned from these summaries? Clearly, student perception of my exams is unfavorable. This is true of both courses. Narrative comments suggest they dislike questions which go beyond the text/lecture material, or which do not reflect time spent upon a subject in class. Next, the most recent (94F) assessment of Astronomy is rather poor overall: this reflects the fact that I taught the course dramatically differently from the past: much more free-form, without the high degree of structure that I usually employ. Clearly, the students disliked this approach—and I'm not sure that I did, either. (Somehow, most of my teaching experiments are not successful!) Overall, however, I would summarize the above results as good—above average—but not outstanding.

A sample (highly biased!) of comments from the written narrative forms, first from the most recent Physics 101 class 94F:

"The prof outlines his lectures nicely. I like the summaries he gives of the major points."

"I thoroughly enjoyed the class in every way. I feel the professor did a very good job of 'scaling down' hard topics and using everyday objects so that students could understand."

"Prof repeats and illustrates the most and/or most difficult material to ensure that students understand it."

"I found his methods to be as close to perfect as possible. I never thought I could be as interested in a science class as I have been here."

And from recent Physics 111-112 class evaluations (94S-95F):

"The teacher is well-prepared and knowledgeable about the subject."

"Takes much care of helping students out of class and was genuinely interested in students' understanding."

"He attempts to make everything clear. His knowledge of the material is great."

"... once we can overcome the intimidation factor of the instructor, he can be very helpful."

"The instructor uses every hour of the class to the fullest ..."

"He has the ability to explain one idea in many ways."

"The discussion/lectures are wonderful and Dr. MacQueen is always making sure we understand."

"... needs to slow down the pace ..."

"You can tell he is excited/interested in the subject, so it makes the student interested, too."

Curricular Revisions

Both the Physics 111-112 and Physics 305-306 courses have evolved over the past three to five years. This evolution has been a result of a) a sharpening of my own perception of what areas in both subjects require elaboration or addition and b) improved awareness on my part of shifts in areas of physics. For example, in Physics 305-306, I now introduce and discuss topics in nonlinear analysis at several points in the course; such topics can now be attacked with numerical computer analysis, which is becoming an increasingly important area in physics. I instigated a more mechanical form of change in Physics 111-112, where this past year we divided very cleanly the study of electrical circuits from the lecture portion of the course and placed it into the laboratory context, where it is particularly well-suited.

On a departmental basis: After my arrival at Rhodes in 1990, I suggested that we carry out a survey of physics alumni over the previous ten years, requesting them to comment on their Rhodes physics education, and on any changes that they would recommend in the way of curricular changes. Respondents confirmed our collective opinion that one weakness in our curriculum was a lack of adequate exposure of the students to quantum physics. As a result, we replaced the current second-year course, which had evolved into mostly topics in classical (nonmodern) physics with a two-semester course in "Introduction to Quantum Physics." Our students thus now receive a more even balance of topics in both classical and quantum physics during their first two years.

Also on a departmental basis, I have encouraged a substantial effort toward enhancing our capabilities for computer simulation of physical phenomena. We have established a Simulation Laboratory for physics students, which has an additional benefit of being a kind of study hall, improving student interaction and camaraderie. In addition, we have greatly enhanced our computing presence in the Introductory Physics laboratory. I am pleased to have played a significant role in the organization and writing of two successful NSF ILI proposals, matched by the college, for this enhancement.

Another example of curricular revision that I led involves the Physics 415L-416L Advanced Laboratory. After a thorough review four years ago by all members of the department, many of the experiments then employed were moved to the lower-level Intermediate Laboratory, and replaced with those being employed by MIT third-year students. Finally, during 1990–1992 I completely revised and changed the experiments carried out in the Physics 101L Astronomy Laboratory. The current lineup includes four experiments employing computer simulation of astronomical events which I have written utilizing a commercial software package, a selection of observational exercises which I have developed, and the utilization of several published workbook exercises. The latter are the least satisfactory; I will work on eliminating the need for the commercial product in the next year.

With a new member joining the faculty next year, I will make a significant shift in teaching responsibilities, taking over the Physics 211-212 Intro to Quantum Physics course second term, and assuming responsibility for the Astronomy program. Lots of work needed here, but especially the IQ course.

Professional Teaching Involvement

I have been a member of the American Association of Physics Teachers (AAPT) for 35 years and attempt to attend the annual winter meeting regularly. This is an excellent forum for teaching innovations, new curricular material, textbooks, and instructional apparatus. For example, we have followed closely the efforts in group learning and Socratic methods reported at the AAPT/TAAPT meetings, and summarized in the *American Journal of Physics*, and, as noted above, have implemented some of the group techniques. In addition, we have viewed several laboratory experiment items at these meetings prior to deciding upon their purchase.

I served in 1995 as president of the Tennessee Section of the AAPT; and we hosted this Section meeting in March 1995. In the past three years I have presented two papers at Section meetings:

"*The Rhodes College Intermediate Laboratory: I*" with E. A. Barnhardt, March 1993. The paper summarized our collective efforts at integrating our second and third year laboratory courses, and fitting the new sequence with the course "Introduction to Quantum Theory."

"*A Particle Track Experiment for the Physics Laboratory,*" March 1994. This paper presents the use of two-dimensional particle tracks for analysis and identification of elementary particle properties.

The Teaching/Research Role
Another measure of teaching results, somewhat more oblique, involves Rhodes physics students' acceptance to and performance in graduate school. Former students over the past four years who entered graduate school are listed below; those students for whom I was research advisor/employer on research grants are marked with *, and those for whom I served as advisor on their senior year honors/directed inquiry study are marked +:

Chad Davidson*+ : Louisiana State University
James Dickens: University of Massachusetts
William Godbold: Florida State University, MS 1994
Bradford Greeley*+ : Johns Hopkins University
Timothy Hamilton*: University of Pittsburgh
Kellee LaCount*: Johns Hopkins University, MS 1994
Michael McPherson: University of Mississippi
Trey White: Ohio State University

In several instances, student involvement in research activities in physics is significant and justifies co-authorship of resultant publications. Joint publications involving students include:

MacQueen, R. M. and B. M. Greeley, 1995, Coronal Dust Scattering in the Infrared, Astrophysical Journal 440, 361–369.

Davidson, C. W., R. M. MacQueen, and I. Mann, 1995, Scattering Models for the Solar Infrared F-Corona Brightness, Planet. Space. Sci. 43, 1395–1400.

MacQueen, R. M., C. W. Davidson, and I. Mann, 1996, The Role of Particle Size in Producing the F-coronal Brightness, in *Physics, Chemistry and Dynamics of Interplanetary Dust, Proc. IAU Colloquium Number 150,* M. Hanner, S. F. Dermott and B. Gustafson, editors (in press).

Oral presentations by students carrying out research work under me include:

V. Savage and R. M. MacQueen, *Effects of a Dust-Free Zone Near the Sun*, National Conference on Undergraduate Research, Troy, New York, April 1995.

C. W. Davidson, R. MacQueen, and I. Mann, *Scattering Models of Solar F-Corona*, International Conference on Cosmic Dust, Capri, Italy, September 1994.

S. Montgomery, *Properties of a Solar Electron Streamer*, National Conference on Undergraduate Research, Chicago, April 1994.

C. W. Davidson, *Comparison of Diffraction and Mie Scattering Models of Interplanetary Dust*, National Conference on Undergraduate Research, Chicago, April 1994.

These examples suggest that at least some students have been motivated sufficiently to compete successfully in the physics arena!

Goals

Objective measures of teaching performance are difficult to generate. One suggestion (P. Seldin) has been to elicit colleague input via a) their review of teaching materials (syllabi, time schedules, tests, and examinations) and b) their in-class observation. A potential source for local evaluators is either or both the University of Memphis and Christian Brothers University physics faculty. I want to discuss this possibility with colleagues at both institutions; it might be possible to establish a sort of "round-robin" system on an annual basis, from which we might all benefit.

A second goal involves a more specific self-evaluation of my testing/exam procedures. Since this is an area where my SIRs are clearly rather weak, I might benefit from specific student (and colleague) input here. I implemented some changes in this area for CY95 and the SIR scores and narrative comments appear to be positive in response (only 111-112 input so far). In any event, I should solicit specific comments from students in this area on the narrative forms this next year. Similarly, my third goal is to solicit specific feedback on the "sporting quiz" use in the Astronomy class.

A fourth goal involves my preserving a sequence of drafts of a term paper in the Dynamics class, to illustrate the role of comments and suggestions in forming the final product.

Finally, I want to encourage other department members, especially the new, relatively junior members, to formulate their own teaching portfolio during the coming year.

Appendices

Appendix A: Course Syllabi
Appendix B: "Sporting Quiz" Description

TEACHING PORTFOLIO
Oliver J. Morgan, S.J.
Department of Counseling & Human Services
University of Scranton
Fall 1995

Table of Contents
1) Statement of Teaching Responsibilities
2) Professional Teaching Philosophy, Strategies, Objectives
3) Description of Curricular Revisions With Learning Resources
4) Student Writing Products
5) Student Course and Teaching Evaluation Data
6) Statements From Peer Colleagues and Classroom Observers
7) Statements by Alumni on Quality of Instruction
8) Listing of Presentations About Curriculum Development
9) Statement of Teaching Goals (1995–1996)
10) Appendices

Statement of Teaching Responsibilities
My primary instructional responsibilities are to teach family therapy and addictions-related courses to both graduate and undergraduate students in the College of Health, Education, and Human Resources. Because I have one permanent course release each semester, I generally teach two content-oriented courses and one section of practicum (skills-oriented) each semester. The fall and spring addiction courses are cross-registered, with graduate and undergraduate students combined in each section, receiving different assignments. I teach one undergraduate family counseling section in the fall and a graduate section in the spring.

Several other courses have been added to my responsibilities on a rotating basis over time. The graduate practicum sections are co-taught and entail both group and individual supervision. I currently teach a graduate section of Developmental Psychology while another department member is on sabbatical, as I taught a course in Psychiatric Disorders when a departmental need arose. Recently, I was asked by several graduate students in the Theology Department to develop a course in Pastoral Psychology and Theology.

Syllabi for the above courses are available in Appendix A.

Professional Teaching Philosophy, Strategies, Objectives
My overall goal, as a teaching professional, is to facilitate a quality learning experience for my students. I believe that this is done in many ways. Building a departmental "culture" and set of performance expectations for students in collaboration with professional colleagues is one way. Giving quality time to faculty-

student interactions, working with students in developing joint learning experiences (e.g., faculty-student research), and engaging in personal-growth-oriented supervision of student learning experiences are others, particularly in the applied, clinical fields of study like counseling and human services. Teaching in structured learning situations such as academic courses is yet another way in which to help students learn. As a full-time faculty member in the Department of Counseling and Human Services, I have engaged in all these forms of teaching and learning.

With regard to classroom teaching in specific courses, I believe that my overall goal, as stated above, entails several auxiliary goals: a) to help students learn the basic material; b) to expose them to the history and important resources in the field; c) to help them connect what they are learning with their own questions/interests, or issues that are currently topical; and, d) to provide them with some facility in engaging the material creatively and critically. I also have a process goal to create an environment in which students can enjoy their learning, willingly engaging the material and having a sense of cooperative learning with each other and with me.

To address these goals, I have tried to structure my courses according to three interlocking themes: Consistent critical thinking and the integration of learning with personal experience are combined with writing across the curriculum in each of my courses.

As the syllabi in Appendix A demonstrate, I am a demanding teacher; my students experience the courses as demanding learning experiences and often speak about them that way. They work hard; that is, they work consistently, coming to every class prepared and often with a written text from their reading. From the first day, I engage students in ways that insure preparedness (e.g., directed questioning, group exercises, article reviews, briefs). By the end of each course, graduate and undergraduate students have between 10 and 15 grades. They have worked consistently throughout the course, have been assessed frequently and in multiple ways, and have needed to use all their learning in order to perform well on their final production (paper, oral presentation, etc.). These methods, I believe, allow students to demonstrate what they are learning (have learned) when they are prepared and at their best; they also provide opportunities for students to learn scholarly habits of mind.

Most of the courses I teach, undergraduate as well as graduate, meet once a week for approximately two and a half hours. Consequently, I have tried to combine a significant amount of reading and writing with a schedule of 14 classroom experiences (per semester) that highlight and complement the readings while using different teaching modalities; e.g., lecture, discussion, directed questions, video presentations, student presentations, thought-provoking exercises, and the like. Both writing assignments and classroom activities are designed to help students integrate the course material with learning from other courses and with their own life experience. The next section about Learning Resources will address this more clearly.

Description of Curricular Revisions With Learning Resources

Toward the end of Appendix A, I have included several syllabi from my first year at the university. The reader may wish to compare these with the more "mature" syllabi for the same courses at the front of the Appendix. Such a comparison will indicate how the expectations, student learning activities, and the readings have changed over time. Each year the expectations and activities have been refined to meet students' needs and to respond to their comments at the end of the previous year's course. Each year the reading selections, classic and contemporary, have been refined and improved.

I am particularly proud of the various assignments and written exercises I have developed to allow students to engage the material personally and critically (Appendix B contains a variety of these Student Learning Resources). Some examples include:

- Graduate student construction of a multi-generational family genogram in concert with interviews of family informants, study of intergenerational theories of family therapy, and keeping a journal of responses to theory-based questions re: family history and dynamics.

- Formats for writing reviews and analyses of articles to be read for class. The undergraduate format consists of six questions that assist in critically analyzing the author's purpose and performance in the article; the graduate format relies on their familiarity with abstracts.

- Viewers' Guides to watching clinical videotapes and learning from them.

- Major course productions are "chunked down" into more manageable pieces that are due throughout the semester, allowing the professor to keep in touch with the student's progress. "Chunks" of the production-in-progress include: CD-ROM projects (review/analysis of the literature), Studies in Contemporary Media, oral presentations or written drafts of material before turning in final written projects, allowing for the professor's feedback prior to final grading.

Student Writing Products

Appendix C contains samples of various student writing productions. Two briefs that were re-submitted after a first grading are included, along with two presentation outlines from graduate students' projects at the end of the substance abuse prevention class.

Student Course and Teaching Evaluation Data

The "Summary Analysis of Student Evaluations" for all years in which student surveys were mandatory (see Appendix D) indicates a general *above average* rating in all three categories measured.

Category	Rating
1. Overall INSTRUCTOR rating	*ABOVE AVERAGE*
2. Overall COURSE rating	*ABOVE AVERAGE*
3. PROGRESS on course objectives	*ABOVE AVERAGE*

While I am pleased at this indicator of teaching effectiveness, a more careful analysis of items within the surveys indicates strengths and weaknesses from which I can continue to learn.

When looking at the aggregate of student surveys, one pattern indicates that I am "prepared for class," that I "demonstrate the importance of the subject matter," and that I "encourage students to express themselves freely." These comments are echoed in peer colleagues' reports of classroom observations. Not infrequently, students also evaluate my teaching style as "stimulating ideas about the subject," while a fair number of students suggest that my teaching stimulates "intellectual effort beyond most courses."

The aggregate of student surveys continues to indicate several areas of needed improvement that remain despite my attempts to improve. This may well indicate a need to participate in OID's mentoring program or to seek some assistance through teaching consultation (see final section of this report, Statement of Teaching Goals). Several items of particular concern to me are indications of *average* or even (occasionally) *below average* performance in teaching, particularly:

- "Explained the reasons for criticisms..."

- Giving exam questions that are either "picky" or "unclear," and

- Showing "concern about student progress..."

I frankly do not understand these criticisms. Sometimes, I wonder if part of this critique is due to the "demanding" quality of the courses. Many of my examination questions are selected from published test files, so that they reflect more general expectations of student performance. In grading written assignments, I have worked to present students with various examples of well-written essays, of various criteria that I use in grading essay material, and I have made myself available so that students can explore further their questions about my criteria. Frankly, while many students enter my courses as weak writers, I believe they leave with greater strengths in this area. However, they have had to struggle to get there. Perhaps these criticisms reflect this struggle.

Statements From Peer Colleagues and Classroom Observers

Appendix E includes reports from peer observations of my classroom style and quotations from chairs' summaries over the past years. I am extremely gratified by the classroom observations and written comments given to me by my professional colleagues. These indicate their acknowledgement of my competence as a teacher. They also seem to address some of the students' criticisms mentioned earlier. They suggest that students are engaged, comfortable, and interested; they suggest that I am accessible. Some comments:

- "Fr. Morgan is a challenging teacher who presents his subject in an engaging, clear, well-organized manner."

- "It was obvious that the students were quite involved in the material and that they felt comfortable participating."

- "The class was fun as well as informative and used a variety of techniques such as lecture, lecture-discussion, media, and small group presentations and discussion."

- "His use of examples was excellent, and he presented himself as an understanding and accessible person."

Statements by Alumni on Quality of Instruction

I have asked several alumni or former students who are currently practicing professionals in the community to write some observations about my teaching based on their previous experiences in my classes. A number of these letters are included in Appendix F.

Interestingly, a review of these letters suggest that—at least for some graduate students—my self-perceptions about being demanding as a teacher, about allowing students to be creative and to integrate their learning into personal issues, and the like are accurate. Some quotations seem relevant:

- "I sought out his class not only because of what I already knew of him as a person but because of what I had heard of him as a teacher—words such as 'thorough, knowledgeable, fair, tough, and interesting' come to mind. 'Easy, boring, and uninspired' are not things you will hear associated with him."

- "I knew through the student grapevine that Ollie Morgan expected his students to work—and not everyone was happy about it. Students looking just to put in time and get their credits are not the ones you will find in his courses by choice—they are likely to avoid him if they can."

- "He is an instructor who pushes his students as far as they can go, and still has them eager to find out what he will be teaching next semester."

- "He actively engages students and has a remarkable way of assessing students' potential and pushing them just a step beyond... [He] encourages each student to make a commitment to his or her course of study. His assignments call for not only an acquisition of knowledge but also an integration of the material both personally and professionally."

- "Fr. Morgan's creativity permeates his work, in the diversity of learning experiences, in class activities, class lectures, and the development of personalized opportunities for learning. With this, he offers respect for each individual."

Listing of Presentations About Curriculum Development

I have been fortunate to work in a department in which curriculum development of our graduate practicum experiences has been a top priority. We presented together the fruits of our collaborative course development in both national and regional conference settings. See Appendix G for a full listing of conference presentations and publications focused on curriculum development.

One spin-off from this larger curriculum development project resulted in a publication and presentations by two of us, centering on curricular methods for integrating freshman into university life:

Eschbach, L., & Morgan, O. J. The freshman goal-setting program: An integrated student development project. Paper presented at the Freshman Year Experience National Conference, Columbia, SC, February 1992.

Eschbach, L., & Morgan, O. J. (1992). Setting goals: An essential life task for freshmen. *Freshman Year Experience Newsletter, 4* (3), 9.

Eschbach, L., & Morgan, O. J. (1994). The freshman goal-setting program: Implementing an integrated student development project. *Journal of College Student Development, 35,* 385–386.

Statement of Teaching Goals

Setting several goals for improving the quality of course instruction suggest themselves from this teaching portfolio.

First I will institute a qualitative *midterm course evaluation process* in each of my classroom courses. I will request that a peer visitor come in to my classes and take some time to process with students their likes and dislikes in the way the course is being conducted. I will also ask that the visitor gather suggestions from the class for improvement. This will give me access to what is working and what is not, and will convey to students my interest in their overall progress.

Second, I will request *assistance from the Office of Instructional Development (OID)* regarding the expectations, quality criteria, and grading of the written assignments for my courses. This kind of assistance may help me to clarify what I do expect from students' writing, and consequently help me to present these expectations more clearly to students.

Third, and for the longer term, I will work with departmental colleagues in our joint desire to pursue curriculum revision and teaching more collaboratively. We have made a commitment to working together in these areas as well as in research. I will work to encourage these efforts, and to join in them with faculty colleagues.

Appendices
Appendix A: Course Syllabi
Appendix B: Student Learning Resources
Appendix C: Student Writing Products
Appendix D: Summary Analysis of Student Evaluations
Appendix E: Peer Classroom Observation Reports
Appendix F: Alumni Letters
Appendix G: Presentations and Publications on Curriculum Development

TEACHING PORTFOLIO
Karen E. Mura
Department of English
Susquehanna University
January 1996

Table of Contents
1) Teaching Responsibilities
2) Teaching and Learning Philosophy
3) Teaching Methods and Strategies
4) Connecting Learning to Students' Lives
5) Developing Critical Thinking Habits
6) Motivating Students to Improve
7) Integrating Computers in the Classroom
8) Evaluating My Teaching
9) Improving My Teaching
10) The Teaching Cell
11) Sharing Teaching Ideas With Others
12) Staying Current as a Teacher
13) Teaching Goals

Teaching Responsibilities
My teaching responsibilities tend to fall into two broad categories: core courses and courses in my specialty, medieval literature. The core courses that everyone in the department teaches are the first-year Writing Seminar (EN 100 with an enrollment of 18 students) and the sophomore year Literature and Culture course (EN 200 with an enrollment of 35 students). Both of these classes are required of all students and include one or more set texts, decided upon annually by the faculty teaching the course. The remainder of the course is shaped by the individual instructor. Courses in my specialty include surveys of medieval literature in translation (EN 320: Literature through the Renaissance, with a cap of 25), upper-level courses and seminars with readings in Middle English (EN 350: Chaucer or EN 390: Medieval Topics, which usually enroll about 12 students), and History of the English Language (EN 310 with 25 students).

While I have taught numerous elective courses over the past five years, I have chosen to focus this portfolio on the three categories of courses defined above. I have invested great effort and poured my soul into developing these courses and believe that they best represent both my passionate commitment to creating a challenging and exciting learning environment for students and my desire to continually evaluate and revise my teaching.

Teaching and Learning Philosophy

I want students to become actively involved and responsible for their own learning and development. This is a crucial component to education because students will have these skills for life, and their personal and professional experiences will be forever enriched. The following six statements define more explicitly the ideas that I believe are fundamental to creating active and responsible learning in our classrooms.

- Learning must be relevant to our students' lives if it is to have a lasting impact.

- We learn and think in new ways when we put our ideas and impressions down in writing.

- Learning occurs most naturally when individual activities build upon and connect to one another, gradually increasing in complexity and subtlety.

- Students who feel positive about their learning efforts learn the most.

- Students gain insight into their own learning when they help their peers to learn.

- Group endeavors and collaborative projects are essential to fully enhance intellectual, social, and personal development.

Teaching Methods and Strategies

My core courses and specialized courses alike have always involved several essential components: class discussion (handouts used to facilitate class discussion are in Appendix A), small group work (see Appendix B for handouts describing group activities and projects), and peer review of student writing (Appendix C contains a variety of peer response sheets). The extent and complexity of these components vary depending upon the level and size of the class, but they remain the backbone of my teaching experience.

In more recent years, my teaching has evolved to include additional elements, most importantly, highly focused library searches (Appendix D contains guidelines for library searches), student portfolios, and student reflective essays (see Appendix E for sets of reflective essays from both my Literature and Culture and Environmental Issues classes). I have found that these new elements enhance the students' level of enthusiasm for and engagement in the course material as well as require students to evaluate their learning and set their own educational goals.

An example taken from my Literature and Culture class reveals how library searches and reading journals help students to engage in active learning and connect material from class to their lives in the world at large. We do a unit on political oppression in Guatemala, using *I, Rigoberta Menchu* as our primary text. The students work in teams to find articles corresponding to the time period covered by the book (1978–82), book reviews, articles about Menchu receiving the Nobel Peace Prize (1992), and current articles dealing with politics, economics, or culture in Guatemala today. We also view a documentary on the lives of the indigenous peoples of Guatemala which includes a narrative by Menchu herself. Finally, the students compose a reading journal describing how the outside materials enhanced their understanding of Menchu's text and attempting to answer the larger question if language is sufficient for communicating human atrocities and suffering.

Connecting Learning to Students' Lives

Since our Writing Seminars are thematically focused, I have experimented with numerous topics, trying in each case to develop a topic that will engage first-year students and relate to their outside experiences. I have taught Writing Seminars on Family Myths and Histories, the Immigrant Experience in America, Banned Books: Censorship vs. Free Speech, and most recently, Environmental Issues: Fact and Fiction.

The Environmental Issues course was most successful, in my estimation, at having students connect their classroom learning with their experiences in the world. Early in the semester, students contacted a local environmentalist, interviewed her or him, and turned this information into a short environmental paper. For the research project, students investigated a regional environmental issue, contacting local authorities as well as relying on books, articles, government documents, and the Internet for information. In the final, reflective essays, students made comments such as "Doing the research paper about wetlands made me concerned about what is happening to them," and "There is a great need to educate and make people aware of the problems in the environment around us if we want to live fruitful lives," demonstrating that their awareness of these larger issues had been heightened. (Appendix E contains the reflective essays for this course.)

In all my classes I strive to introduce current issues and articles from my own reading and research that relate to the material being studied. Some recent examples I have used include articles on the movement to award reparations to the descendants of former slaves after reading Frederick Douglass's autobiography, pamphlets and articles about the Holocaust denial movement after reading *Maus* by Art Spiegelman, and articles about local Pennsylvania school boards and the banning of textbooks for the Censorship class. (Appendix F has examples of current articles.)

Developing Critical Thinking Habits

A primary goal for all of my classes is to encourage and develop critical thinking habits in my students. This was one of the motivating factors that led to my newly configured Literature and Culture class on the topic of slavery and oppression. While the readings for this course vary from semester to semester, they all focus on some historical or present-day experience of oppression.

In conjunction with this thematic focus, I have students write weekly journal entries in response to particular questions. As the semester progresses, these journal questions become more complex and require more advanced levels of analysis and synthesis from the students. For instance, one journal question for the second week of the semester was "Describe the personal characteristics of Frederick Douglass that you think MOST contribute to his strength of character and determination to flee slavery." By week ten, the students are faced with a question such as "Based on your readings and class discussion, do you think the Holocaust was the only true genocide in history?" or "Can language adequately convey experiences of suffering and oppression?" In order to develop a well-supported argument, students at this point in the semester must draw from numerous sources, synthesize their ideas, and express them clearly. (For a semester's worth of sequenced journal questions, see Appendix G).

Motivating Students to Improve
One new method to motivate students to improve that I am developing and refining is having students design final portfolios which will represent their best work. The students select their best formal and informal writing from the semester, according to carefully determined guidelines, create a title page and table of contents for it, and compose an introduction highlighting what they have learned in the class and introducing the work in the pages to follow. (See Appendix H for portfolio guidelines.) This gives students a chance at the end of 14 weeks to look back over earlier work (something they rarely do) and assess it for themselves in order to make their selections.

In all classes, I allow students to rework any paper, providing they meet with me first to discuss rewriting strategies. I then collect the original final version along with the rewritten one in order to assess the changes that were made. Allowing students this second chance does more than just improve their grade; it encourages them to think again about their paper, usually after some time has passed, and to see it in a new light. (Appendix I has samples of first versions and rewritten papers.)

Finally, I have students work in teams on group presentations or lead class discussion, so that students have a way to demonstrate knowledge and skills that extend beyond classroom discussion and writing. Sometimes the groups choose material that is related to, but outside, the course content. For example, students in my History of the English Language class prepared a class "lesson" on any topic related to language study. They had to select an article to assign to the class to read, prepare an annotated bibliography on their topic for students to keep as a reference, present their information using some multimedia material, engage their classmates in active participation, and end with questions to spark class discussion and evaluation.

Integrating Computers in the Classroom
My most extensive attempt to utilize computer technology in the classroom began in Spring 1994. I incorporated the Daedalus Integrated Writing Environment in my Literature and Culture classes. As with any new pedagogical attempt, I quickly learned what worked and what did not. The class discussions varied wildly from day to day, sometimes remaining focused on the reading and issues at hand and sometimes straying completely from the topic. The fact that students could post messages to the electronic discussion using a pseudonym seemed to some to be a license for rude or even vulgar comments. However, subsequent attempts to use Daedalus in my classes were much more successful. First, I removed the pseudonym option so that students wrote under their own names. Secondly, I initiated each class discussion by posting particular questions for that session. (Transcripts of several Daedalus discussions can be found in Appendix J.)

Evaluating My Teaching
Student evaluations are gathered each semester at Susquehanna by using the IDEA Short Form. While this form provides limited feedback due to its brevity and applicability to a wide range of courses, two of the students' self-ratings provide meaningful evidence of teaching effectiveness. (Complete IDEA Short Form summaries are in Appendix K.) The following summary provides median scores (on a 1–5 scale with 5 high) for two important core items:

"Overall, an excellent teacher."				
Writing Seminars	F95	F93	F93	F92
	4.5	4.3	4.3	4.3
Literature and Culture	F95	F94	F94	S94
	4.2	4.2	4.3	3.8
"Would like instructor again."				
Writing Seminars	F95	F93	F93	F92
	4.2	4.1	3.9	4.0
Literature and Culture	F95	F94	F94	S94
	4.0	3.8	3.8	3.4

The ratings for my medieval classes are slightly lower than for my core courses (ranging from 3.5–3.9 for the first question and 3.3–3.8 for the second). I believe this results from several factors: I usually teach only one medieval class per year, while I teach two or three core classes per year; the medieval classes vary greatly in terms of content and level of difficulty, ranging from works read in translation to fourteen weeks of readings in Middle English; many medieval classes have fewer than 15 students so I have no scores for them since the data are considered statistically unreliable.

When students were asked at the end of the semester "What did you like best about this [Literature and Culture] class?" typical comments included:

- "Dr. Mura was creative with her teaching methods . . . it made the course more memorable."

- "Dr. Mura was always willing to try new things with the class if it seemed that what we had been doing was not working. When she/we found something that worked well, she would keep it."

When students were asked "How have your feelings about literature changed?" some replies from recent Literature and Culture students were:

- "I learned that literature is *not* just reading and interpreting pieces of literature, but expressing them orally and by writing."

- "I have even noticed I'm spending more time in bookstores."

(Appendix L contains narrative end-of-semester evaluations.)

Improving My Teaching
Anonymous narrative evaluations solicited by me at both mid-semester and the end of the semester provide specific and relevant feedback for teaching improvement. At times, I find it possible to make significant mid-semester changes to facilitate student learning. Some recent instances of this include:

- Changing journal due dates from Mondays to Wednesdays.

- Letting students select their own group members for projects and peer reviews.

- Distributing journal questions before starting a text instead of part way through reading it.

In addition to feedback from students, I have always sought input from other professors about how to enhance my teaching. A Council of Independent Colleges–sponsored Teaching Portfolio Workshop has had a profound impact upon developing and improving my teaching. Immediately upon returning from the summer workshop, I began to redesign my Literature and Culture course, developing a thematic emphasis, adding weekly reading journals, having students do process papers, and introducing the final portfolio component.

Finally, I have found my syllabi to be not only effective teaching tools but also clear indicators of my evolving teaching efforts. I include past and current syllabi in Appendix M to illustrate this. Early syllabi were complete but rather skeletal. They typically described the course, requirements, grading system, writing assignments, class discussions, important due dates, and weekly reading assignments. My recent syllabi are fleshed out, now explaining the process papers, rough draft workshops, small group projects, and voicing my commitment to an open classroom environment, free of intolerance.

The Teaching Cell

Five of us at Susquehanna formed a "teaching cell" in order to meet weekly and talk about teaching. The cell members represent different disciplines: history, biology, accounting, management, and English. We have continued to meet every week for the past one-and-a-half years. We regularly discuss and share materials from all aspects of our classes, including syllabi, group work evaluation, grading essay exams, and much more. I cannot state strongly enough how this group of trusted colleagues has profoundly influenced my teaching; we can share openly with each other all of our teaching successes and failures.

One outgrowth of the teaching cell that has been extremely helpful is classroom visitation. For the past two semesters, we have visited each other's classes and then discussed our impressions and given suggestions for change. This visitation works most effectively when we have a clear idea of the instructor's goals for the class in general and for that particular class day. Therefore, we share syllabi and class assignments before visiting the class itself. One new awareness I gained after a Fall 1995 visit was my need to address more consciously within individual class periods the various learning styles of my students. Some discussion days suited best the aural learners in the class but did not address enough those with other learning styles.

Sharing Teaching Ideas With Others

After the CIC workshop, Peggy Holdren, Instructor of Education at Susquehanna, and I began talking with faculty on campus about teaching portfolios, giving a presentation at a faculty meeting, planning a TGIF to discuss the concept in more detail, and planning additional teaching-related initiatives on campus throughout the year. We also wrote the AAL grant application to acquire funds for the Teaching Portfolio Workshop.

In addition, I have organized or helped plan two Faculty Workshops at Susquehanna on teaching-related topics, one on sexual harassment in the classroom and one on teaching innovations and initiatives at Susquehanna. I have also organized and helped to present two TGIFs, one on Teaching Portfolios and one on evaluating group work. I spoke about using reading journals to develop writing ideas for a Writing Intensive Courses Workshop. In addition, I have been co-organizer of the Teaching Portfolio Workshop.

This spring, I will present papers which address pedagogical issues at two national conferences. I will copresent with Linda McMillin, Assistant Professor of History at Susquehanna, a paper on "Medieval Studies as an Interdisciplinary Program for Undergraduates" and I will present a paper on "Teaching *Piers Plowman* to Undergraduates." Finally, for two years (1995–97) I am a member of the CIC Faculty Task Force, a selected group of professors from around the country. We have the unique pleasure of conversing with each other about teaching, helping to plan the national Faculty Workshops, and leading one of the discussion sessions.

Staying Current as a Teacher

I stay current in the field of medieval studies by reading journals, attending conferences, presenting papers at conferences (seven papers in the past five years), and connecting with other medievalists on listservs and via e-mail. The summer of 1995 I had a unique opportunity to spend five weeks with 28 medievalists at the NEH Chaucer/Langland Institute. This institute has had a profound impact on my scholarship and teaching, primarily because the focus of the summer was integrating these authors into the undergraduate curriculum. Much time was devoted to discussions of pedagogy, teaching medieval literature in general education courses, the differing challenges of teaching medieval literature in translation vs. in the original language, and many other topics. As a result of this institute, I taught *Piers Plowman* in my 200-level War and Worship course and am planning to teach a Chaucer/Langland course. The presentation that I made is an outgrowth of both my teaching experience this past fall and my participation in the summer institute.

Teaching Goals

My ever-present teaching goal is for my courses to continually evolve to reflect my personal learning and growth. Some immediate, concrete goals follow:

1. Obtain written observations of classroom visits from colleagues.

2. Obtain feedback from colleagues about my teaching materials.

3. Include some letters from former students in my teaching portfolio.

4. Clarify my teaching objectives and criteria for assessment on all future syllabi.

5. Include some shared decision-making with students about class expectations and assessment.

Appendices

Appendix A: Class discussion handouts
Appendix B: Handouts for group activities and projects
Appendix C: Peer response sheets
Appendix D: Guidelines for library searches

Appendix E: Student reflective essays from Literature and Culture and Environmental Issues classes
Appendix F: Current supplemental articles
Appendix G: Sequenced journal questions
Appendix H: Final portfolio guidelines
Appendix I: Sample student papers
Appendix J: Daedalus discussion transcripts
Appendix K: Student evaluations
Appendix L: Student narrative evaluations
Appendix M: Sample syllabi

TEACHING PORTFOLIO
Charles P. Rose
School of Law
Wake Forest University
Spring 1996

Table of Contents

1) Statement of Teaching Responsibility
2) Reflective Statement
3) Course Syllabi, Handouts, and Exams
4) New Teaching Techniques
5) Peer Evaluation of My Teaching and Teaching Materials
6) Student and Alumni Evaluation of My Teaching
7) Student Achievement
8) Future Teaching Goals
9) Appendices

Statement of Teaching Responsibilities

I am fortunate in that my teaching responsibilities include a course in each of the three years of law school. I am responsible for two sections of forty students each in the first year criminal law course (3 semester hours). The challenge in criminal law, an entry level course, is to teach basic skills of analysis and persuasion as well as the substantive law. I teach one section of evidence, a second year, 4 semester hour, required course, to approximately 75 students. The evidence course seeks to expand the student experience from thinking like appellate lawyers to thinking like trial lawyers. I teach federal criminal law, an elective, 3 semester hour course, open to second and third year students. Federal criminal law concentrates on the relationship between state and federal jurisdiction of criminal cases as well as the theoretical foundation of certain crimes not covered in the first year course.

In addition to traditional courses, I have been faculty advisor to the National Moot Court team for the past nine years. The role of faculty advisor involves instruction through intense critical evaluation of student performance. I work with two teams of three students each. Students practice making moot appellate arguments in preparation for an intramural competition. In addition to interaction between the student and teacher during the practice argument, there is a period of evaluation following the argument.

Reflective Statement
Philosophy
"Give me a fish and I eat for today. Teach me to fish and I eat for a lifetime." Early in my teaching career this quotation struck me as apropos to what I was

trying to do with my students. The quote captures the tension that exists between the student's desire to "get" the blackletter rules and the teacher's desire to train an advocate who can reason and persuade. Implementing this philosophy presents a challenge when teaching students who enter law school with a variety of goals and abilities.

Objective

My objective is twofold. I want to make the material sufficiently sophisticated to satisfy the student who wants to learn at the levels of analysis, synthesis, and judgment. At the same time, I feel a responsibility to see that virtually every student knows the basic principles and analytical models within the subject matter area. The first goal is accomplished by the use of hypotheticals in class discussion and feedback on student exams. The second objective is accomplished through an intentional introductory lecture to each unit of material, emphasis on analytical models for specific legal problems, and periodic outline review sessions.

The tension between my objectives requires a choice which confronts every teacher: depth vs. coverage. My teaching has evolved into a style which emphasizes depth over coverage. I am comfortable with this choice for two reasons. First, legal concepts are, for many people, difficult to grasp at a knowledge level because there are many concepts in each area and most of the concepts deal with issues new to the student. Second, most issues discussed in class involve several interrelated analytical steps making the background for analysis, synthesis, and judgment a challenge. Because the material is new and the analysis complex, students need time to confront, digest, and work with the information if they are to learn at either an information or an understanding level.

Strategy

My strategy for implementing my philosophy and objectives has two major components. In selecting material I seek to raise with the students significant issues in five to six discrete areas of the course material. At the end of each unit of instruction, the student should be able to identify the significant legal problems or issues in that unit and articulate persuasive arguments on various sides of each issue. The methods I use include lecture, discussion of hypotheticals, group conferencing, and feedback to students.

The self-defense unit in criminal law provides a good example of the strategy. A recurrent issue in the criminal law course is whether an individual's culpability ought to be measured subjectively or objectively. The unit on self-defense begins with a discussion (lecture in disguise) to develop the elements of self-defense as well as the rationale of the defense. This part of the instruction accomplishes the goal of making sure that as many students as possible have the information needed to deal with a self-defense issue. Once the elements and rationale of the defense have been presented, the students discuss a case involving the relevance of evidence of the battered woman's syndrome in self-defense cases. Rather than being asked to recite the facts, holding, and rationale of the case, the students are asked to assume the role of an appellate advocate and make arguments for and against a position as if they were arguing in an appellate court. To advance effective arguments for and against the relevance of the evidence requires an understanding of the debate concerning objective vs. subjective measures of culpability.

Course Syllabi, Handouts, and Exams
Syllabi
Appendix A includes copies of syllabi from my courses in criminal law and evidence. The introductory portion of each syllabus provides basic administrative information about course objectives, examination format, grading, and any additional student responsibilities. The criminal law syllabus excerpt below illustrates the body of the syllabus.

ASSIGNMENT GUIDE
CHAPTER 1, Basic Culpability Doctrines.
  A. Traditional Concepts.
    1. TOPIC: Mens Rea.

    ASSIGNMENT: Casebook pp. 1–14 [Cases to be briefed: *Faulkner, Yermian, Hood*].

    QUESTIONS:

    [*FAULKNER*]

    What did Faulkner set out to do?

    What are the elements of the crime charged in *Faulkner?*

    What facts did the trial judge tell the jury they must find to convict?

    Upon what authority does Barry rely in deciding against the government on appeal?

    What is the holding of *Pembliton?*

    Why does Barry reject the arson and homicide precedents?

    How do Barry, Fitzgerald, and Keough differ as to the "foresight of consequence" required for criminal liability?

The syllabus is designed to help the student organize the subject matter by identifying a topic for each unit of material. The bold headings in the criminal law syllabus parallel and reinforce the textbook organization of the material. This is useful because I have found that students tend to spend all of their time studying the individual rules while ignoring the overall structure of a given unit of material.

The topic entry is followed by an assignment for that topic. Because students become frustrated when a class gets behind and material is not covered on the day assigned, the topics are not assigned for particular class periods. The rule of thumb, identified in the introduction, is that the daily assignment requires preparation of material fifteen pages beyond the point in the material at which the preceding class ended.

Perhaps the most important part of the syllabus is the "Questions" section. Following the assignment for each topic there are several questions designed to help direct the student preparation for class discussion. This technique also increases the efficiency of the learning process by helping the individual student master information without either consuming valuable class time or remaining lost.

Finally, the syllabus for criminal law, because it is a first-year class, identifies a series of cases in parenthesis following each assignment. The student is responsible for briefing each of those cases using the student's own briefing technique. The briefs are randomly collected by row (seven per day) and critiqued, but not graded, by the instructor. This technique gives the first year student feedback on the development of the student's ability to read cases, and it gives the teacher feedback about what concepts students find difficult to grasp.

Handouts

Appendix B includes two representative class handouts. The homicide handout is used in the criminal law course, and the analytical models handout is used in the evidence course.

The homicide handout includes two different charts. The first three pages represent an organization of the law of homicide in three different contexts: common law; Pennsylvania model; and Model Penal Code. I prepared those pages to help the student organize the law of homicide. The final two pages were prepared by my former student, Eric Groves, and represent an organization of the material from a different perspective. Eric was having difficulty with my organization and asked me to help him develop his own. In the process, it occurred to me that I tended to think of the material in the context of moving from the rules to the fact pattern while Eric tended to think of the material by moving from the fact pattern to the rules. Eric finished his chart and, since it is clear to me that students approach material in a variety of ways, I distribute both charts.

The evidence handout illustrates an analytical model for working with a relevancy problem. The rules here are intricate. To save class time for discussion of application of these rules, the handout is designed to help the student learn the information and organization he must have to engage in the analysis and application of relevancy principles to fact patterns.

Exams

Appendix C includes examples of examinations from my courses in criminal law, evidence, and criminal procedure. The format of the criminal law and evidence exams is identical. Each exam has four parts: 1) 20 true/false questions; 2) 10 multiple choice questions; 3) Five short answer questions; 4) Two major essay questions. The design of the true/false and multiple choice sections is to present a fact pattern and ask the student a question that requires application of some concept learned in the course. I use an objective component in these exams to give the student experience with this type of question in preparation for the multi-state bar examination and to increase the amount of material I am able to test. The short answers are to test information. The essay questions seek to assess how well the student can analyze and discuss clearly the solution to a legal problem using material covered in the course.

The federal criminal law exam format is a traditional all essay law school exam. The questions are similar to the essay questions asked in the essay portions of the criminal law and evidence exams. These students are generally well-grounded in learning information, and I am interested in how well they can analyze specific problems.

New Teaching Techniques
Group activities

I use group activities to facilitate learning in at least two ways.

Small group units. In each of my classes for the past year, I have organized the class into small groups of four to five students based on where they sit in the classroom. I use these groups in two ways. First, if a student is having difficulty with a recitation, the student may call upon his group for help. That student's group (and in fact all of the groups) then caucuses and helps develop a response. Sometimes I may ask a question and have the groups spend four or five minutes, in-place, talking within their group about the solution to the problem posed.

The small group, in-class discussion units were designed to take the edge off of the increasingly competitive environment among law students. The student feels less intimidated with the group available for support. The technique demonstrates to the student that he can learn from his classmates through discussion. In my view, students spend too much time in the solitary memorization of outlines. Perhaps group discussions in class will lead to more discussions outside the classroom.

Criminal law group assignments. In my criminal law class I often make two group assignments (one on premeditation and deliberation and one on insanity). For the premeditation and deliberation assignment, the class is broken into four equal groups of ten students each. Two groups are designated prosecution, and two groups are designated defense. They are all given the same homicide fact situation involving an intended killing. Each group is assigned to meet outside of class to create a five minute excerpt from a closing argument that its side might make to a jury. The group is to identify the best three facts for its side on the issue of premeditation and deliberation as the basis for the argument. Each group then appoints a representative to make the five minute presentation in class.

The premeditation and deliberation exercise serves several purposes. It serves the same function as the small group discussion units. It also allows the students to learn from each other in a more organized setting than the small group units. The assignment allows students to learn in a setting that is more realistic and less academic than the traditional classroom approach. Working with colleagues in groups is an important skill for students to develop. Finally, trying one's hand at even a small part of a jury summation is a welcome change to traditional instruction for first year students.

Examination feedback

An oft-heard criticism of legal education is the lack of feedback received by students. Examination review discussions with second- and third-year students left me with the impression that often the students know the information taught but, due to poor test-taking techniques, do not demonstrate what they know. A first-year student who never reviews an exam with a professor will often make the same error for three years.

Several years ago I gave an exam with unusually poor performance and decided to give an individual written critique to each student. I now do this with every first-year exam and as many upper level course exams as possible. As I read each exam I am intentional about making written comments on the examination booklet. Then I distribute to each student a memo [Appendix D] which critiques the exam.

The memo generally has at least four parts. Part one is a general discussion of the exam answers. This section is a good opportunity to provide positive feedback to students. Law students are constantly being critiqued, and they complain about the lack of positive reinforcement. If a test is difficult and the students do especially well, that is a cause for celebration by the teacher and the students should know that. The section also gives me an opportunity to correct wrong impressions formed during the term and to draw parallels between common analytical errors made by students and a more effective analytical approach. Part two merely reproduces the question for the convenience of the student. Part three will include a sample answer to the question. Sometimes I will include a "school solution" drafted by me, and sometimes I will include, anonymously, a very good student answer. I prefer a student answer so other students can compare their own work with someone who shared the experience. Part four will include a copy of the individual student answer with my comments made during grading. It is important to individualize the comments even if you must write the same comment 50 times. A student will assume the general critique applies to someone else. A copy of his answer with comments forces the student to examine his own performance.

Peer Evaluation of My Teaching and Teaching Materials

I have asked my law school colleagues, Miles Foy and Suzanne Reynolds, to evaluate my classroom instruction as well as my teaching materials [syllabus, examinations, etc.]. Associate Dean Foy is the academic dean at Wake Forest. He and I collaborated on several teaching workshops for adjunct professors at the law school. Dean Foy's evaluation appears in Appendix E. Professor Reynolds was my student and is now a colleague. Professor Reynolds' evaluation appears in Appendix F.

In her evaluation Professor Reynolds comments:

His constant focus on the student has a number of consequences. One, he looks at the material he assigns not as object but as vehicle. He has analyzed very carefully what he thinks is important for the student to learn and uses the material in order to teach those points. By viewing the material in this way, he chooses wisely the parts to emphasize and remains flexible. . . . Also, because he focuses on the students, he listens to their answers better than most of us do. . . . Finally, his students know that the drive behind Professor Rose is his desire to give them the skills and the judgment to be good lawyers. Because they know it, students work hard for him and are proud of performing well for him.

Student and Alumni Evaluation Data
Student evaluations
Appendix G includes sample data from student evaluations in my courses between 1990–1993.

A. Summary of Student Evaluation Responses to Question 9.

Question 9 on the student evaluation form asks: "In view of the above considerations, what was the teacher's overall teaching effectiveness?" A = excellent; B = good; C = Adequate; D = Poor. The chart below indicates the average response to question 9 over several years in my courses.

Course	% Response A	% Response B
Criminal Law [1989–1993]	ave. 83%	ave. 13%
Evidence [1990–1992]	ave. 87%	ave. 11%
Criminal Pro [1990]	ave. 92%	ave. 6%

B. Selected Comments: The following are student comments extracted from evaluations over the past several years:

"Encourages small group discussions. Varies from the casebook with mini projects now and then. Welcome relief!" [Criminal Law §3, 1991]

"Lots of 'role playing' and hypotheticals—an effective system for generating enthusiasm and thought about the subject." [Criminal Law §3, 1991]

"His style of lecturing is provocative and always interesting. Very articulate— demanding of students, challenging but never abusive. Strikes the right balance between challenging and nurturing. Excellent teacher in the highest sense of the word 'teacher.'" [Criminal Law §3, 1991]

"Making of arguments, handouts, and outside class discussions were good. Excellent teacher, stimulates interest, and challenges students. Clearly explains material. Presents a relaxed atmosphere, so students aren't uptight or worried about going to class." [Criminal Law §4, 1991]

"Socratic method and hypos were exceptionally well-directed so that they stayed on track. Rose is one of the most outstanding professors I've had. He can make any subject difficult by his questions in class yet still reduce the major concerns to some well-reasoned concepts." [Evidence, Fall 1991]

"The practice pointers in class were great—both as pointing out the importance and practical side of the material and making it interesting. Great professor—very interested in students—which is the highest praise that I think a professor can be given."

Jurist "Excellence in Teaching" award
I received the Jurist "Excellence in Teaching Award" at the law school in 1983, 1985, 1990, 1993, and 1996. The award was established in 1979 and is awarded by a vote of the members of the graduating class as a recognition of excellence in teaching.

Alumni evaluation
Appendix H includes several unsolicited letters from alumni commenting on my teaching.

The following excerpts from unsolicited alumni letters illustrate the effectiveness of my teaching as it contributes to the work for which my students train.

A law clerk for a federal district court judge, after commenting on a case she was working with, wrote:

"... Even though I do not like the end result, I am confident that the reasoning is sound. That confidence comes from knowing that I had a remarkable professor for criminal procedure. I do not have that same confidence with every case I work on.

In addition to the knowledge I gained in criminal procedure, I use my evidence knowledge almost daily. I feel confident that I can understand the philosophy behind the rules and can find my way around the rules, even if I can't remember each and every one off the top of my head." [Allison (Moore) Grimm]

A practicing attorney in Charlotte wrote:

"You, Professor Rose, epitomize what a teacher should be. You not only have a vast knowledge of the subject matter, but you exhibit that rare concern for students' well being. Whether by constantly striving to discern the effectiveness of your lectures, stopping someone in the halls to say 'did you understand what I meant by...,' or by graciously taking time away from your work in your office to go over and sit on the couch with a student struggling with a point of law, life in law school, or whatever— you make a difference in Wake Forest Law School students' educational experience." [R. Harding Erwin, Jr.]

Student Achievement

I cite three examples of student achievement as evidence of good teaching.

1) I have served as faculty advisor to the Wake Forest National Moot Court Team for the past several years. Wake Forest has traditionally enjoyed a strong reputation for its moot court program in a region which is very strong. During the 1986–87 academic year, one of the teams I advised won the national championship. Two of the three team members argued in the final round of the competition and won the awards for best oralist and runner-up best oralist at the national level. In 1993–94 and 1994–95, Wake Forest had a team advance to the quarter-finals at the national level, and in 1993–94 the team won runner-up best brief nationally.

2) I have worked with three different students who had failed the bar examination. In each case I reviewed the failing examination with the student; helped develop a study strategy for the second exam; evaluated practice answers; and provided encouragement. In each case the student had difficulty recognizing the need to study the structure of the material as well as the individual rules. On two other occasions I worked one-on-one with students who had been readmitted to the law school after failing to meet the academic requirements. All five of these students have passed the bar exam and are pursuing successful careers.

3) Professor Suzanne Reynolds was my student during my early years at Wake Forest. She enrolled in all of my courses and still refers to examples from those classes. Upon graduation, she became a successful practitioner with a large Greensboro law firm. Approximately 14 years ago, Suzanne joined the law faculty and became a colleague. During her early years as a teacher, I had a chance to help her with her teaching. She often refers to our "Wendy's lunch" as a big step in her development as a teacher. That lunch was an informal lunch at which we talked about preparing for class and developing an organization for presenting the material. The discussion focused on being intentional about teaching structure as well as rules. It has been my good fortune to help Suzanne develop as a fine attorney and an excellent law professor.

Future Teaching Goals
Continue to develop group learning techniques
Because my experiment with group learning techniques is a new experience, I want to continue to work with and refine the technique. Evaluations indicate that students respond favorably to the technique. Over the next two years it is my goal to introduce one new group learning exercise in each of my courses. The goal is modest because the technique is time-consuming.

Develop a teaching evaluation form directed to alumni
Preparation of this portfolio has piqued my interest in alumni evaluation. Alumni are in an excellent position to inform our decisions on ways teaching might be improved to help students do what they are being trained to do. Over the next three years it is my goal to develop an evaluation form to be used to survey graduates concerning the effectiveness of my instruction in preparing them for law practice.

Work at a more even-handed treatment of students
It is a goal of mine to become more aware of subtle ways in which a teacher unconsciously sends signals of approval or disapproval of student recitation. With an increasingly diverse student body I believe it is important that professors provide good role models of even-handed treatment. This goal might be satisfied by attending professional workshops or seminars, by peer evaluation, and by learning about literature on the point.

Appendices
Appendix A: Course Syllabi
Appendix B: Handouts
Appendix C: Examinations
Appendix D: Examination Feedback
Appendix E: Peer Evaluation—Miles Foy
Appendix F: Peer Evaluation—Suzanne Reynolds
Appendix G: Student Evaluations
Appendix H: Alumni Evaluation

TEACHING PORTFOLIO
James M. Ryan
Biology Department
Hobart and William Smith Colleges
Fall 1996

Table of Contents
1) Introduction to the Portfolio
2) Teaching Philosophy
3) Statement of Teaching Responsibilities
4) Teaching Strategies and Methods
5) Representative Syllabi, Assignments, and Laboratories
6) The Link Between Research and Teaching
    Honors and independent study
7) Evidence of Teaching Effectiveness
    Student feedback and evaluations
    Student placement
8) Future Teaching Goals
9) Appendices

Introduction to the Portfolio
This portfolio is designed primarily as a self-assessment device to allow me to improve my courses and enhance my teaching. Instead of exhaustively describing each course, I will concentrate on four courses that show my range of teaching styles and that demonstrate my teaching philosophy.

Teaching Philosophy
I am a firm believer in the liberal arts philosophy of education. First and foremost, a liberal arts education should form the basis for a lifetime of intellectual growth, and only secondarily does it provide career training. In order to accomplish the former, we as educators have to encourage our students to be curious about their world by providing them with an atmosphere that supports inquiry. At the same time we must provide them with the analytical skills necessary to satisfy that curiosity. Some students come to college without clear career goals in mind and wish only to sample from the intellectual banquet laid before them. Others come with specific goals and career objectives already articulated. I feel that the best way to meet the needs of both students is to foster a sense of learning for learning's sake (i.e., a liberal arts education). I came to Hobart and William Smith Colleges because they share that philosophy and have a strong commitment to undergraduate teaching and research.

My goals as an science educator in a liberal arts institution are to:

- serve as a role model for learning and thereby pass on to each student my excitement about learning (not just about biology, but learning in general)

- serve as an escort through the confusion of information available to them

- serve as an expert in a specific discipline of study: biological science

- help nonscience students become scientifically literate citizens in an increasingly technological world

- build confident and competent future scientists

I believe the best approach to accomplish these goals is through active participation in the investigative process that is science. Our students' high school education has, for the most part, focused on the products of scientific investigation (i.e., the facts). A college education must build on that foundation by emphasizing the process of scientific inquiry and take them beyond the results of one study into the beginning of another. By this I mean that students must learn how to pose interesting questions, how to access relevant information, and how to integrate conflicting data into a coherent body of knowledge—in short, how to do science. In my view, the most productive learning experiences come when we treat our students as colleagues in the investigative process. Rather than present questions for which we already know the answers, we must enter unexplored territory and work together as a team to find the answers. In doing so, students learn not only the answer but the process by which the answer is obtained and thereby share in the sense of discovery that is the beauty of science.

Statement of Teaching Responsibilities

Currently, I teach the following courses: Vertebrate Anatomy (Bio. 224) and Field Biology (Bio. 330) are electives designed for upper-class biology majors, while The Body Human (Bio. 101) is primarily for nonmajors. Every other summer I co-teach an off-campus program called "Across the Great Divide." This term off-campus takes 15 science students on a trip of discovery through the western United States. In the recent past I have also co-taught the large majors Introductory Biology course (Bio. 110), the first year component of the general curriculum called "Ways of Knowing," and a bidisciplinary course, Math Models in Biological Systems (BiDis. 219), co-taught with a member of the mathematics and computer science department.

In general in the sciences, each course meets three times a week and has two lab sections that meet for four hours once a week. Class sizes range from 80+ first year students in the Introductory Biology course to 15 students in the off-campus program "Across the Great Divide." Typically, majors courses in the Biology Department have between 24–26 students per class.

Teaching Strategies and Methods

The teaching methods I employ in a given course depend greatly on the type of course being taught. For example, in the larger Introductory Biology course we teach using a standard lecture format. This is necessitated by the large size of the class. However, in Field Biology (an upper level Biology course) and in the summer program "Across the Great Divide" I use a project-based approach. By this I mean that the bulk of the class and lab time is spent designing and implementing a series of field projects. With the realization that different classes require different teaching styles, I will describe below four courses that I feel demonstrate the range of my teaching styles.

Vertebrate Anatomy

I have taught the Vertebrate Anatomy course every year since coming to Hobart and William Smith Colleges. It is a course designed not only to give students a solid background in classical comparative anatomy, but to incorporate embryology, functional morphology, physiology, and phylogeny. Whenever possible, I include examples that use modern approaches and techniques for understanding how evolution has designed organisms, while at the same time pointing out the need to understand how the organism uses these structures to function in its environment. The lectures incorporate the most recent research findings in the field by requiring students to read and discuss current research articles. The exams are a combination of short-answer and essay questions that force students to make connections between the topics covered on different days (no multiple-choice).

I also involve the students in the design of the labs. Each lab has a set of goals to be covered that day. In addition, one or two students from the class are responsible for setting up a comparative anatomical demonstration (or prosection) for the other students in the course. The demonstration topic and materials are provided, but it is up to the students to research the topic, set up the demonstration, and write up the handouts to present to their classmates. This approach has met with great success and enthusiasm on the part of the students. Students often tell me that the lab material they understand the best is the demonstration topic for which they were responsible. In 1994 I implemented a pre-course and post-course assessment to determine if my goals and objectives were being met. This consisted of two types of questions given out the first day of class and again on the last day of class. One set of questions asked for information about the key concepts in the course and the second set asked the student to rate their abilities on a list of skills from one to five. Obviously, I did not expect students to be able to answer any of the concept questions before taking the class. Differences between pre- and post-course scores allowed me to assess any improvement made during the term.

Field Biology

In my Field Biology course I take a different approach to both lecture and lab. Students in this course have no textbook. In its place they are given copies of recent journal papers on a wide variety of topics, including optimal foraging theory, predator-prey interactions, neuroendocrine regulation of behavior, and molecular evolution (copies of some 1989 lecture notes and the articles assigned are enclosed in Appendix B). The students are responsible for coming to class ready to discuss these papers in detail (not unlike some graduate seminars). This gives undergraduates an introduction to the primary literature and experimental design. The entire lecture is devoted to an open discussion of the research topic. In 1995, I tried a new approach. The class worked together to design and conduct an environmental impact assessment of the Colleges' Hanley Preserve. Students had to research the literature, map habitats, design ways to assess habitat quality, and write an impact statement suitable for publication.

At first this approach is intimidating to the students because it presents a radical departure from the traditional science course. However, by the second or third week the students have taken an active role in the lecture discussions and are beginning to ask difficult questions of one another. My role at this point is to help focus the debate and to provide additional information from areas outside their reading. While the students may learn fewer "facts" using this approach, they have a much better understanding of the key concepts that form the basis of the field. Furthermore, the students' self-confidence in their ability to master difficult concepts increases throughout the course. For me this is truly one of the most rewarding aspects of teaching.

The lecture exams in Field Biology are also nontraditional. I ask several essay questions that are based loosely on the papers we have discussed in class, but the majority of the essay questions are from research papers they have not read (Appendix C). The students must take our class discussions a step further. Often there are several correct ways to approach each problem, and grading is based on whether they can take what they already know and apply it, in a logical manner, to a novel set of circumstances. After one of these exams, I never again hear, "What do we have to know for the exam?"

The lab component of this course is discovery-oriented. For the first half of the term students learn modern field data collection techniques (at the Colleges' Hanley Preserve), procedures for statistical analysis of that data, and the proper style for scientific writing. During the second half of the term, students break into small groups and design novel field projects. Each project must ask a discrete question that has not been researched previously and provide adequate methodology for answering the question. This culminates in a paper written in a form suitable for publication (Appendix E). The aim is to provide the students with real world experience and to give them an idea of what goes into the collection of the data, which they have been reading about in lecture. The papers (four per term) force them to place the experiment in an historical context (What information leads to this question?) and requires that they explain the significance of their findings. This approach has worked well for teaching Field Biology; the students enjoy the course and its challenging format.

"Across the Great Divide" summer program

Every other summer for the past six years, a colleague in the Geoscience Department at Hobart and William Smith and I taught an off-campus program in the western United States. The "Across the Great Divide" program consists of three courses: Geology of the Western U.S., Ecology of the Western U.S. (Ryan), and Water Resource Issues in the West (co-taught). We developed this program over a three-year period in an effort to provide science students with an opportunity to study off-campus. The program actually began during spring term. We assigned a series of books to read prior to departure and gave oral exams on those readings at the end of spring term. Students met us in Salt Lake City and the courses began. The western ecology and western geology courses were designed to complement one another. In addition to learning the key concepts of each course, we wanted students to see how the underlying geology determined, in part, the distribution of plants and animals on its surface. It is one thing to lecture on the alpine zone or the stresses desert plants face, but there is absolutely no substitute for being there and seeing things first-hand. The same is true of the geology: You can describe an anticline, but it makes much more sense when you are standing on one. In short, that is the philosophy of the course. The Water Resource Issues of the West course is an Environmental Studies course designed to introduce students to the ecological role that water plays in the desert environments of the west and the politics of water "management." We had all read several books concerning water issues in the west including *Cadillac Desert*. At each site we conducted streamside experiments on water quality and listened to local experts speak on both sides of the debate.

In all, we visited five western states and traveled and camped over 5,000 miles in six and a half weeks. The students had specific research projects to do at each of eight major sites, which culminated in writing assignments or short data presentations (Appendix H). For six weeks we all worked very hard from 6 a.m. to 9 p.m. daily with only three days off. This program was one of the finest teaching experiences of my career. I say this because in this type of setting, faculty camping with students in close quarters for six weeks, we grew to become a community of learners not bound by the traditional separation between professor and student. We saw each other as members of a team with a common purpose and worked together in every aspect of the program. We all pitched in with daily chores and the collection of data for our field projects. It was very exciting to see students who had never camped or hiked before become confident field biologists. It allowed me a greater chance to become involved in their personal and academic growth.

The Body Human

This course is designed for those who do not plan on majoring in the sciences, but who have an interest in biology. The goals of this class are: 1) to entice those students who remain undecided about majoring in biology into the field, 2) to demonstrate to those who think they can't do science that science is not about memorizing facts but is a part of their everyday lives, and 3) to create scientifically literate citizens who can recognize the difference between science and "pseudoscience" in an increasingly technological world.

My goal has been to choose topics that I know will impact the lives of my students in their immediate future (if they haven't already). Examples of topics are: genetic engineering and gene therapy, the causes and experimental treatments of cancer, nutrition and diet, reproductive technologies, the workings of the immune system and AIDS. In addition to the basic biology of each topic, we discuss the most current findings and the economic and social implications of this knowledge. My goal is to present all sides of each issue objectively and encourage the discussion of alternative points of view. Only when they have all the data present can they evaluate the issue properly and make an educated decision about what is best for them.

The labs for my The Body Human focus on how biologists think: how a biologist asks questions, conducts experiments, and evaluates her/his results and not on what the specific results say. My aim here is to take the mystique out of doing science. Each of us reasons scientifically every day only often we don't recognize it as such. When the car fails to start in the morning, one might reason that the battery is dead. To be sure, one turns the key and turns on the headlights. If the lights come on, the battery is fine and another hypothesis is required. This simple example is science in its most fundamental form: a problem, a hypothesis, and an experiment.

I designed or modified eight new labs for this course (Appendix D); each is designed to build the students' confidence in their ability to think critically and creatively. As one example, the AIDS simulation lab gives students a safe and effective way to see just how quickly a disease can spread in a community. Students are given a test tube of clear fluid which represents their bodily fluids. They are asked to remove a small amount of fluid and exchange this aliquot of fluid with others in the class (bodily fluid exchange). At the beginning of the exercise one student was unknowingly given a tube with a very different clear liquid than the others (the infected tube). Since they exchanged liquids with one another, any person receiving an aliquot from the infected tube also became infected. After a set number of exchanges they are asked to add to their test tube a second clear liquid which reacts with the infected liquid turning it bright red:

the AIDS test. They must now work backwards from these exposure tests to determine who was originally given the infected tube and plot the spread of the infection in this population. These novice epidemiologists are shocked to see how quickly disease can spread, and I then ask them to change the parameters to model a different type of disease and we repeat the process. The students have a lot of fun with this lab, but I believe the message stays with them.

The Link Between Research and Teaching
Science is a process, and therefore requires active participation. A student who never has the opportunity to do a novel experiment will never know if she/he *is* a scientist or simply well-educated about science.

As an undergraduate I did two independent study projects that ultimately resulted in publications in research journals. Those early experiences were critical for my decision to continue my education at the graduate level. Since arriving at the colleges, I have had the pleasure of being the advisor of over 22 independent study and honors students in the past nine years. In the Biology Department independent study, students must do novel research and present their results in a research paper as well as an oral seminar to the entire department (and any members of the public that choose to come). Working closely with one or two students on a shared research project provides the best opportunity for individualized education. Not only does student research offer students an educational opportunity that is uniquely their own, but they build self-confidence in the process. I have watched very shy, academically average students transform into articulate self-assured young adults in the course of an independent study. In fact, several students have applied for and received competitive funding from Sigma Xi, the Scientific Research Foundation (Appendix F). Others have gone to national and regional scientific meetings, such as the National Council on Undergraduate Research, Rochester Academy of Science, and the Eastern Colleges Science Conference. In addition, I currently have three book chapters in press with a total of eight undergraduate student co-authors and two manuscripts in the works with an additional five student co-authors.

Finally, I am not alone in my belief that research and teaching are fundamental to a high quality undergraduate education. Recently I have received three grants that support research with undergraduates: Whitehall Foundation Grant-in-Aid, National Science Foundation grant (co-authored with my colleague Joel Kerlan) for collaborative learning through research-based projects in the anatomy and physiology courses, and a Research at Undergraduate Institutions grant from the National Science Foundation to support three years of research that involves undergraduates.

Representative Syllabi, Assignments, and Laboratories
Detailed syllabi and course objectives are given out to the students the first day

of class (see samples in Appendix A). Generally, these syllabi spell out my teaching philosophy, objectives, reasons for teaching this class, a list of lecture topics, a detailed exam schedule, a laboratory schedule, and a description of how the final grade is computed. I am a strong believer in providing students with a well-planned course. A comprehensive syllabi gives students an overview of the course as a whole and allows them to see the connections between lectures, readings, and laboratories. I also spend a fair amount of time discussing my academic expectations for each of them. It's been my experience that when I set high standards for academic performance I am rarely disappointed.

All biology courses have a four-hour laboratory in which we try to test some of the ideas and concepts we are discussing in class. Laboratories are a time when students actually get to put theory into practice and *do* science. I have developed a wide variety of laboratory experiences for my students. As mentioned above, in the project-based courses (Field Biology and Across the Great Divide) I have several labs that require the students to help design a series of experiments that will test some hypothesis about the way the natural world works. We often spend several class periods honing the design to make it the best we can. We then carry out our design in the field and report back on the data we have gathered.

In The Body Human my approach is different because I have students who have had less biology background. Here the focus is on taking the mystique out of science by having them understand how science is done. I have also developed several labs that demonstrate concepts relevant to their lives (such as an AIDS simulation, and bacterial testing). I have included several lab exercises that demonstrate this approach in Appendix D.

Evidence of Teaching Effectiveness
Student feedback and evaluations
The following table of responses to student course evaluations and supporting documentation in Appendix G are used as indicators of teaching effectiveness. Sample questions and the percent of students responding to each question are summarized in the following table. In addition to these quantitative measures I have included several unsolicited comments that speak directly to the goals I have articulated above. As noted previously, my goals include building student confidence in their ability to do science and making science accessible to non-majors. These comments are representative:

From a student taking Vertebrate Anatomy:

> "I really appreciate the time you spent with me making sure that I under-·
> stood the course material. I wish more professors were as enthusiastic as you
> about teaching."

From a student who did honors research with me:

"I wanted to thank you for all that you have done for me.... You gave me some much needed confidence in my academic work."

From nonmajors who took The Body Human:

"Thank you also for making the biology material so easy to understand. I enjoyed your class so much that if I had had this class with you earlier, I would have probably majored in biology."

"He obviously loves what he is doing and wants us to love biology as well. He is an excellent teacher and I'm glad I've taken a class with him as I'm not a biology major and will probably never take more biology."

"I dreaded the thought of an 8 o'clock class, but after I got here, I had no problem staying awake because you made things like 'mitosis' (things I never thought could be interesting) seem important for me to know."

"...his enthusiasm was catching."

The following table summarizes the mean scores for Vertebrate Anatomy, Field Biology, and The Body Human over the years indicated. The four key questions shown below were chosen by the Committee on Tenure and Promotion from a standard course evaluation form because they deal specifically with the quality of teaching. Field Biology was taught in 1991 and 1995.

VERTEBRATE ANATOMY 92–95 (n = 88)

Sample Question	*Percent Responses*
How would you rate the overall quality of teaching in this course?	78% Excellent 22% Very good 0% Good-Fair-Poor
Does the instructor stimulate thinking?	83% Most times 17% Sometimes 0% Infrequently or Never
Did you perceive the instructor to be helpful when you had difficulty with the course material?	91% Very helpful 4% Usually helpful 5% Never asked for help
Does the instructor put material across in an interesting way?	96% Most Times 4% Sometimes 0% Infrequently or Never

FIELD BIOLOGY 1991 and 1995 (n = 42)

How would you rate the overall quality of teaching in this course?	88% Excellent 12% Very good 0% Good-Fair-Poor

Does the instructor stimulate thinking?	93% Most times
	7% Sometimes
	0% Infrequently-Never

Did you perceive the instructor to be helpful when you had difficulty with the course material?	100% Very Helpful
	0% Usually-Never

Does the instructor put material across in an interesting way?	100% Most Times
	0% Sometimes
	0% Infrequently-Never

THE BODY HUMAN last taught 92–93 (n = 38)

How would you rate the overall quality of teaching in this course?	80% Excellent
	16% Very good
	4% Good
	0% Fair-Poor

Does the instructor stimulate thinking?	81% Most times
	9% Sometimes
	0% Infrequently-Never

Does the instructor put material across in an interesting way?	6% Most times
	4% Sometimes
	0% Infrequently or Never

Did you perceive the instructor to be helpful when you had difficulty with the course material?	91% Very helpful
	9% Never asked for help

Student placement

As shown in Appendix F, I have advised many independent study research and honors projects over the years. Many of these students are now in graduate schools, medical schools, or working toward careers in biology-related fields. For example, one student is now in medical school at Rutgers University and another has just finished her veterinary school training. Several others are in graduate programs, such as Penn State, Duke University, and RPI. Many of the others have begun careers in biology ranging from environmental law to neuroscience research.

Future Teaching Goals

Generally, I am pleased with what I have been able to accomplish in the classroom over the past eight years. However, there are a variety of teaching methods that I would like to try during the next academic year that I believe may enhance student learning.

- I plan to continue to use the environmental impact assessment as a project in my Field Biology class design. By working together on a project that is both relevant and important I hope that these students will gain first-hand knowledge of the ecosystems of the Finger Lakes region and at the same time produce a document that will be of value to others.

- I plan to include more outside-of-class projects in several courses. For example, I will ask students to complete a set of questions before coming to class the following week. These weekly question sets will ensure that all students have done the readings and thought about the material we plan to discuss the following week.

- I plan to increase the amount of student writing in my courses by requiring drafts and providing plenty of written and verbal feedback on student papers.

- I plan to continue to begin each term with an assessment of the students' skills as they relate to my course objectives. This assessment will be followed by a similar one at the end of the course that I hope will allow me to see if I have been successful in achieving my objectives.

- I plan to incorporate student portfolios into my upper division biology classes.

- I plan to invite colleagues to observe and comment on my teaching.

- I plan to continue my emphasis on providing research experiences for undergraduates using funding from my NSF grant. I also plan to submit at least one research paper each year co-authored by Hobart and William Smith undergraduates.

Appendices
Appendix A: Course Syllabi and Objectives
Appendix B: Sample Lecture Notes and Materials
Appendix C: Sample Exams
Appendix D: Laboratory Exercises I Have Designed
Appendix E: Examples of Student Papers
Appendix F: List of Independent Study and Honors Students
Appendix G: Summary of Student Teaching Evaluations for All Courses in 1990–95
Appendix H: Course Materials for "Across the Great Divide" Summer Program

TEACHING PORTFOLIO
Kenneth L. Stanley
College of Business Administration
Valdosta State University
Winter 1995

Table of Contents
1) Statement of Teaching Responsibilities
2) An Evolving Teaching Philosophy
3) My Teaching Values and Beliefs
4) My Changing Instructional Style
5) Student Evaluations
6) Course Syllabi
7) Future Goals & Agenda
8) Appendices

Statement of Teaching Responsibilities
Although a tenured professor on Valdosta State University's College of Business Administration faculty, my primary responsibility is administrative as Dean of the College. This administrative position has relegated my teaching responsibilities to the status of "part-time instructor" in finance.

In recent years, I have taught infrequently: during Spring Quarter 1994, I taught two sections of the basic finance course (FIN 335) to a total of 42 undergraduate students (19 in Finance 335A and 23 in Finance 335B). In Fall Quarter 1994, I taught the graduate finance course (MBA 735). Finance 335 is the senior college core course for all COBA students; for all but accounting and finance students, this course represents a student's only direct exposure to finance in the curriculum. MBA 735 is a required graduate course in our small MBA Program. These were my first teaching assignments since Winter Quarter 1991; they may be my last until Fall Quarter 1996 when I am scheduled to again teach MBA 735. When coming to VSU in 1984, I was told that deans were expected to teach at least one course per year. In recent years, administrative duties (e.g., Executive Director of the South Georgia Institute) and special projects (e.g., fundraising) have been used as justifications (or excuses) for teaching less and less.

Since coming to VSU, most of my teaching assignments have involved other agendas. Initially, I taught introductory accounting courses in response to faculty shortages. Later, with the advent of two off-campus business programs, I taught the core finance course (Finance 335) in these off-campus programs; my rationale for taking on these assignments was that if COBA faculty were to teach off-campus, then I should also be willing to do so. More recently, my sections of Finance 335 were taught utilizing the prototype classroom equipment for the computer graphics technology that would eventually be available in the renovated Pound Hall, my hope being that this would set an example for other COBA faculty.

Finally, the two sections of Finance 335 taught Spring Quarter 1994 were experimental in the sense that one was taught rather traditionally while the other focused on experiential learning techniques, again, with a hope that other COBA faculty might also begin experimenting with alternative teaching methodologies.

An Evolving Teaching Philosophy

Until recently, I was quite satisfied teaching finance tools and methodologies in the first, or basic, finance course. My teaching philosophy was rather simple: teach finance tools and concepts. I was equally satisfied that I was a "good instructor" if students could demonstrate—to *my* satisfaction—competence with basic finance techniques: the ability to perform ratio analysis, understand valuation concepts, do capital budgeting, be sufficiently confused about whether or not dividends and/or capital structure mattered, etc.

Over the last several years, however, a combination of influences have caused me to reexamine my earlier philosophy: repeated exposure to the quality movement, the AACSB's continuing improvement philosophy, the extensive literature on the importance putting customers first, Stephen Covey's *Seven Habits of Effective People* and *Principle-Centered Leadership*, to mention just a few. As a result of these various influences, my philosophy has evolved into something quite different.

Rather than focusing solely on finance tools and techniques, I now believe there may be some professional success attributes (e.g., oral/written communications, teamwork, a respect and appreciation for cultural diversity, logic, a tolerance for change and uncertainty, appreciation for the international dimension of business, moral/ethical decision-making, appreciation for learning as a life-long activity) that may be more important to a student's lifelong professional success than just functional area knowledge. Equally important in my evolving philosophy is the belief that our job as teachers should focus more on helping our students learn things rather than finding ways to grade them.

Accordingly, my teaching philosophy is evolving into using finance as a vehicle for teaching/demonstrating these professional success attributes.

Embracing and operationalizing this new philosophy has led to a new set of questions: What is the proper balance between functional area and professional success attribute material? Recognizing that one course cannot teach the entire spectrum of professional success attributes, which ones should be emphasized in this particular finance course?

Since my teaching philosophy has yet to become fully operational, it may be useful to share my teaching values. These values will help guide the evolution of an appropriate teaching philosophy in the months and years ahead.

My Teaching Values and Beliefs

Teachers have the opportunity and responsibility to positively impact the future of our society as we share our knowledge and values with our students. As teachers, we must continuously strive for excellence in every facet of our personal and professional lives. The following statements in random sequence reflect my current beliefs about my role as a teacher:

1) I believe that I have an obligation to work harder as a teacher than I expect my students to work as students.

2) I believe that as a teacher I have the responsibility of identifying a set of concepts appropriate for the course that a student should master.

3) I believe that learning is an equal partnership between students and the instructor.

4) Furthermore, I believe that students through their class-related activities (e.g., reading assignments, project participation, homework) have a shared responsibility with the instructor in providing an environment leading to a positive learning experience.

5) I believe that students should be given every opportunity to master the appropriate concepts, and that this mastery is more important than the grade a student receives.

6) I believe that there is a set of professional success attributes which should be integrated into the educational process which are as important, long-term educational goals as concept mastery.

7) I believe that as a finance teacher I have an obligation to demonstrate the integration of finance concepts and techniques across the business curriculum.

8) I believe that as a teacher I must treat all students with respect.

My Changing Instructional Style

Historically, my favorite teaching method has been the lecture method used with homework problems and short, problem-oriented cases. Of course, all of this culminated in exams which were used to determine grades—hopefully, these grades were appropriately distributed so better students could be rewarded, and I could justify my rigor to my colleagues. I enjoyed teaching the first finance course (a "difficult" and, often, "feared" course) to both undergraduate and graduate students. It was fun to teach the use of difficult concepts and/or techniques and to explain how these were used in the "real world." This became my preferred course and instructional style because 1) I received good evaluations and 2) it was easier for me than other courses and/or methodologies. This instructional style was justified by convincing myself (and others) that this was the most efficient technique/style for teaching basic principles.

Currently, I am using more and more experiential projects in my courses. This results from my philosophy that these experiential projects provide a richer learning environment for both functional area knowledge and professional success attributes. Individual and team projects are used primarily to 1) illustrate and reinforce finance concepts, 2) integrate professional success attributes into the course, and 3) integrate finance with the other functional area courses in the business curriculum. I anticipate that these experiential projects and exercises will become a larger portion of the course as experience teaches me what projects work best.

Student Evaluations

Course and instructor evaluations are required in every COBA course. A copy of the evaluation instrument used within COBA is contained in Appendix B.

During Spring Quarter 1994, my Finance 335 evaluations were conducted at approximately the midterm of the quarter. Results of the COBA evaluations are not made available to instructors until after the end of the term. MBA 735 course instructor evaluations were conducted at the end of the course. Appendix C summarizes my course evaluations for both courses and compares these results with evaluations performed Winter Quarter 1991. Based on these evaluation scores, I have plenty of room for "continuous improvement"! I was rather surprised that the MBA 735 ratings were even lower than the Finance 335 ratings!

In addition to the COBA evaluation instrument, teams in the Finance 335B [Spring 1994] section and MBA 735 were asked to prepare a course evaluation as one of their team projects. These teams also met with the course facilitator(s) to discuss specific recommendations. Many of the recommendations coming from these reports were, indeed, incorporated into the course. These team reports may be reviewed in Appendix D.

Course Syllabi

Course syllabi for Finance 335A (Traditional Lecture Course) and Finance 335B (Experiential Course) offered Spring Quarter 1994 and MBA 735 offered Fall Quarter 1994 are contained in Appendix A. Although taught with very different instructional styles, the two Finance 335 sections contained common themes of the generally accepted topics found in most introductory finance courses: financial analysis, valuation theory, capital budgeting, and an introduction to financial markets. Since there is little in the Finance 335A (Traditional Lecture Course) that distinguishes it from literally hundreds of introductory finance courses taught in every business curriculum, the remainder of this section is devoted to a brief description of the methodologies used in Finance 335B (Experiential Course) which make this course rather different. Some of these differences were then incorporated into MBA 735.

In Finance 335B the students' grades were determined totally by team and individual projects. These projects were graded on an acceptable/unacceptable basis, and the students' grades were determined by a combination of 1) points earned on acceptable projects 2) class attendance, and 3) peer evaluations by other students on a specific team. There were no tests used in grade determination. The original premise for this instructional design was that students would be motivated to learn the requisite finance material as they completed actual projects.

In hindsight, the most successful project in both Finance 335 and MBA 735 was the Completed Loan Application Project. Teams were required to prepare an actual loan package and negotiate a loan with a local bank lending officer at Valdosta community banks. Both the students and the local loan officers seemed to think this was a very worthwhile project. Of course, MBA 735 was a much more difficult case than the one used for Finance 335.

From an instructor's perspective, another successful project in Finance 335 focused on students preparing memos on a variety of financial problems and issues. Although students seemed to feel the workload associated with these six memos (and the three computer exercises) was excessive, it was obvious to me that the students became much more proficient at actually writing these memos. The assignments were successful in helping students develop better written communication skills. This was again used in MBA 735 with the same student reaction.

One final example should suffice in giving a flavor for the experiential courses: Students watched the movie *Wall Street* as a basis for distinguishing between legal/illegal and ethical/unethical activities related to the securities markets. I felt that this movie is an effective, enjoyable, entertaining way to bring to life some legal and ethical issues associated with financial markets. Both the undergraduate and graduate students seemed to agree.

Examples of the student products (and reactions to some of these projects) are contained in Appendix E.

Future Goals and Agenda
Based on my recent teaching experiences, I will be working to incorporate still more of the successful elements of this approach into my next teaching assignment (MBA 735: Financial Management) to be taught Fall Quarter 1996:

1) Team projects will continue to be used for class projects, and a corporate mentor project is also planned for the course.

2) The memo format will be used with fewer assignments. This ties into the oral/written communication professional success attribute objective.

3) The ethics section of the course will be expanded. Prior to watching and critiquing the movie *Wall Street*, a set of background readings will be assigned to better identify the issues.

4) A stronger component of international finance will be incorporated into the course.

5) Students will be required to submit a student portfolio of all their work as a requirement of the course.

6) Recognizing that this teaching portfolio is a continuing process, the next update will take place in January 1997 after the conclusion of the next MBA class. I anticipate that this update will contain a section on external evaluation and/or colleague evaluation.

Appendices:
Appendix A: Course Syllabi
Appendix B: COBA Course/Instructor Evaluation Instrument
Appendix C: Course/Instructor Evaluation Results
Appendix D: Team Project Evaluations
Appendix E: Examples of Student Work

TEACHING PORTFOLIO

Maggie M. Sullivan
Doctoral Candidate
Department of Speech Communication
Southern Illinois University
Spring 1996

Table of Contents
1) Teaching Responsibilities and Strategies
2) Philosophy of Teaching
3) Evaluation of Teaching
4) Additional Preparation in Instructional Pedagogy
5) Future Goals
6) Appendices

Statement of Teaching Responsibilities and Strategies

As an instructor for a university-required course in public speaking, I encounter students with varying degrees of apathy and apprehension. This challenges me to present a course in which students can learn, improve, and ideally enjoy. As a full-time instructor at Eastern Illinois University and as a graduate teaching assistant at Southern Illinois University, I have had full responsibility for the classes I teach. I prepare my own syllabi. I write and deliver lectures. I design and prepare tests. I create and facilitate in-class activities, and I plan and evaluate class assignments. Though textbooks change and certain mandated assignments change among institutions, the basic foundation for a public speaking course remains the same. Appendix A shows the syllabus for the course I am currently teaching. The goal of the class is to increase students' competence and confidence in creating, organizing, and delivering messages in public settings. My responsibility, therefore, goes beyond conquering communication apprehension. My mission is to teach skills and methods that create well-reasoned, well-researched argumentation and explanation. I am responsible for teaching students skills needed to deliver an oral presentation, manage speech anxiety, work with groups, and listen critically.

Presentation

I teach basic presentational skills involved in speaking in front of an audience. This area includes voice, gesture, and eye contact. Students are expected to give three to four graded oral presentations. Additionally, I have students give several impromptu speeches over the course of the semester. These give the students experience and practice in quick thinking and public performing.

My students also view videotapes of speakers from speech classes at other institutions. This allows the class to see what is effective and what is not effective in similar speaking situations. They get an opportunity to evaluate and critique others, which in turn causes them to look more closely at their own performances.

Speech anxiety and audience adaptation

One of the most noted fears among adults in our society is that of speaking in front of an audience. My responsibility is to make students aware of the commonality of this fear. Further, my charge is to teach them how to cope with speaker apprehension. The impromptu speeches help with this task. We also discuss how nervousness can generate positive energy in a presentation. I find the best strategy in managing speech anxiety is to develop an appreciation and awareness of the sensation. Everyone experiences uneasiness, and in the public speaking course, everyone can empathize. Students in this course learn to be respectful audience members as well as competent speakers. The course teaches students the importance of sensitivity and awareness when one considers one's audience. Messages are often dependent upon the individuals to whom they are addressed.

Group decision-making

Other teaching responsibilities in this course include addressing group decision-making and interpersonal communication. I devote half of each class period to lecture material and the other half to group work or to an entire class activity. Regardless of the content of the exercise, the students engage in active interpersonal communication, through which, either consciously or unconsciously, they use their ability to explain, argue, and reason.

Listening and writing

Quite obviously, an introductory course in public speaking involves more than performing in front of a group. The course teaches students the role that listening plays in the communication process. By developing critical listening adeptness, students are forming skills that benefit and describe a responsible citizen. The course also emphasizes the importance of good written communication. Appendix B includes a writing assignment I use in a 100-level public speaking course. Effective writing is a precursor to effective speaking. I am therefore responsible for evaluating the students' word choices and language devices as well. These are irreplaceable ingredients in public speaking.

Philosophy of teaching

As a student, I learned through interaction, application, and association. I also use these approaches in my teaching. I believe students learn by interacting with each other as well as with the instructor. I facilitate dialogue as much as possible during each class period. Each class takes on a culture of its own, and I adapt classroom discussions for the particular culture of each section. As student comfort increases, students are more likely to contribute to discussions and to offer personal opinions and experiences related to the course. By hearing such experiences, students are able to apply material to real life. Personal narrative and story telling are wonderful agents for cooperative learning. The understanding of how book terms actually explain and reflect real life is truly enlightening.

My father was a theater professor for 23 years. He frequently taught courses for nontheater majors that fulfilled university requirements. I so often heard people say, "I had your Dad for one class three years ago and he still says hi to me by name." Now as a college teacher myself, I understand and appreciate such a skill and such a sincere interest in students. In higher education, there are often ethical concerns surrounding student/teacher relationships. However, it is possible to show empathy and concern for my students without crossing any line of professionalism. Indeed, it is essential.

Overall, I create a classroom in which I encourage all students to share and communicate ideas, experiences, and opinions. I want students to enjoy the class. I urge them to contribute, and I lead them by example.

Evaluation of teaching

A thorough evaluation of one's teaching includes three types of assessment: student, colleague, and self. I place a high value on student comments because I find them to be useful in my own reflection of my instructional performance.

Student evaluations of my teaching are contained in Appendix C. These evaluations were collected on a campus-wide standardized survey. Students rate me strongest on "enthusiasm for the course," "interest in the students," and an "openness to student participation." I believe it is interesting and important to note these evaluations are from students enrolled in a general education required course. The average response to "self interest in the subject" was a .5 on a 5.0 scale. That's a tough crowd, as they say in show business. Appendix D includes representative examples of anonymous student evaluation narratives regarding my course and instruction.

I also value opinions and observations of colleagues within the discipline. Surely, I can grow from what I see others do and from what others see me do. Appendix E includes statements from several colleagues who have visited my class and observed my interaction with students. The feedback and suggestions I receive from them are instrumental in evaluating my instructional skill and strategies. Similar to the student evaluations, my colleagues' remarks list enthusiasm and concern for students as strong points in my teaching. I am constantly learning and improving by the advice, praise, and even criticism of my peers. Their comments cause me to reflect on my strengths and weaknesses, another valuable form of evaluation.

Self-reflection is a way for me to assess my choices in grading, evaluating, and interacting with my students. I enjoy experimenting with the way I present material. I give considerable thought to my performance each and every day I am in the classroom. After completing a lecture, I go back through my notes and make revisions. If something seemed to work well within the discussion, I make a note.

If I need to adjust the time frame of the lecture, I do so. If the class discussion provides additional examples or insight that I had not previously included, I add them. I also alternate the activities I use in class. There is no time to complete as many of them as I would like. This way I am able to try several different exercises.

Additional Preparation in Instructional Pedagogy

In addition to pursuing a Ph.D. in Speech Communication, I have additional training through course work in college teaching methods, college student profiles, and the college culture. I am devoted to becoming an effective teacher in higher education. I continually work to improve my ability and make the learning experience pleasant and perhaps even fun for my students. Every day I engage in quality discussions with colleagues about occurrences in my classes. The feedback and reciprocal comments are educational. I receive innovative ideas and genuine suggestions through this informal, but useful dialogue. In addition to this, however, I have colleagues observe my performance regularly and offer specific recommendations for improvement.

I am a member of the Central States Communication Association. The annual convention creates an enormous amount of excitement and anticipation for the remainder of the semester as well as for future semesters. I return from such events with renewed enthusiasm and a revitalized commitment to teaching.

Future Goals

My future aspirations include becoming an educator with a doctoral degree. After completing my Master's degree, I taught for two years at Eastern Illinois University. That initial experience with communication education was so positive, I decided this is truly the career in which I belong. Upon receiving my doctorate, I hope to work at an institution where my teaching is valued and my research interests are respected. I want to continue to study student/teacher relationships and classroom culture. I look forward to learning more about myself and my profession. I look forward to opening apathetic freshmen eyes to the phenomenon of human communication. I look forward to working with enthusiastic, undergraduate speech majors. Mostly however, I look forward to polishing my pedagogical skills and insights semester after semester. Number 548 of *Life's Little Instruction Book* reads: "Seize every opportunity for additional training in your job." I do that every day I walk into the classroom.

Appendices

Appendix A: Course Syllabus
Appendix B: Vivid Description Assignment
Appendix C: Student Standardized Survey Evaluations
Appendix D: Student Evaluation Narratives
Appendix E: Letters/Statements From Colleagues

TEACHING PORTFOLIO
Tammy Tobin-Janzen
Biology Department
Susquehanna University
Spring 1996

Table of Contents
1) Teaching Responsibilities
2) Teaching Philosophy
3) General Classroom Strategies
4) Course Syllabi
5) Student Research
6) Additional Teaching Activities
7) Teaching Assessment
8) Teaching Improvement
9) Future Teaching Goals
10) Appendices

Teaching Responsibilities

I am responsible for teaching five different upper-level undergraduate biology classes. Genetics (BI:201) enrolls roughly 50–60 biology sophomores every fall. This year it was taught as part of the introductory biology sequence for the first time. My other two lecture courses, Microbiology (BI:312) and Immunology (BI:400), are both biology electives with annual enrollments of 10–25 students. Microbiology Laboratory (313) and Immunology Laboratory (401) are elective laboratory courses that require past or current enrollment in the lecture courses and regularly enroll between 10 to 16 students.

I am also developing a new lecture course in virology (BI:500) that will be taught to 16 upper-class biology students next fall.

Teaching Philosophy

Lectures should introduce concepts in a fashion that conveys excitement, while providing the training necessary to prepare students for their chosen fields. Students should not be intimidated by the presentation, as over-whelmed students will not learn. There is a great deal of material to be learned in the introductory levels of any course, but if the material is taught in such a manner that students are able to relate to it, they will not only more readily retain the information; they will also be more likely to interact in class, and to independently seek out related topics. Both lectures and assigned readings should include current articles that stress the daily relevance of the course material being presented, and historical readings that show just how far we've come.

Since students learn in many different ways, I am currently developing courses that use a variety of approaches, not only to teach biology, but to evaluate student learning as well. These approaches stress critical thinking and problem solving, rather than just memorizing facts, involve both group and individual assignments, and allow students to progress through a series of project drafts. I make frequent use of student-led peer evaluations, as I feel that students learn as much from teaching each other as I learn from teaching them.

Enthusiasm in a biology program should not only be found in lectures and demonstrations, but also in laboratories that are challenging while still teaching basic experimental skills. Laboratories should prepare students to solve problems of many different sorts. They provide an excellent opportunity to incorporate instruction on topics that often don't fit into any particular niche in classroom instruction. These topics include, but are not limited to, items such as interpretation and presentation of experimental results in both oral and written forms, experimental design, the use of computers in data analysis, and laboratory safety.

Computer literacy is a requirement that cannot be excessively stressed in modern science. It is vital for students to be exposed to computers in scientific applications from the very beginning of their course work. The World Wide Web contains databases and resources that provide valuable ancillary course information.

The goal of a good science program should be to develop in students the intellectual and technical skills necessary to begin answering scientific questions for themselves. Undergraduate research is an invaluable tool to be used in this process. It allows students to apply all the knowledge and laboratory skills they learned in a structured classroom or laboratory setting to a particular scientific question. In an independent project, there is the added excitement of knowing that the research is novel, not just an exercise to learn a new technique. Through successfully solving an original research problem, a student tends to develop self-confidence and a desire to learn even more. In addition to being a great teaching tool, research keeps an educator current in the field. If an instructor is not current, it is difficult to maintain the high degree of enthusiasm necessary to be an effective teacher.

Finally, an isolated professor seldom teaches well. Competent teaching and research can only be accomplished through the contributions of a diverse, but cohesive group of peers, and through the use of student comments to constantly evaluate course outcomes. Student comments should be encouraged throughout the semester in informal conversations, as well as through formal evaluation forms at the end of a semester.

General Classroom Strategies

In order to convey information to students without overwhelming them, I have found it very useful to provide the students with typed outlines of my lectures (see Appendix A) which include copies of any detailed figures that the students will need. These handouts are also made into transparencies or slides that are used to organize my lectures. With these outlines on hand, students can spend more time listening to important concepts, and less time writing down every little detail that comes out of my mouth. This approach also allows me to cover concepts in more detail, as I do not have to wait while my budding Rembrandts try to draw reasonable facsimiles of cell architecture.

It is important to stress the relevance of biology in students' everyday lives. In microbiology (BI:312), we take 15 minutes at the end of class every other week to discuss "microbes in the news." In this format, students earn credit for discussing any papers they have read, or news stories they have seen that involve microbiology. Last year, topics of discussion included everything from new strains of bacteria found in hot springs, to food poisoning incidents on cruise ships. In immunology (BI:400), lecture topics include "why do I get colds?" and AIDS biology.

New biological discoveries are making the news every day, and in order to remain current and exciting, my courses need to reflect these discoveries. In all of my courses, I keep current by reading journal articles, and relevant information is incorporated into my lectures, and/or added to the class reading lists.

Course Syllabi

My course syllabi (see Appendix B) reflect many of the different techniques that I use for teaching and student evaluation, and several of those approaches are highlighted on a course-by-course basis in the section below.

Genetics (BI:201)

The first half hour to hour of each two-hour class is spent explaining concepts and formulas. Then the students break up into groups of three to five to work on graded in-class assignments. This approach gives me time to interact with students immediately following the lecture, as the students try to apply the material from class to sample problems. The problems are handed in at the end of class and are graded before the next class period. This allows me to determine if there were any glaring problems with comprehension of the material, which can then be addressed at the beginning of the next lecture.

I presented a "way cool biology database of the week" (see Appendix C for some representative databases) to my genetics students every week this fall, and was stunned by the positive response. By the end of the semester, students were coming to *me* with new databases, and one of my students even found a database site where he could make virtual fruit fly matings (he called them "cyber-matings") to supplement his real fruit fly experiments, which had gone awry.

Microbiology (BI:312)

Activities are incorporated that break down the barriers between lecture and lab whenever possible, as most science concepts rely on both. I often begin a lecture, then say "Oh, to heck with this; let's go to the lab!" In lab, students actually look at living microorganisms while we discuss their biology. For example, it is much more effective to have students observe a bacterium while it is swimming, than to expect them to remember the statement "spirochetes swim with a corkscrew-like motion." Likewise, students who have actually done a Gram stain are more likely to remember that Gram positive bacteria are purple.

Immunology (BI:400)

Group activities—rather than quizzes—are used to assay student performance between tests. One of my more successful events was "Immuno-Jeopardy," where students answered questions in groups and were graded based on the amount of money their group had won by the end of the class period. The final group activity for students was to present any area of immunology to any group of nonpeer, nonscientists. Some of the more creative products included a bedtime story about "Tommy T-cell" and a puppet show that showed how macrophages attack and eat invading bacteria (if you have never seen one sock puppet eat another, you have not truly lived!).

Laboratory courses

I am slowly adding to my repertoire laboratories that require students to devise their own experiments to answer scientific questions. This approach not only teaches students techniques, but also how to think critically about science. In Genetics Lab (BI:201), students use the Ames Test to determine if commonly used substances (like toothpaste, beer, and tobacco) are carcinogenic. In Microbiology Lab (BI:313), students learn a variety of techniques early in the semester; then use those techniques to identify unknown strains of bacteria.

Finally, peer evaluations of student work are an integral part of many lab assignments. In Immunology Lab (BI:401), the first class period is dedicated to describing how a good science paper should be written (see Appendix D for the biology department's criteria for grading papers) and how to make helpful comments when reviewing papers. Following that session, students evaluate each other's first drafts, and I evaluate only the second drafts, as well as the reviewer's first-draft comments. Students have a much clearer understanding of how to write a good paper once they have gone through the process of grading a bad one.

Student Research

The importance of student research in an undergraduate science education cannot be underestimated. Independent research allows students to begin to ask scientific questions for themselves, rather than just performing "canned" experiments with known answers during defined laboratory experiments. Over the past year and a half, I have collaborated with seven undergraduate researchers who are all attempting to determine genetic mechanisms that underlie the regulation of the mammalian immune response. Jennifer Wells and Elise Knappenberger used their research experience with me to fulfill university honors thesis requirements, and Meredith Libby received departmental honors for her work. See Appendix E for copies of student papers.

Often the outcomes of student research are not as tangible as papers or presentations. My first research student, Jennifer Wells ('95), is not only the first member of her family ever to go to college, but she is now pursuing her Ph.D. in biology at the University of Maryland, Baltimore. Her independent research experience was a critical factor in her decision to pursue graduate work. From this year's crop of five research students, two (Jason Guilford and Jennifer Wilhelm) are applying to graduate school, and two (Meredith Libby and Elise Knappenberger) have been accepted to vet school.

Additional Teaching Activities
In order to serve the Selinsgrove community, I have participated in several high school science education programs. Every fall, Susquehanna University sponsors a Science In Action Day, during which several hundred high school teachers and students come to campus to learn science techniques that high schools do not normally teach. As part of the program, I have developed a "Solving Crime Using Biology" unit (see Appendix F) in which students determine which suspects have performed the heinous murder of the year. Last year, biology faculty members were accused of murdering Barney, and this year we had to determine if Wile E. Coyote had indeed managed to kill Roadrunner. The students are given sheets that tell the alibis and motives for each suspect. Then they test blood found at the crime scene for blood type and DNA type to determine "whodunit."

I have also served as judge for several high school science fairs and have supervised a high school research project. See Appendix G for letters pertaining to these activities.

Teaching Assessment
Student assessment: IDEA forms
The following table summarizes the 1994–95 student evaluations of my courses (my only year of teaching) based on the IDEA Short Form that Susquehanna University uses. I have chosen to summarize my scores for "factual knowledge," "principles and theories," "thinking and problem solving," and "overall, an excellent teacher." Gaining factual knowledge is critical to all science courses, while learning principles and theories is important because it indicates that I have been successful in conveying "the big picture." The analysis of my ability

to stimulate thinking and problem solving indicates how successfully I am teaching critical thinking. The final scores give me an overview of how successful I am as an educator.

	Factual	*Principles*	*Thinking*	*Excellent Teacher*
BI:201	4.2*	4.1	3.9	4.5
BI:312	4.8	4.6	4.0	4.8
BI:313	4.8	4.6	4.4	4.8
BI:400	4.8	4.8	3.7	4.7
BI:401	Course too small to get evaluated			
BI:500	New Course			

*The scores for each course show the average raw score (1 = low, 5 = high).

Student assessment: anecdotal comments

I always encourage students to comment on my teaching techniques on the back of their IDEA forms in order to get a more diagnostic picture of my teaching effectiveness. The comments are always very useful and have indicated that many of my teaching strategies are quite effective. See Appendix H for complete copies of student comments.

My course outlines have met with unanimous approval, and have helped to organize my lectures as well as encouraging my students to listen. Representative student comments include: "I liked the class very much. The handouts for lecture were great—made class easier to follow—enabled me to listen more rather than always missing certain sections in my mad rush to take notes. Overall—two thumbs up!" "The handouts/outlines for each lecture are extremely helpful!! It gives me the chance to look at what Dr. Tobin-Janzen is planning for the lecture—it helps keep me on track because I know what is important & what is not important."

Students also seemed to enjoy the varied class activities that I have employed. About in-lecture lab activities, one student wrote, "I think integrated lab/lectures were very helpful in reinforcement. Some concepts were easier for me to understand because of being in lab..." The microbiology poster sessions were a "super idea, since they get the students out into the 'real world' of microbiology," and Immuno-Jeopardy was "fun and a great way to remember info for the exams."

Microbes in the News was successful in getting students to make connections to their lives. Students wrote "I like Microbes in the News not just as extra credit but because it lets you see how micro is related to everyday stuff" and, "The best part of this class was Microbes in the News. It was good to take a break from straightforward lecture to discuss current issues."

Teaching Improvement

My attempts at improving my teaching have centered around three basic areas: response to student comments, participation in a small teaching cell, and participation in a teaching portfolio workshop.

Response to student comments

Student comments (both elicited and spontaneous) have given me tremendous insight into what works in my courses and what doesn't. After my first semester of teaching, most of my students commented that they would like more frequent tests in class, so I began to give four semester exams rather than three. I found that the increased number of smaller tests allowed students to learn the material at a much more reasonable pace.

I am also changing my immunology textbook since the nicest comment about last year's text was "the book had good figures." Most of my students read the text for the first week, then gave up in disgust. This year's text is written much more clearly and does a much better job of describing the big picture, rather than wallowing in facts. Also, it still has good figures.

Teaching cell activities

Since I came to Susquehanna University, I have been part of a small group that meets once a week to discuss teaching strategies. The other group members are Mary Cianni and Jerry Habegger from Business, Don Housely from History, and Karen Mura from English. The teaching cell has provided a place for me to fly some of my more radical teaching ideas past a forgiving, critical audience that frequently has very valuable suggestions to improve my courses. In particular, I have incorporated case studies into my genetics course, have developed an anecdotal student evaluation to complement the IDEA form, and have broken away from the strict lecture mode employed by all of my professors in the past.

In August 1995, our teaching cell organized and hosted a Teaching Fair that featured teaching strategies that work. As part of this workshop, I described my use of Immuno-Jeopardy to bring life to the classroom. Following that presentation, several faculty, including Jeannie Zeck from English, indicated that they used Jeopardy to teach many different aspects of their courses and that it was successful in all cases.

Teaching portfolio workshop

I participated in a teaching portfolio workshop in order to clarify my teaching goals, and to determine whether my teaching methods are adequately fulfilling my goals. As a result of this workshop, I have developed a series of future goals to improve my teaching performance. These goals are outlined in the next section.

Future Teaching Goals

I think that my teaching evaluations make it quite clear that while I teach facts quite well I still need to work on developing students' critical thinking abilities. I have three major areas where I will address this need. Beginning in spring semester 1996, I will incorporate more investigative-style laboratories into my courses. For example, rather than doing an in-class problem set, genetics students could spend time following my natural selection lecture planning how to use fruit flies to study natural selection. Then they could use that approach in lab that week.

I am also in the process of co-authoring a regional interactive genetics database with James Pollack, Toni Oltenacu, Martha Mutschler, Charles Aquadro, and Dean Sutphin from Cornell University, and Barbara Ward from Delaware Valley College. This database will contain interactive projects that will stimulate critical thinking outside of class. Additionally, the database will have simulations, videos, and pictures of mutant organisms that will provide another medium by which students can learn genetics. (See Appendix I for a copy of the funded grant for this project.) This database should be ready for use by fall semester, 1996.

More rewrites will be incorporated into my courses. In immunology lab this spring (1996), third drafts of papers will be allowed in order to address my comments. Additionally, while students know the minimum requirements for an acceptable biology paper (see Appendix D), they often seem to miss the qualities that raise a paper from being simply acceptable to being very good. I plan to search the literature to find published papers that exemplify both examples and have the students read both papers. We will then discuss which paper is which, and why this is the case. Examples of "A" and "D" papers from this spring's labs will also be used as models in future lab courses.

By spring of 1997, students working in my lab will be expected to present the results of their independent research projects at regional conventions, such as the ones sponsored by the Pennsylvania Academy of Science and the Council of Undergraduate Research. Truly outstanding performances will be presented as posters at national immunology conferences.

Finally, I will improve the methods by which my course outcomes are evaluated. An additional, anecdotal form for student evaluations will be used beginning this spring (see Appendix J for a copy of the form under consideration for use). This form will give me more diagnostic information than the IDEA short form currently does. Furthermore, the anecdotal form has a specific section that will allow me to analyze the effectiveness of the student peer review system that is used to grade immunology papers.

Starting next semester, I also plan to get my department head, Jack Holt, to sit in on my classes. Additionally, as part of our teaching cell activities, members of my teaching cell will begin regular class visitations. These peer evaluations should prove very helpful to my course development.

Appendices
Appendix A: Sample Lecture Outline
Appendix B: Course Syllabi
Appendix C: "Way Cool" Biology Databases
Appendix D: Biology Instructor's Grading Criteria
Appendix E: Samples of Student Papers
Appendix F: Science in Action Day Handouts
Appendix G: Letters From Local High Schools
Appendix H: Anecdotal Student Comments
Appendix I: Interactive Genetics Database Grant
Appendix J: Anecdotal Student Evaluation Form

TEACHING PORTFOLIO
Joseph A. Weber
Department of Family Relations and Child Development
Oklahoma State University
Fall 1996

Table of Contents
1) Statement of Teaching Responsibilities
2) Overview of Teaching Philosophy
       Learning From the Past
       Understanding the Present
       Reaching Out to the Future
3) Teaching Strategies and Methods
4) Evidence of Instructional Effectiveness
       Student Evaluations and Feedback
       Teaching Honors and Awards
       Research and Service Activities
5) Measures of Student Achievement
       Student Placement
       Honors Earned by Former Students
       Publications and Presentations by Former Students
6) Teaching Improvement Activities
7) Future Teaching Program Goals
8) Appendices

Statement of Teaching Responsibilities
Since 1991 my major responsibility has been to teach the undergraduate and graduate-level gerontology courses. Undergraduate students in the FRCD-gerontology degree plan option are required to take the developmental life span courses in middle years (FRCD 4533) and later years (FRCD 4543). These courses are offered every other semester and are also required courses for students in the sociology-gerontology degree plan option and for students who are interested in receiving a minor in gerontology. The undergraduate gerontology courses average around 30–40 students a semester.

Graduate-level gerontology courses include Research Literature and Theory in Gerontology (FRCD 5423), Orientation to Gerontology (GRAD 5883), Ethics and Aging (FRCD 5470), and Grandparent-Grandchild Relationships (FRCD 5750). These are courses which can be used as required or elective hours to fulfill the requirements for receiving a graduate certificate in gerontology. Graduate courses are taught in an informal seminar format, and enrollment averages around 10 to 15 students. Additional teaching responsibilities have included undergraduate preparations in Family Life Education (FRCD 4823) and Adult Learning (FRCD 4353); and a required graduate course for all FRCD majors at the master's and doctoral level in Family Science Theory (FRCD 5523). Brief course descriptions and past enrollments are included in Appendix A.

Overview of Teaching Philosophy
Simply stated, my philosophy of teaching is to stimulate thinking, demand excellence, and prepare students for a world we will hardly recognize in the future. Much of the information students learn today will be outdated in three to five years. The demand on teachers to be current and to allow students to think creatively is no easy task.

I view teaching as a process of educating and encouraging future scholars. In order to help prepare future professionals for a world of technological and social change, I have adapted a philosophy of "scholarship and integration." This particular philosophy incorporates into the classroom and encourages students to 1) learn from the past, 2) understand the present, and 3) reach out into the future.

1. Learning from the past
When students first begin a course, there is always a certain amount of common knowledge or skill level that must be mastered. There are always certain concepts, assumptions, and theories that are the underpinnings for a particular field of study. The field of family science and gerontology has a rich tradition of past research and theory. To understand current family issues such as caring for relatives with Alzheimer's disease, grandparents who are raising grandchildren, or mid-life career and family changes, students have the opportunity to read and discuss past theoretical frameworks and research-based journal articles. Not only are scholarly publications studied, but students are also required to read contemporary novels which address gerontological issues. In the Middle Years (FRCD 4533), students read Bill Cosby's *Time Flies* and the Pulitzer-winning novel by John Updike, *Rabbit at Rest*. Students can begin to understand the physiological changes and dilemmas facing middle age adults as Bill Cosby discusses this part of the life cycle as a long distance runner who often has to "run , run, run without knowing why." This is such an enlightening experience that some students give the book to their parents to read. As one student announced in class, "I can't wait for my parents to read the Cosby book. I wonder if they are going through some of the same dilemmas." Selected course comments by students are included in Appendix B. In the Later Years (FRCD 4543) students read *Friends*, a novel which details the friendship between two nursing home residents. These novels give students a unique perspective of the middle and later years of development through the eyes of the characters who are facing family and personal issues of aging.

2. Understanding the present

In order to help students take abstract information and integrate it into the realm of scholarship, I have incorporated into my undergraduate and graduate courses a research component. This integrative process allows students to see that theory and research are important in understanding current trends and applying the information to future scenarios. But most importantly, research can be fun and exciting. Teaching from this perspective helps students develop critical thinking skills which are important in problem solving in a rapidly changing society. In 1994, two undergraduate students and one graduate student helped analyze student interviews of middle age adults as part of a course assignment (FRCD 4533). The students (with a little direction and encouragement) submitted an abstract which was accepted, and they presented a paper entitled "Looking For a Sense of Direction in Mid-Life" at the American Society on Aging annual meeting in San Francisco (March 1994). In 1995 three undergraduate students and one graduate student presented papers on the "Adult Day Treatment Concept" and "Grandparenting" at the American Society on Aging annual meeting in Atlanta (March 1995) and the Oklahoma Council on Family Relations annual meeting (April 1995). In 1996 one graduate student presented a paper on "Ethics and Aging" at the American Society on Aging annual meeting in Anaheim (March 1996) and a class project on a "View of Mid-Life" was presented at the Oklahoma Council on Family Relations annual meeting (April 1996). Selected national and state conference program agendas with student papers listed are presented in Appendix C. Helping students reach their maximum potential is a key ingredient teachers must cultivate. Involving undergraduate and graduate students in professional activities and associations will help build future professionals.

3. Reaching out to the future

Many students enjoy learning and becoming competent scholars. In an information society which is changing daily, students demand knowledge that is not only interesting but will prepare them for future success in a world which their grandparents would hardly recognize. In my undergraduate and graduate courses, I invite former students who are now community professionals to share their expertise with a class. This often gives students a current, historical, and applied perspective of gerontology. One example is a former student who has started her own company to assist and provide direction for families with an Alzheimer's patient. I have invited Linda to come to the Later Years class (FRCD 4543) for the last four years. When Linda comes to class, she discusses the rewards of working with Alzheimer's families and how she turned an academic interest into a career success. Another former student (Diane), who has lectured in my Grandparenting course (FRCD 5750) the last two years, is an expert on grandparent raising grandchildren. Diane was enrolled in the Grandparenting course in 1992 and developed an interest in grandparents raising grandchildren. This interest led Diane to organize a Grandparents Raising Grandchildren support group and to complete her thesis on this topic. She also presented a briefing at a legislative day at the Oklahoma state capitol. Course lectures and discussions by former students are presented in Appendix D. Listening to former students this allows students to see that the field of gerontology is exciting and can provide rewarding professional and personal opportunities which are constantly changing.

Curriculum Revisions

My philosophy of teaching has changed considerably over the years. Looking back to 1978 when I taught my first undergraduate courses to today, I realize that my teaching philosophy and my approach to teaching has evolved. I used to lecture, trying to cover as much material as possible, while now I am more interested in the quality of information presented and guiding students through a problem solving process of learning. I feel the best way to do this is through the scholarship of integration from the past, the present, and the future.

A review of my course syllabi and outlines shows that my teaching style and approach to scholarship has changed. Courses taught previous to 1990 were an exercise in structured lectures while courses since that time have become more of a free flow of ideas and dialogue between students and professor. This includes active participation by students in applying theory and research to practical situations which will be discussed further in the Teaching Strategies and Methods section. The main reason for revising my curriculum centered around two major factors. This included listening to student feedback and incorporating ideas generated from attending professional association workshops and seminars on teaching. In Appendix E, I have enclosed an example of a pre-1990 syllabi (Later Years, FRCD 4543) and six examples of current syllabi from three undergraduate courses (Middle Years, FRCD 4533; Later Years, FRCD 4543; Family Life Education, FRCD 4823) and three graduate courses (Research Literature and Theory in Gerontology, FRCD 5423; Orientation to Gerontology, GRAD 5883; Grandparent-Grandchild Relationships, FRCD 5750).

Teaching Strategies and Methods

A variety of teaching/learning methods are used to help students successfully master the subject matter presented. Because students have different learning styles, I have deliberately incorporated a multimethod approach to teaching. My ultimate goal is for students to think critically and to be able to discuss/communicate their views. Undergraduate courses are usually more structured than graduate courses in order to provide students with a background in terminology and theoretical concepts. Graduate courses, on the other hand, are taught in a more relaxed format. Regardless of the students' level of education, I try to build a sense of professional companionship among all students in the classroom. Classes are set up to provide an experience for students to formally and informally express their views, expand their knowledge base, and re-evaluate their career and professional goals.

The types of multimethod techniques used in undergraduate and graduate courses include a combination of lectures, class discussions, group discussions, interviewing projects, journal article reports, and class presentations. These strategies are used to help students become consumers of information in gerontology. One unique assignment I have incorporated into the curriculum is an experience which involves taking field trips to agencies and interviewing service providers for the elderly. This gives students an opportunity to learn first-hand the types of professional opportunities available in gerontology. Provided in Appendix F are a sample of several lesson assignments.

Evidence of Instructional Effectiveness
Student evaluations and feedback
Evidence of instructional effectiveness include quantitative results and qualitative student comments from teacher evaluation forms. Student evaluation summary sheets and selected comments are included in Appendix G. Sample questions and mean responses on student evaluations over the last three years are summarized in the following table:

Student Ratings of Faculty
Comparison of mean scores from all of Dr. Weber's
undergraduate (UG) and graduate gerontology (GG) courses
and all other (OTH) courses
Mean scores on a 4-point continuum (SA = 4, A = 3, D = 2, SD = 1)

Sample Questions	Mean 1994 UG	GG	OTH	Mean 1995 UG	GG	OTH	Mean 1996 UG	GG	OTH
1. Instructor was well prepared and organized	3.3	3.3	–	3.0	3.5	3.1	3.2	3.9	3.1
2. Instructor explained & presented material clearly	2.8	2.9	–	2.8	3.2	2.9	2.9	3.7	2.8
3. Instructor enjoyed teaching this course	3.6	3.8	–	3.4	3.6	3.8	3.6	4.0	3.4
4. Instructor increased my understanding of subject matter	3.5	3.3	–	3.5	3.5	3.4	3.5	3.7	3.0
5. Overall faculty rating	3.2	3.4	–	3.1	3.5	3.6	3.4	3.9	3.1

Teaching honors and awards

My effectiveness as a teacher has been recognized by my students and colleagues through several honors and awards received. In 1994 and 1995, I was nominated and selected by the Department of Family Relations and Child Development to represent the College of Human Environmental Sciences for the Regents Distinguished Teaching Award. In letters of support one student said, "Dr. Weber relates to students well and has a genuine concern for the students' professional growth. The personal interest he shows students assisted me in my decision to major in gerontology." A colleague who has observed my teaching writes, "I have been very impressed with the quality of instruction Dr. Weber facilitates for both undergraduate and graduate students in our college. He is very adept at gearing examples and terminology to fit the needs of the group to which he speaks and is a rich source of current information." Additional letters of support and recommendation for the Regents Distinguished Teaching Award are included in Appendix H.

In 1995 I was honored by the College of Human Environmental Sciences at the annual awards event as the Outstanding Graduate Student Mentor. In letters of support for this award one student wrote, "Dr. Weber encourages students to go beyond their potential and continually strive for excellence." A faculty member said, "Dr. Weber is actively involved with graduate students in his department and our college. He supports the activities of the graduate student association in the college and engages in positive mentoring experiences with FRCD graduate students on a consistent basis." Selected student and faculty letters of support are included in Appendix I.

Measures of Student Achievement

Student placement

As shown in Appendix J, many of my undergraduate and graduate students have found employment in a variety of fields related to gerontology. Several former students have continued in higher education and presently have positions at universities such as the University of Central Oklahoma, Ball State University, and East Central Oklahoma University. Other students have been very creative and presently have positions with the Oklahoma Area Agency on Aging, Eldercare, Stillwater Senior Center, Stillwater Adult Day Care facility, Reflections Adult Day Treatment Center, and various nursing home positions, to mention a few. One of my doctoral students, Dr. Linda Mitchell, was interested in the support services Alzheimer's families received. After graduation she started her own company, Glow Inc., to meet the needs of families who have a relative with Alzheimer's.

Honors earned by former students

Several of my former students have received various honors and awards related to teaching and research scholarship. My first doctoral student, Dr. Chalon

Anderson, University of Central Oklahoma, was awarded a summer (1991) internship at the National Institute on Aging. Diane Morrow-Kondos, my first master's student to be awarded a graduate certificate in gerontology, submitted her thesis manuscript (1993) for review competition to Sigma Phi Omega, National Gerontology Honor Society. Diane's thesis won the best manuscript award in the United States. Another master's student, Jenny Hesser, has been active in classroom teaching and manuscript development. Jenny was selected as the top master's student (1993 and 1994) in FRCD for the Phoenix Award competition for graduate student excellence. Jenny's file was reviewed and she was selected as one of the top five master's students at Oklahoma State University both years. One of my present doctoral students, Kathy Cooper, was selected (1995) to represent the department of FRCD in the Phoenix Award competition. A new doctoral student of mine, Deborah Waldrop, was selected (1996) to receive the Oklahoma State University President's Scholarship for graduate student scholastic achievement. I have felt honored to mentor these and other students throughout my college tenure. A student's success is a reward I dearly treasure.

Publications and presentations by former students
Involving students in manuscript development, professional association involvement, and journal article submissions are ways to encourage students to continue their educational scholarship long after they have graduated. Student involvement in co-presenting research and theme topics on gerontology issues at state and national professional association meetings is invaluable in their teaching scholarship. Students have co-presented with me at conferences in Philadelphia, Chicago, San Francisco, Atlanta, and Ft. Worth. Students have also been involved in submitting manuscripts for publications. Manuscripts are presently published or currently under review in such journals as *Educational Gerontology, Southwest Journal of Aging, Journal of Religious Gerontology, Journal of Housing for the Elderly, Journal of Alcohol and Drug Education, Art Therapy,* and *Family Perspective.* A list of presentations and publications with former students are presented in Appendix K.

Teaching Improvement Activities
Striving for excellence is a goal most teachers want to achieve. I have tried to upgrade and re-evaluate my teaching scholarship since I first stepped into the classroom. The process is continually evolving as I search for better and better ways to share scholarly information with my students. Over the years I have participated in several university/college-sponsored workshops and attended several national forums on teaching excellence. In the summer and fall of 1990, I attended two seminars sponsored by the College of Human Environmental Sciences at Oklahoma State University on "Student Learning Styles" by Dr. Gary Price and "Techniques for Developing Effective Instruction" by Dr. Lawrence Aleamoni respectively. Attending these seminars helped me view the classroom

as a dynamic environment for intellectual stimulation. This was just the start as I began to search out more and more resources on teaching effectiveness. During the next several years I attended workshops on "Teaching Critical Thinking" by Dr. Richard Batteiger (Fall 1990) and "What We Would Really Do If We Loved Our Students" by Dr. Chip Powell (Spring 1991). Recently I attended a series of three workshops on "Creative Teaching Techniques" at the Association for Gerontology in Higher Education in Ft. Worth, Texas, in March 1995. These workshops gave creative ways to present research-based information and issues on aging in the classroom. I have already revised course activities and incorporated several hands-on techniques into the classroom learning experience to generate excitement and enthusiasm in students. See Appendix L for documentation of teaching improvement activities.

Future Teaching Program Goals
Striving for excellence in teaching is a goal I feel must be achieved. Student scholars need to be challenged and stretched to reach their full potential. Teaching excellence and teacher dedication allows students to go beyond their limits. A necessary goal I have set for myself is to continue to develop, update, and revise teaching strategies and content-based material to reflect our information global society. Specifically, my goals are:

1) Invite colleagues to critique my classroom teaching style (Fall 1997).

2) Involve students in the development of a student-teacher evaluation instrument (Spring 1997).

3) Develop new courses and revise present courses in emerging areas and theme issues in gerontology such as ethics and aging, theories of aging, and family concerns of aging (Summer 1997).

Appendices
Appendix A: Course Descriptions and Enrollments
Appendix B: Examples of Student Comments on Evaluation Forms
Appendix C: Conference Programs Citing Student Papers
Appendix D: Course Lectures and Discussions by Former Students
Appendix E: Course Syllabi and Outlines
Appendix F: Lesson Assignments
Appendix G: Summary of Student Evaluations
Appendix H: Letters of Support From Students and Colleagues
Appendix I: Student Letters Supporting Outstanding Mentor Award
Appendix J: Student Placement
Appendix K: Publications and Presentations
Appendix L: Teaching Improvement Activities

TEACHING PORTFOLIO
Clyde E. Willis
Department of Political Science
Valdosta State University
Fall 1996

Table of Contents
1) Teaching Philosophy
2) Teaching Responsibilities
3) Advising
4) Teaching Methods
5) Syllabi and Materials
6) Student Evaluations
7) Administrative and Peer Review
8) Related Activities
     For Students
     For the University
     For the Community
9) Professional Improvement Activities
10) Goals
11) Appendices

Teaching Philosophy

My philosophy of teaching revolves around the conviction that the task of education in general and teachers in particular is to encourage and enable students to escape self-tutelage and be able to critique themselves and society in a healthy way. I subscribe to Immanuel Kant's definition: "Tutelage is our inability to make use of our understanding without direction from another. And this tutelage is self-tutelage when its cause lies not in lack of reason but in lack of resolution and courage without direction from another." Kant went on to admonish us to "Know ourselves! To have courage to use our own reason!"

This philosophy informs my observation that by the time students reach the university curriculum they have created a form of self-tutelage by believing that they must not appear to others as if they are "learning" anything. Which is another way of saying they cannot appear ignorant or stupid. It is like the feeling one gets when in a large city for the first time. One cannot, by any means, stare at the tall buildings, else the natives will know right away that you are a tourist, a stupid tourist, of course. The reluctance to appear ignorant, or touristy if you will, is the most glaring obstacle to an otherwise excellent educational opportunity. The ultimate consequence is that students want a system that allows them to "succeed" without exposing their shortcomings (particular with writing requirements), on the heels of which often follows a teaching strategy calculated to teach without offense: Students are afraid to confess ignorance, teachers are afraid to expose ignorance—even in the name of eradicating ignorance.

My main teaching goal is to disabuse students of the notion that they should somehow know everything, and that learning must be a embarrassing experience. Students can and must experience the fact that confessing ignorance is the first step in gaining knowledge. If college is a new experience, it by definition must be strange, even unknown to a degree. Indeed, an educational experience—something experienced anew or for the first time—must by definition be somewhat uncomfortable. If it is not, then it is a redundancy, a waste of time. However, it does not have to be a distasteful occasion.

I firmly believe that most students are full of ideas and opinions that are suppressed—many for years—out of a simple fear of being wrong. The student's fear of inadequacy, coupled with the corollary impression that others do not feel likewise, becomes the single most debilitating aspect of a student's university career. The teaching methods and strategies I have developed and employ are calculated to counter this pervasive diffidence. In order to learn, students must get past the anxiety of becoming vulnerable to the learning experience. My primary concern as a teacher is to coax, nudge, and support students in this effort. There are two principal ways in which I attempt to achieve this strategy: writing and active learning, discussed in the section on Teaching Methods.

Teaching Responsibilities

I teach, along with all members of the political science faculty, a survey course in American government which is required of all university students in Georgia. I also teach public law courses, such as U.S. Constitutional Law, to political science majors who are in large measure planning to attend law school. I also teach public law courses to students with a major in Legal Assistant studies who are planning legal careers with law firms or governmental agencies upon graduation. I teach public law courses in the graduate MPA program and a college level American government course via satellite to selected high school students who will receive college credit. A complete list of courses taught during the past three years is found in Appendix A.

Recently I directed six students in directed study courses (POS 485) and two internships (POS 486). Directed study and internship activities are voluntarily assumed by faculty members in addition to a regular teaching load.

I developed a new course (POS 328) in trial advocacy. This course grew out of the mock trial program developed during the past year which has become and will continue to serve as an adjunct to the course in trial advocacy. (See Appendix A for a copy of the New Course Proposal and syllabus.)

I was selected to teach in a pilot in long distance learning during fall term 1994. The Georgia Board of Regents began offering on a trial basis American government to qualified high school students as part of the post secondary option that makes college courses available to students who have not only qualified for college work while still in secondary school, but who could travel to and from the university campus during regular hours. The course I am teaching utilizes both telephonic and satellite technology to take the courses directly to the high schools in Georgia.

Student Advising
Student advising is considered very important at VSU. I currently have approximately fifteen formal advisees who are either political science/pre-law or legal assistant majors. I receive many of the inquiries from prospective students about the various public law programs at VSU. Moreover, my legal experience as a practicing trial lawyer for over two decades has attracted many students from all over the university for advice and consultation on law and law-related careers.

Teaching Methods
My teaching method is composed of four major components: writing exercises; active learning exercises; reader-response approach to analysis; and one-on-one sessions.

I emphasize the value of writing by having the students write in nontraditional ways. For example, I stress the personal involvement in writing; instead of having students simply essay about what the author "actually" said or meant or what some commentator thinks, I have students answer questions typical of the following: 1) What did *you* expect that the author had to say about anything? 2) Were *your* anticipations fulfilled? 3) If so how? 4) If not, what would you suggest the author say? An example instruction guide that I use to assist students in writing an essay on Madison's *Federalist Number Ten* can be found in Appendix D.

The hermeneutical technique of using various reader-response approaches to reading and understanding texts is another specific strategy I use to help students gain self-confidence as they learn substantive material. For instance, I insist that students read primary works rather than secondary works regardless of whether the author is James Madison or Plato, Richard Nixon or John Locke, and focus on their response rather than that of some commentator. When students realize that they do not have to relate to everything through a medium—parent, teacher, or other so-called experts—they not only gain an empowering self-confidence, they also become highly vested in their education.

The active learning activities involve simulation of the processes contained in the subject matter. This is most apparent in courses like judicial process and trial advocacy. But students also emulate other processes of government that implicate the Congress, the Presidency, and the public. For example, in the American government class, students in pairs or groups will emulate a congressional committee hearing or a presidential staff meeting.

A particular strategy that I employ to achieve my philosophical concern that students lack self-confidence is to conduct as many one-on-one sessions with students as possible. This relationship with students allows us to focus on their individual strengths and weaknesses. For instance, I do not simply assign several written exercises, grade them, and turn them back to the student. I work individually with students on one written exercise as they do multiple revisions to make points that build on each other at different levels. An example of this which consists of a progressive work by a legal assistant student—in this case successive drafts of a legal memorandum—in POS 316 is found in Appendix B.

Course Syllabi and Materials
Appendix C contains course syllabi and course descriptions for each course I currently teach or have taught during the period covered by this portfolio. My syllabi seek to explain to students not only what is objectively expected for completion of the course, but my teaching philosophy and strategies for accomplishing goals for the term as well. In constructing my syllabi I have consulted with colleagues at VSU and elsewhere. I have also used model suggestions contained in the pattern syllabi for political science courses published by the American Political Science Association.

Appendix D contains a letter to my students entitled the *How, Why, and What of Writing.* This piece seeks to help students understand the personal aspect of writing and how it is essential to internalizing the objective world in such a way that the students become *of* the world as well as *in* the world. This exercise implements my teaching philosophy by helping students overcome the self-consciousness that invariably attends "putting oneself on the line." In other words, realizing that new experiences—especially writing about them—necessarily causes discomfort, students become comfortable with feelings of discomfort, thus receiving much more benefits from each new experience.

Student Evaluations
During the academic years at Union College in Barbourville, Kentucky, I consistently received student evaluation objective scores above the average for the Social Science Division. During my first year at VSU, I was also well-received by the students. For the Fall Quarter, I received the highest student ratings for the undergraduate survey course and for the upper-level courses offered political science majors. The scores received for fall and winter terms, which show that I have continued to receive student evaluations well above average, are summarized as follows:

Term	Course	Rating	Dept. Avg.
Fall	POS 200-B American Government	4.75[1]	[2]
	POS 200-I American Government	4.36	
	POS 315 US Constitutional Law	4.80[3]	
Winter	POS 200-G American Government	4.68	4.29
	POS 200-I American Government	4.78	4.29
	POS 316 US Constitutional law	4.69	
Spring	POS 200-F American Government	4.81	3.97
	POS 200-H American Government	4.66	3.96
	POS 322 Judicial Process	4.80	n/a
Summer	POS 776 Labor Law	4.72	n/a
	POS 485 Sem: Law & Literature– Trial Advocacy	5.00	n/a

Responses are: 5 = highest score, 1 = lowest score. Copies of the survey questionnaires follow the survey data for each term in Appendix E.

[1]Highest in the department for survey courses.
[2]Department data not available for this period.
[3]Highest in the department for an upper-level course.

A summary of the subjective comments made by students as part of the evaluation process are set forth in Appendix E along with copies of the complete student evaluation forms. Some student comments that reveal success in implementing my teaching philosophy are:

- Dr. Willis is very profound when it comes to explaining the material of this course. He does an excellent job giving the reasons why behind the facts stated in the textbook. He takes teaching this course a step further by being very communicative with the class and going into detail. He also shows how the material studied in this class relates to the society and world we live in today.

- Dr. Willis was very helpful during the quarter and was always available if we needed him.

- Most enthusiastic professor I've had at VSU. He really tried to relate the material to real situations. Encouraged critical thinking based on sound logical arguments. Excellent instructor.

- Dr. Willis genuinely cares if a student is learning in his class. I have had only one other instructor during my college career that I feel I learned as much from.

- Excellent, but a little scattered. I benefited a lot because constitutional law is very important in my profession. Dr. Willis provided a foundation-building format and built strongly on it. I feel prepared to handle complex issues.

- Dr. Willis is a patient, caring, and knowledgeable instructor. It was a joy to be in this class.

- Dr. Willis is a very good instructor. Dr. Willis took up a lot of time with us as a class and individually.

- I feel that Dr. Willis is an excellent instructor. He shows and is concerned about the students.

- Very enthusiastic. Encourages participation and is extremely helpful outside of class.

Administrative and Peer Review

My teaching performance has been reviewed by my immediate administrative supervisors for the past three years. Most recently, my department head stated that

> Dr. Willis made an outstanding beginning to his academic career at VSU. He was extremely well-received by the undergraduate students, and this is reflected in the fact that his student ratings for one section of POS 200 and his ratings for the upper-division course were the highest in the department for those categories. He is intelligent, dynamic, and energetic in the classroom. Students are constantly in the office seeking his advice, and he freely gives of his time.

An earlier comment by one of my supervisors states: "Clyde has made a very positive contribution to social sciences and Union College in his first year. I don't think we could have found a better person for the position." Appendix M contains copies of these reviews and a letter from a colleague that states: "Clyde's Intro to Criminal Justice stirred one student to change to that major, and the honesty of the issues discussed in Administrative Security was appreciated. Also Clyde's integrity and abilities in the classroom were mentioned more than once."

Regarding my performance in teaching via the long distance network, the Director of the Long Distance Program at VSU made the following comment to the university president regarding my performance: "Site facilitators at all of the distance sites have told me how much the students love Dr. Clyde Willis. He is doing an excellent job teaching the post secondary option political science class. From what I have seen and heard, you could not have picked a better professor for this class." (See Appendix A for copy of this memorandum.)

Related Activities: For Students

I advise VSU's local chapter of Phi Alpha Delta, the international pre-professional legal society. In that role I have assisted the program in a variety of ways: discussion of topics and issues of interest to the members, advising, scheduling, recruitment, etc. A major undertaking associated with Phi Alpha Delta was the organization of a mock trial team at VSU. In the mock trial program students learn how to analyze and organize a random set of facts into a presentable, persuasive argument. They also learn trial and advocacy procedure as they perfect communication and analytical skills presenting cases in simulated courtroom trials.

The mock trial program is part of the national program sponsored by the American Mock Trial Association headquartered in Des Moines, Iowa, that conducts an annual national competition. The team competed in the Annual Capital Classic Mock Trial Tournament at the University of Maryland at College Park, and the American Mock Trial Association Regional Tournament in Atlanta, where it received a bid to compete in the national AMTA tournament in Milwaukee. The team, which received an Outstanding First Team Award at Milwaukee, was proud to have three of its members receive individual honors at all three competitions. I organized and directed a Southeastern American Mock Trial Invitational Tournament. The mock trial program is extracurricular for both students and teacher. See Appendix F for news articles and memoranda relating to this activity.

I am the faculty advisor to the *Spectator*, the university's student-newspaper. In that role I advise the faculty and student staff on legal advice involving a wide range of activities from advertising contracts to freedom of the press issues.

I was the moderator for the spring Student Government Association elections held in Powel Hall. I advise the Student Government Association and the SGA Senate. The SGA conducted presidential impeachment proceedings and it has considered various issues impacting the right of expression and association. See Appendix F for news articles relating to this activity.

I conducted a two-day, twelve-hour Seminar-Workshop on Computer Assisted Legal Research (CALR) for students who had not been able to cover the topic in the Legal Research course (POS/LA 325). Some faculty also attended the seminar-workshop. Evaluations rated the instructor 3.75 on a scale of 4 = Excellent, 3 = Good, 2 = Fair, 1 = Poor for knowledge, preparation, communication, and overall effectiveness. See Appendix F for a letter of thanks from the Continuing Education Center and copies of participant evaluations.

I proposed and assisted the successful nomination of a student in my constitutional law class for the Annie Powe-Hopper Award. This is the university's most distinguished annual award. The winner must exemplify the tradition of VSU and those traits of character, dignity, and scholarship associated with the best of university traditions. See Appendix F for news articles and my nominating petition relating to this activity.

While at Union College, I served as a judge at intercollegiate academic tournaments. Appendix F contains a letter of thanks for participating in that activity.

Many of the students who attend my classes participate in the trial advocacy program and seek advice from me plan to attend graduate and professional schools. Consequently, I am frequently called upon to write letters of recommendation. Appendix F contains sample letters of recommendation that I have recently completed on behalf of these students.

Related Activities: For the University

I have served on a variety of committees for both the political science department and the university as a whole. I serve on 1) the department's committee which has commenced to make the assessment of its undergraduate program in Legal Studies. I wrote the "Statement of Purpose" and "Outcomes" as a member of that committee; 2) the department's promotion and tenure committee; 3) the faculty search committee; 4) the department's committee to review and revise the questionnaire form used by students in the Survey of Student Opinion of Instructor & Course; 5) the department's committee to study the role of adjuncts and make policy recommendations to the chair; 6) the university's committee on the faculty handbook; 7) advisor to the faculty grievance committee; 8) distance learning policy subcommittee on training; and 9) the Pew Higher Education Roundtable, as one of three representatives from the College of Arts and Sciences at VSU. (See Appendix G for a sample of my participation in committee affairs.) At Union College during the 1992–93 academic year I served on the self-study committee that prepared the report (with documentation) for a SACS accreditation review, and also the committee on committees as chair.

I participated as a panelist in a public forum on "Politics, Privacy, and the Press," an explanation of media ethics through film and panel discussion at VSU. The event was supported in part by the Georgia Humanities Council and the National Endowment for the Humanities.

I conducted a half-day seminar-workshop for the VSU Odum Library staff on how to use Georgia Law on Disk, a CD-ROM electronic legal research service produced by the Michie Company.

I presented four student-faculty lectures at Union College in Barbourville, Kentucky. The lectures were: "Limited Government: Who is Limited and Who is Not," part of the Union College Lecture Series and later published under the title of "The Paradox of Limited Government: A Topsy-Turvy World"; "The Hermeneutics of Literary Criticism"; "Battleships, Pepsi-Cola and College Dictionaries: A Notion of Democratic-Capitalism"; and "Mr. Civil Rights: An

Essay/Lecture In Tribute to Justice Thurgood Marshall." Copies or summaries of these lectures are included in Appendix G.

Related Activities: For the Community
I presented a program to the Valdosta Bar Association on the various aspects of the Legal Assistant Studies program. The presentation covered three major aspects: the B.A. degree, the opportunity for selective education by law office personnel, and the opportunity for continuing legal education courses and programs offered jointly by the Political Science faculty and VSU's Continuing Education Department.

Service to the community-at-large is a major commitment of the University and one I take very seriously as well. I presented a four-evening workshop-seminar on electronic legal research to the South Georgia Association of Legal Assistants; I presented a similar two-day workshop to attorneys from bar associations in South Georgia (see Appendix H); and also I directed a student-led mock trial before the South Georgia Association of Radiologists that dealt with medical malpractice. I also presented two half-day seminars at the South Georgia Medical Center entitled "The Medical Community Meets the Legal Community." Each of these programs has been approved for continuing education credits by the various agencies respectively in charge of legal assistants, lawyers, and radiologists.

Professional Improvement Activities
I was awarded a faculty development grant by the VSU Center for Faculty Development and Institutional Improvement. This grant allowed me to attend and participate in the faculty/coach workshops and seminars while attending the National Intercollegiate Mock Trial Tournament at the University of Milwaukee. These workshops and seminars covered various aspects of mock trial advocacy competition as well as administrative aspects of the American Mock Trial Association. Included in the activities were: discussion of appropriate course materials, types and manner of supporting lab experience, and consideration of problems encountered by existing programs. A copy of my grant proposal and final report along with a letter of congratulations—when I locate its whereabouts—from the Dean of the College of Liberal Arts are contained in Appendix I.

I attended three course-related legal seminars. One seminar was on ethics in the legal community, another on criminal law, and one on the legal rights of workers in the modern workplace. Most of my courses in public law, particularly the courses in trial advocacy and judicial procedure, have an ethical component which was facilitated by the ethics seminar. The seminar on workers' rights was very germane to my graduate course in labor law. Programs from these seminars can be found in Appendix I to the extent I have been able to locate them among my papers.

I do not draw my classroom lectures from textbooks alone. I engage in independent, original research for the specific purpose of delivering at least a few lectures each term that are not contained in the typical textbook treatment. Many of my lectures are taken directly from my research effort. During the past three years, I have engaged in different forms of research, writing, and professional presentation that were directly related to and helpful in my course preparation. Examples of these, which can be found in Appendix H.

• I participated in a conference that related to my American government class. This was a constitutional conference in Atlanta for South Africans sponsored by the U.S. Information Agency. The purpose of this conference was to present to a delegation of twelve South Africans from wide-ranging political and economic positions various aspects of the American constitutional system. I presented a paper on the constitutional evolution of the American presidency. This 3,200-word paper was entitled "The Genesis and Evolution of the U.S. Presidency: A Constitutional Perspective." This paper reviewed certain aspects of the process by which a very undemocratic government evolved into a very democratic government while emphasizing the continuing limitations on democratic processes with the conclusion that it is most critical to focus on where political society is going rather than where it has been, and relying on short constitutional documents that are written in very broad and general terms is the best way to get there.

• Also related to my American government course is a 4,100-word essay entitled "The Paradox of Limited Government: A Topsy-Turvy World" which was accepted for publication in the edition of *American Review*, a publication of the Institute for American Studies at Rand Afrikaans University in Johannesburg, South Africa. The essay argued that the general use of the term *limited* as applied to government suggests that the concept has today become the opposite of what it originally meant. If democracy is a self-regulating (i.e., self-governing) society in which all members participate and disagreements are settled by the democratic process (i.e., majority vote), limiting either the scope or authority of government obviously defeats the very rationale of democratic government.

• "Judicial Interpretation: Distinctions Without Differences" is an essay I wrote for inclusion in *Perspectives in Politics: From Aristotle to Present*, Peterson, Argile, and Allen, eds. (Dubuque: Kendall/Hunt Publishing Company, 1994). This essay has generated several lectures and written assignments for my American constitutional law course. The essay reviews the attempt to employ an objective method of textual interpretation employed by judges in deciding cases. The review reveals an attempt by some to construct a meaning of law that is external to the judge's subjectivity. The article uses the interpretative approaches offered by former Associate Justice William Brennan and former United States Attorney General Edwin Meese to make the argument that while each approach can be distinguished, there is no essential difference as far as avoiding judicial subjectivity is concerned. In other words, each interpretative method ultimately rests in part on judicial subjectivity, just different versions.

The article admonishes the reader to make subjectivity a manifest part of the interpretative process that will lead to a responsible accounting of its effect rather than a simple and hazardous denial of its existence. Since, as Justice Blackmun states, the verbal expressions are just the point of beginning, we must, following Plato as he stated in *Rehetorica*, argue that the juror's oath "I will give my verdict according to my honest opinion," means that one will not simply follow the letter of the law. This means that we must pursue the analysis of judicial subjectivity.

The article, as well as the lectures it has generated, provokes students to see and understand a given set of facts from radically different perspectives. This leads to an analysis of the considerations and processes appropriate to presenting a constitutional or legal argument.

Goals

- During the next academic cycle, I want to improve and expand my syllabi and course materials to better reflect and strategically articulate my educational philosophy.

- By the end of the next academic year I want to have received some formal training in teaching via satellite technology and write an article that addresses a broad policy issue in that teaching technology. One possible issue concerns the extent we may be sacrificing authentic human communities at a time when they are most needed.

- I want to complete my research and writing on an article that critiques James Madison's *Federalist Number Ten*. This work is directly related to my American government class inasmuch as I routinely assign students the task of writing an interpretative essay on Madison's work.

- I want to introduce a course in legal philosophy into the public law curriculum.

- I want to complete work on my manuscript, *Phenomenology of Judicial Decision-making*, and use the work as a foundation in teaching a seminar on Theories of Legal-Literary Criticism.

Appendices
Appendix A: List of Courses Taught
Appendix B: Samples of Student Work
Appendix C: Course Syllabi and Materials
Appendix D: Student Learning Aids
Appendix E: Student, Admin., & Peer Evaluations
Appendix F: Student-Related Activities
Appendix G: University-Related Activities
Appendix H: Community-Related Activities
Appendix I: Professional Improvement Activities

TEACHING PORTFOLIO
Janie H. Wilson
Department of Psychology
Georgia Southern University
Fall 1996

Table of Contents
1) Teaching Responsibilities
2) Animal Laboratory Experience
3) Teaching Philosophy
4) Teaching Techniques
5) Course Syllabi
6) Student Papers
7) Student Evaluations of Teaching
8) Faculty Evaluations of Teaching
9) Student Support
10) Teaching Enhancement
11) Professional Organizations for Teaching
12) Future Learning and Teaching Goals
13) Appendices

Teaching Responsibilities
Introduction to Psychology (Psy 150) provides an overview of the history and areas of psychology. It is an undergraduate course required of our majors but is often taken by nonmajors, and the average enrollment is 35 students. This course should stimulate interest in the discipline of psychology. Indeed, many of our majors chose this discipline as a direct result of an interesting and encouraging Introduction to Psychology professor.

Psychological Statistics I (Psy 280) and II (Psy 380) offer an overview of statistical methods used in psychological research, and both of these undergraduate courses are required of our majors, with an average enrollment of 22 students. In addition to teaching the calculations associated with statistics, I believe that an understanding of the theories upon which the calculations are based is important. In Psychological Statistics I, we discuss descriptive statistics, correlations, and linear regression, and students prepare a project using regression analysis. In addition, I conduct workshops on the use of QUATTRO, a computer graphics program. During Psychological Statistics II, we focus on t-tests, analysis of variance (ANOVA), Fisher's protected t-test, Tukey's HSD, chi-squared, and Mann-Whitney U, and students complete a project using ANOVA and Tukey's HSD. I also teach students MYSTAT in Statistics II in order to prepare them for their upcoming Research Methods class.

Research Methods (Psy 382) is a required undergraduate course with an average enrollment of 15 students designed to teach the basics of experimental design and APA style. A literature review followed by an original research project and APA-style paper are also required. In my class, students give ten-minute oral presentations of their research projects, and these talks are videotaped so the students can evaluate their own performances. In addition, students work closely with me to prepare professional posters of their research projects, which were displayed in the Psychology Department.

Physiological Psychology (Psy 457) is designed to teach students how psychology and biology can be combined. In addition to learning lecture and text materials, students are required to complete an APA-style paper about a brain disorder of interest to them and teach the class about their subject for ten minutes at the end of the quarter. This class is primarily for undergraduates, but graduate students are also encouraged to register, with an average enrollment of 20 students.

Careers in Psychology (Psy 210) is a required undergraduate course with an average enrollment of 18 students. Speakers from various areas of psychology and related disciplines summarize the responsibilities, joys, and difficulties of their careers. Students also learn about graduate school, job opportunities for different levels of education, and how to write a résumé.

Animal Laboratory Experience

Research Experience (Psy 391) offers students first-hand involvement in research. In my laboratory, we study Fetal Alcohol Syndrome using rats. For the past several quarters, six to nine students have worked with me in the lab, with a total of about 30 students. In this research experience, students learn about animal care, breeding, scoring behaviors using videotapes, entering data into the computer, and organizing notebooks of all of our work. They get an idea of what it would be like to choose this area of psychology before they have to make the decision. If they think that they would like to work with animals in their careers, I recommend that they take a *Directed Research (Psy 492)* in my lab. In this course, the student and I design a research project for which I donate rats, (s)he gathers literature, tests rats, and writes a paper. To date, two students have completed directed research with me. These courses are not required, but they provide an excellent opportunity for students to learn about animal research through participation.

Teaching Philosophy

The instructor's knowledge in a given area is necessary but not sufficient for effective teaching; students must be actively motivated to learn new material. This often entails moving beyond lecturing at students for the duration of the course and focuses on involving students in the learning process. Whenever possible, demonstrations of psychological phenomena should include the students themselves—learning through participation. Student participation is particularly important within the realm of research, and every effort should be made to provide simple, intuitive experiments from which students can learn the fundamentals of sound research. As learning progresses beyond this foundation, students themselves should be encouraged to design and implement studies in a supportive atmosphere. One of the most important components of encouragement is evaluation throughout the research process; therefore, the instructor should be available and willing to offer constructive criticism and praise. Under no circumstances should the student be discouraged from his or her endeavors.

Within the classroom, lectures should be presented in an enthusiastic manner, with an enduring understanding that the information is new to the students if not to the instructor. By the same token, lectures should be updated consistently with current research findings in any given area. Lectures should be highly organized; students cannot be expected to grasp the instructor's view of the material unless this organization is directly apparent. An additional aid in the classroom is rapport. It has been my experience that a relaxed atmosphere of human understanding does not detract from the learning experience but rather enhances it. Students who feel free to ask questions, comment, and even disagree with a concept will leave the class with a deeper understanding of the material. The objective is to teach as much new and relevant information as possible, and instructors should strive to enhance the process as well as the product of learning to provide a positive educational experience.

In all classes, outside assignments enhance learning. For some classes, such as psychological statistics, homework provides students with necessary practice in order to understand procedures and theories. In an introductory psychology class, students can be asked to complete simple assignments designed to build interest in the discipline such as counting the number of times they see sexual content in commercials or trying to interpret a friend's behavior. In physiological psychology, thought-provoking questions can be considered overnight and discussed during the next class meeting (e.g., Why do we not have very large heads? . . . discussed in the context of evolutionary theory). In a class on research methods, students can conduct their own simple experiments individually or in groups and even write their procedures and results in APA style, all of which provide solid examples of the material in their text. Most students will not simply read a textbook each evening, but they will complete tasks they consider useful and fun.

Both in and out of the classroom, student management is crucial to successful teaching. Expectations of student performance and accomplishments should be clear at all times. Consequences of failure to perform well and accomplish necessary tasks also must be clearly defined. These consequences should remain consistent across all students within a class. In order for management policies to be upheld, decisions about consequences cannot be made on a case-by-case basis. This type of preferential treatment encourages students to fabricate reasons for failing to perform adequately. It also places the professor in the role of confidant for personal issues the student may not wish to share; thus, students' privacy is compromised. Within all matters of student management, consistency and respect should be of primary concern.

Finally, it is my responsibility to continue to learn about teaching and maintain a positive attitude toward my students. Attending conferences and workshops dedicated to enhancing instruction is critical to my development as a professor. These experiences provide new teaching procedures and fresh insights into the needs of my students. In addition, it is my responsibility to present teaching material or techniques to my colleagues to enhance their ability to mature in their careers or view some aspect of teaching from a new perspective. With colleagues and personally, it is my responsibility to avoid making global attributions of poor student abilities or motivation. Indeed, it is my role as a teacher to foster these qualities.

Teaching Techniques

Team teaching provides an excellent opportunity to expand professors' knowledge and solicit peer review of teaching. I recently taught Careers in Psychology with Dr. Bill McIntosh. Judging by our own perceptions and student evaluations, team-teaching was a success, and we have requested that we again work together in this course. In addition, I have requested to teach Clinical Neuroscience with Dr. Lisa Sherwin. My strengths include anatomy and function of the human nervous system, and Dr. Sherwin will concentrate on the clinical aspect of the course. I am certain that we will learn a great deal from each other, and the students will learn Clinical Neuroscience from a broader perspective.

Students should practice research in most psychology classes. In Introduction to Psychology, Statistics I and II, and Research Methods, I engage students in experiments to actively demonstrate the principles of psychology as a science. Students have enjoyed in-class experiments on:

1) possible differences in the visual and gustatory inputs from three brands of cola as well as their relative "fizziness"

2) tests of the tastes and smells of three brands of peanut butter

3) the effect of caffeinated versus decaffeinated coffee on retention of lecture material

4) the effect of listing negative thoughts or positive thoughts on a rating scale of mood

In Research Methods, I found that students were not addressing many of my written concerns on their introduction sections, so I canceled class one day and made one-hour appointments for each of them individually. They were asked to bring to my office outlines of their papers composed of the topic sentence from each paragraph. I then spent one hour with each student reviewing my comments and rewording or reorganizing the paper. In this way, they were able to ask questions as we worked, and I was able to see potential problems in comprehension when they occurred. All of the students left with a clearer understanding of how to improve their papers. When asked for feedback at the end of the course, one student wrote, "The most helpful [exercise] of all was when you sat down and discussed our research papers with us."

Dr. Bill McIntosh shared with me a demonstration of perceptual set using music played backwards. The music does not have meaning until (Satanic) words are suggested, after which it is impossible not to "hear" the suggested words. I used this demonstration in my last Introduction to Psychology class, and it was very powerful. Unfortunately, many students were convinced that the "words" I gave them were really in the music, and they believed that Satan was speaking to them. Thus, I will compose a non-Satanic set of words for the same piece of music and let them "hear" that any type of meaning can be imposed.

Also in Introduction to Psychology, when covering adolescent physical and social development, I brought my 13-year-old daughter to class to discuss her life. The students appreciated her clear and honest answers to their many questions. I also intend to videotape my 3-year-old son completing tasks used to demonstrate Piaget's early stages of intellectual development for use in my next Introduction to Psychology class.

I have adopted a new animated cartoon computer program to demonstrate complex physiological functions, and I hope that it will supplement lecture material and promote understanding in Physiological Psychology and Clinical Neuroscience.

Course Syllabi

Appendix A is composed of the syllabi used in courses at Georgia Southern University. In my syllabi, I communicate to the student that a) We will treat each other with courtesy and respect within the classroom in order to encourage free expression of ideas; and b) There is no attendance policy because students are adults and must make their own decisions about how to spend their time. If they are absent, they must get notes from two colleagues in the class before asking me specific questions about the lecture.

In my syllabi, I also remind students that they are in charge of their success in the class:

"One final note: At this stage in your education, you must learn to empower yourself. You are in charge of your life. It is your responsibility to complete your work as specified and turn it in on time. In order to perform well, you must read and listen carefully at all times to know what is expected of you. I trust that you will allow yourself to devote your energy to this class and your university career."

Student Papers

Writing is possibly the single most important skill for success in academia; therefore, students should be required to complete writing assignments in every class, and they should complete a research paper in most psychology classes. To enhance the learning process, at least one rough draft should be submitted for review prior to turning in the final paper. When students are working on a research project which involves conducting their own experiment, I require several rough drafts. Students should become familiar with the review process and become comfortable with molding their work into a superior final product. Original drafts and final copies of two student papers in Appendix B provide examples of suggestions for improvement and students' interpretations of my comments.

Student Evaluations of Teaching

Evaluations by my students are consistently positive. I believe that my students realize that I enjoy teaching them and sincerely want them to perform well. Ratings of courses and instructor are based on a five-point scale, with 1 representing "poor" and 5 representing "excellent." These data are representative ratings from each course:

Course	Evaluation of Course	Evaluation of Instructor	Organization	Respect
Psy 150	4.48	4.61	4.52	4.58
Psy 280	4.25	4.50	4.69	4.62
Psy 380	4.75	4.75	4.44	4.19
Psy 382	3.82	3.56	4.22	4.11
Psy 457	4.06	4.12	4.38	4.50
Psy 210	4.62	4.72	4.79	4.83

Several areas of importance to me in teaching are not reflected in the numerical evaluations but are represented by anonymous student comments. In response to an item asking what students liked most about the class, students in my Winter 1996 Statistics and Research Methods classes responded:

"our teacher was fair"

"teacher's enthusiasm"

"We were given many opportunities to make good grades to make sure we had learned the material and could apply our knowledge."

"She has a positive attitude and is willing to help anyone at any time."

Faculty Evaluations of Teaching
Appendix D is composed of evaluations of my performance and as an assistant professor at Georgia Southern University, my current position.

Activities in Support of Students
I am willing to work with my students outside of class in order to enhance comprehension of the material. I encourage my students to call me at home if they have any questions regarding classwork. I have never found this to be a burden, and I intend to continue offering my home number to all of my students.

Several years ago I sponsored six students at Columbia College to give oral presentations of their research papers at the Carolinas Psychology Conference. This year, I am sponsoring four students at Georgia Southern University. Two of the students are from my Research Methods class, and two students are from other professors' classes. All of the students' abstracts have been accepted for publication and presentation at the conference and are found in Appendix E.

I have been the advisor for Psychology Club for the past two years, and we are a very active club both on campus and in the community. As the advisor for this club, I have the unique opportunity to be involved in student accomplishments outside of the traditional role as professor. These interactions have been positive, and I hope to serve the students in this capacity for as long as I am needed.

I actively advise 23 students for the Psychology Department as well, and many of my advisees come to my office or call me in the evenings to ask for advice about classes and their future careers.

I attended a two-day workshop on distance learning to learn how to use the equipment associated with this new technology. Distance learning provides an excellent service to students who otherwise would not have access to university classes, and I want to be ready to teach psychology courses as needed for Georgia Southern University's several off-campus sites.

Teaching Enhancement
I normally attend the Southeastern Conference on the Teaching of Psychology at Kennesaw State College. I learned an interesting technique for my statistics classes: My students were surprised and delighted to receive M & M's so they could each prepare frequency distributions of the colors found in their packages. I learned a) a demonstration of regression to the mean for Statistics I, b) a first-day, stress-reduction exercise for Research Methods, and c) how to divide students into "jigsaw" groups to promote retention of material through active learning. At the 1996 conference, I presented an Introductory Psychology technique on "backmasking" and have been asked to lead a discussion next year on a topic I suggested: empowering students.

I was intrigued by the concept of "jigsaw" groups, and I would like to share this teaching technique with my colleagues. As a result, I have arranged with Dr.

Jeffrey Buller of Dean Newson's office to teach a new-faculty workshop entitled, "Jigsaw Groups: Active Learning."

I attended a faculty workshop, "Alternatives to Lecture," sponsored by Dean Newson's office. This workshop reinforced the idea that the best way to learn is to teach, and as a result, I have reaffirmed my goal to strongly encourage and reinforce student teaching in all of my classes.

I am serving on master's thesis committees for Angelita Nicholson and Elisa Sullivan. The title of Ms Nicholson's thesis is "A Projective Technique to Identify Aggressive Men," and she will conduct her thesis defense this year. The title of Ms Sullivan's thesis proposal is "Visual Discrimination and Benzodiazepines."

Professional Organizations for Teaching

I am a member of the American Psychological Association (APA), Division Two: Teaching of Psychology. This division publishes a journal of teaching techniques to enhance classroom instruction. In one publication, I learned how to deal effectively with a confrontive student, and our relationship so improved that the student has recently asked me to write a letter of recommendation for her. In another edition of the journal, I learned an interesting way to help my students approach statistics tests using a battle analogy. In part, the article suggested that students be told to first read the entire test before beginning, then divide the tasks and conquer the material one step at a time.

I have been a member of Faculty for Undergraduate Neuroscience (FUN) since 1992 and will continue my affiliation with this organization. One of the objectives of FUN is to provide funds and leadership for undergraduates to attend professional meetings, and I have supported this endeavor. In addition, FUN is dedicated to reviewing undergraduate texts to ensure quality materials for a superior education. As a member of FUN, I was asked to review three first-draft chapters of an undergraduate neuroscience text. It was a valuable experience, and I look forward to being involved further in the development of undergraduate educational materials.

Future Learning and Teaching Goals

1) I will continue to encourage students to attend professional meetings such as the Carolinas Conference when they complete research projects, and I will accompany them to provide guidance and encouragement.

2) I will continue to speak with students about graduate school and help them to explore this option if they are interested in extending their formal education.

3) I plan to conduct more in-class analyses of my teaching. I will administer an exam on the first day of class and again in the final week of Psychological Statistics II.

4) I will write a grant for the development of an undergraduate physiological psychology laboratory to give students more opportunities to learn valuable material and techniques.

5) I will continue to attend the Southeastern Conference on the Teaching of Psychology each year to learn new techniques and renew my commitment to teaching.

6) I will remain positive when dealing with my students, and I will always support their endeavors. I recognize that students are future teachers and researchers, and to dampen their enthusiasm would be to deny them the opportunity to succeed.

Appendices
Appendix A: Course Syllabi
Appendix B: Student Papers
Appendix C: Student Evaluations of Teaching
Appendix D: Faculty Evaluations of Teaching
Appendix E: Student Abstracts for 1996 Carolinas Conference

12

AFTERWORD

Linda Annis

It has been my personal good fortune since 1991 to be an active participant in the movement to make the teaching portfolio an integral part of higher education's efforts to improve teaching and personnel decisions. I have written my own portfolio, been the on-site campus director of an extensive teaching portfolio project, made many presentations, and written extensively on the topic. In addition, I have served as a mentor to more than 125 faculty members on a variety of campuses as they prepared their own teaching portfolios.

It is this latter activity that has given me the most personal pleasure. By serving as a mentor who works intensively and individually with each faculty member as they prepare their portfolios, I have been privileged to get a unique insight into the many strengths of and strong dedication to good teaching among so many faculty in today's institutions of higher education. This experience has intensified my pride in being a member of this broad fraternity of teaching faculty.

Having served as a mentor to so many, I am now beginning to get feedback about the many successes resulting from the development and subsequent use of a teaching portfolio. These reports may come in the form of a post card, phone call, or chance meeting at a conference. Whatever the form, I find these responses heartwarming and reinforcing. They have actually brightened my spirits for days. A few of these reports are included here.

Very early in our work with portfolios, it became clear that they would be useful in applying for awards regarding teaching because they so clearly documented good teaching with empirical evidence. I have worked with faculty who have received university awards for best teaching, statewide awards for teaching in their discipline, and even large federally funded grants for teaching-related projects. All have attributed their success largely to the documentation in their portfolios. One professor who received a statewide award for "Foreign Language Teacher of the Year" wrote to me:

> *A friend of mine who was on the selection committee said it was my teaching portfolio that did the job. The selection committee was so impressed with the way the portfolio documented my teaching that they had no other choice than to vote for me.*

Many professors attribute their improved student evaluations to their work on a teaching portfolio. For example, a professor at a major medical school in the southwestern United States wrote me at the end of the first semester following his preparation of a portfolio. He said, "I just received my teaching evaluations for the spring semester. I was so proud that I wanted to share the good news!"

Still others have reported that they are achieving success in submitting proposals for conference presentations and journal articles for publication, often for the first time, when they report on their experiences in applying the teaching portfolios to their specific disciplines. Two academic librarians at a small liberal arts school in the Midwest wrote:

> *We are delighted to have been selected to present at this particular conference, which for our profession is a highly prestigious one. We are equally delighted that one of the "Future Goals" that we defined in our portfolios last spring has become a reality.*

"Future Goals" with time frames, which are often the last section in a portfolio, really do work.

Feedback from professors indicates that the teaching portfolio is a very effective vehicle in finding a job, especially in a tight market. One faculty member I worked with had been moving all over the country in a long series of one-year teaching positions as she attempted to get a regular position. The year after I helped her prepare her portfolio, she sent me a post card proclaiming, "It worked! I now have a *tenure-track* position in a department and school that I love!" (I will always treasure that post card.)

Perhaps one of the most unique uses for a portfolio occurred recently when I was working with a brand-new faculty member with a newly minted Ph.D. She was the first member of her family to go to college, not to mention the first to receive an advanced degree. She reported to me at our third meeting that her mother had been wondering what she did with her time as a professor. The previous night she had described her teaching portfolio preparation to her mother in a phone conversation. Her mother asked her to send a copy of her portfolio so she could have a better understanding of how her daughter spent her days. (This might even be considered a new form of a report card.)

Lastly, at a conference, I discovered a completely unexpected use for the portfolio when I happened to run into a faculty member I had worked with a year earlier. She was delighted to see me and reported how useful preparing a teaching portfolio had been for her. It turned out that this process had made her aware for the first time that she was burned out as a professor. She had changed jobs and was now very happy in her new position as a dean. At first I was somewhat taken aback by this story, but upon further reflection I saw it as another success story for portfolio use. She was more fulfilled in her new job, and the students she would have had enjoyed the benefits of a different professor.

All in all, the anecdotal evidence for successful use of teaching portfolios is overwhelmingly positive. And, importantly, since it is almost impossible to prepare a teaching portfolio without coming up with at least one, and probably many more, ideas for improving teaching, I strongly believe that the ultimate beneficiaries of the portfolio movement are our students. Every professor who prepares a portfolio influences many students in each class over all the terms of their career. As a veteran of many years in higher education, I see the portfolio as a win-win concept for all involved—professors, administrators, and most of all, our students.

APPENDIX

KEY POINTS
ON REVISING A PORTFOLIO

Peter Seldin and John Zubizarreta

All portfolios are works in progress, revised periodically to capture genuine improvement in teaching and its impact on student learning. This appendix offers a portfolio with numbered items that correspond to the list detailing revisions made after considerable self-reflection and collaboration with a mentor.

Descriptions of specific revisions and important observations are keyed to numbers in the margins of the earlier portfolio draft.

1. Note: name of faculty member, department, and institution.

2. *Revision:* date of portfolio is added for clear baseline for improvement.

3. Note: detailed table of contents.

4. *Revision:* author added a listing of the appendix items for clear indication of amount and type of evidence included.

5. *Revision:* author separated teaching responsibilities, philosophy, and strategies into distinct categories. Philosophy became a stronger, more discreet feature.

6. *Revision:* author added course titles, numbers, levels, sizes, and whether required or elective. Information about *what* he teaches is clearer and more specific, especially for accreditation purposes, if needed.

7. *Revision:* this is the start of philosophy section (*why* he does what he does as a teacher).

7a. Key paragraph identifies values to which he is committed as a teacher. This paragraph is the linchpin for much of what follows, and the author refers to the stated values often.

8. *Revision:* start of the section on strategies and methods (*how* he handles teaching responsibilities).

9. Specific examples of how he offers personal attention.

10. Specific examples of varied methods. Author does not just *say* he uses varied methods but gives clear examples of what he does.

11. Refers to use of student portfolios to enhance learning. Makes reference to syllabi as offering further details, keeping information selected, compressed, and factual.

12. Use of specific, detailed examples to illustrate point.

13. Section on respect for scholarship ties in with 7a above. Author gives clear examples of how his own continued learning has affected his courses.

14. Again, ties in with 7a above, revealing coherence among sections of the narrative and strengthening validity.

15. Section on shared research and writing with students relates to 7a above.

16. Specific examples (not generalities) throughout portfolio.

17. *revision:* student evaluations: a) added number of students per course; b) added course titles; c) added more depth by citing the six core questions on student rating forms at his college and the mean score received on each question in each of his courses; d) graphically compressed information into a succinct chart.

18. *Revision:* cut down on the number of student comments but retained focus on values articulated in philosophy.

19. Again, a link to values detailed in 7a.

20. *Revision:* title changed to "Statements from Colleagues and Alumnae." In revised version, the section includes peer review reports, solicited and unsolicited letters from colleagues, chair, dean, faculty development specialist, and alumnae.

21. *Revision:* name and position of person is added in each of three cases for specificity; actual letters are in appendix.

22. Provides further evidence of *what he does* in the classroom.

23. Goal: to keep himself and course fresh. Changes in syllabi over time provide evidence that he succeeds.

24. Further elaboration of how syllabi have changed (altered readings, methods, goals, assignment, assessment techniques). Goes beyond generalities. Specificity is essential.

25. Provides highlights of handouts used in class. Materials themselves are placed in appendix.

26. *Revision:* in the section on workshops attended, author spells out how attending each specific workshop or conference has improved his teaching and student learning, providing evidence of changes in various appendices.

27. Goal section: notice the inclusion of completion dates wherever appropriate. In revision, goals are updated.

28. Appendices: notice detailed listing here. In revision, author chose to move to "Table of Contents" for more immediate impact of evidence.

Also, in revision, author added a separate section on "Products of Student Learning." In earlier draft, such information is scattered in different locations. In revision, evidence of student learning is highlighted in discreet section with description and analysis of students' work and accomplishments. Included are items such as: a) representative excellent, average, and poor essays in successive drafts with teacher's comments; b) sample student presentations at conferences or publications under teacher's mentoring; c) selected senior honors projects directed by the teacher; d) descriptive list of successful student practicums or study opportunities outside the classroom.

The entire portfolio is placed in a three-ring binder with tabs for appendices. Bulkier evidence such as videotapes or posters are listed and annotated in an appendix and made available upon request. Descriptive and analytical narrative too lengthy for the narrative section is relegated to an appendix, keeping the reflective portion of the portfolio to about ten pages.

The dynamic quality of portfolio revisions suggests that the author can maintain the portfolio without continually adding to its size. The focus of revision should remain on cogent, qualitative analysis for improvement.

TEACHING PORTFOLIO
1

John Zubizarreta
Department of English
2
Columbia College

┌ **Table of Contents**
│ Teaching Responsibilities, Philosophy, Strategies
│ Collaborative Scholarship with Students
3 │ Student Evaluations
│ Letters from Colleagues
│ Teaching Awards
│ Syllabi, Reading Lists, Assignments, Handouts, and Exams
│ Teaching Improvement
│ Teaching Related Activities and Committee Work
│ Letters for Students
│ Future Teaching Goals
4 └ Appendices

5
6 **Teaching Responsibilities, Philosophy, Strategies**

 Each semester, I teach four sections of English courses, with three preparations (an average of eighty-three students per semester), and I currently advise nine majors. I have taught specially developed seminars in two May terms, and I have volunteered twice to teach Orientation 190 and Leadership 190. In Spring 1990, I directed a senior honors project and served as second reader of another. In Spring 1991, I again directed a project. In Spring 1992, I supervised an independent study for an outstanding Bulgarian student; at Columbia College, independent studies are considered volunteer work in addition to a full teaching load.

7
 In my relations with students, I have learned that conscientious mentoring is a necessary dimension of careful teaching. Delivering information in the classroom, administering tests, and computing information are superficial acts of teaching which the uninspired but competent teacher can perform. But the outstanding professor knows the value of working patiently with students on personal levels. In the intellectually productive relationship that develops between student and mentor, the teacher advocates the student's whole learning as the student learns not only academic information but social and personal skills that enhance learning. In a sense, the professor teaches more than content; he or she teaches habits of thinking, habits of being. Students discover in the process of engaged learning the rewards of controlled inquiry, the value of reasoned discourse, the delight of intellectual curiosity, and an earned respect for knowledge. Faculty who work vitally with students encourage learning on various levels and contribute to students' lifelong commitment to truth in knowledge.

 Excellent teaching must inspire and be inspired. The authentic aim of education is not information—a mean goal—but truth. In order to discover the truth in knowledge, students must insist on the best from teachers. They must demand not only course content and common assessment but the uncommon interactive mentoring that results in genuine learning. The teacher must teach not train. Students must learn, not "perform competencies." Students must know that more should happen in their education than what happens in ordinary classrooms. The outstanding professor extends the teaching moment and inspires students to learn beyond the classroom, beyond facts, beyond "assessment instruments."

┌ I believe that I have lived up to my own standards of teaching. In subsequent categories and
7a │ appendices, I take care to demonstrate my effectiveness in the classroom and in teaching related
│ activities and my strong commitment to continued development of teaching, to close contact
│ with students, to innovation, to rigorous scholarship, and to the shared act of learning that
└ inspires both teacher and student.

8
 First, I routinely make time for conferences with students to offer them valuable personal attention. Students need such attention in order to learn important skills that carry over to their

careers. In composition classes, I meet with students in small groups to teach them word processing or other tactics of writing. For example, I may allow three students to "shadow" me as I underline significant passages in a story, write comments in the margins, make connections among sets of details, and compose a short essay on the computer screen. The small group conference provides an atmosphere of trust and sharing that teaches the students crucial habits. Other times, I meet individually with students to help them revise and edit essays, showing them personally how good writers work. 9

Second, I use various presentations to engage students in several forms of learning. I particularly encourage discussion, asking students questions, inviting them to participate in vital discourse. I also use portfolios as springboards for dialogue, reading compelling entries aloud so that students become accustomed to analyzing, defending, and challenging ideas. Occasionally, I assign oral reports, use films or slides, and invite guest speakers in order to vary classroom activities. In an honors course in Spring 1991, for instance, I asked a colleague to share with the class a conference paper dealing with a subject we had discussed. She described the process of writing the paper, the many revisions, the discoveries she made in successive drafts, the experience finally of reading the paper at a conference. The students were fascinated with learning that even professors struggle with writing, and they were so delighted and encouraged that they pestered me all term to invite another professor. I believe the students learned something that day that far exceeded the information of the course 10

Third, my use of student portfolios enhances learning. The descriptions of the portfolio in my syllabi record my methods, and enthusiastic student evaluations testify to the effectiveness of portfolios in encouraging students to develop and test critical thinking and writing skills. One example sufficiently demonstrates the value of portfolios. In my World Literature class of spring 1990, I began to notice in an Iranian student's folder a number of informal entries on an unfamiliar modern Persian poet. I encouraged her to present an oral report to the class, and later she wrote a research paper on Forugh Farrokhzad. In the spring, I collaborated with the student in presenting a workshop at a national conference on teaching methods, highlighting the use of portfolios in teaching intercultural students. Finally, with the help of my student's translations, I have published a paper on Farrokhzad in a prestigious journal. Clearly, portfolios effectively prompt students to practice essential skills without penalties and inhibitions, and the close intellectual relationship that develops between students and teacher is extremely rewarding to both. 11 12

Finally, I pride myself on being both teacher and scholar, and I try to teach students respect for scholarship that transfers to other courses and to their professional lives. Professors should be active scholars, and teaching should be informed by research and professional development. My syllabi change regularly to reflect my own continual learning and interests within my discipline. For example, as I developed a scholarly interest in modern Hispanic literature, I incorporated such writers into various courses. When I began teaching at a women's college, I studied more female writers and adjusted my syllabi accordingly. In fact, in summer 1989, I was awarded a fellowship with USC's Institute for Southern Studies, enabling me to study women in Flannery O'Connor's fiction, a topic I now teach in special May terms. I am devoted to the interaction of scholarship and effective teaching, and I try to inspire students with the value of accurate, original research. My beliefs about scholarship and teaching are discussed further in my address at the college's Faculty Convivium; the text is included in Appendix A. 13 14

Collaborative Scholarship with Students

A rewarding aspect of teaching has been my involvement with students in producing scholarship that reflects genuine collaborative learning. No student evaluation conveys the extent of learning and influence that results when a professor and student engage in shared research and writing. Both are enriched by the experience. 15

Appendix A contains a copy of my address at the first Faculty Convivium, a series of talks highlighting faculty research on campus. In order to inaugurate the convivium uniquely, I focused on collaborative ventures between faculty and students, citing three examples of my own involvement with students in presenting workshops, reading papers at conferences, and writing for publication. In February 1991, an Iranian student and I presented "The Written Portfolio: A Collabora- 16

16 tive Model for Intercultural Students," a workshop at the Enhancing the Quality of Teaching Conference in Charleston, SC. With the student's translations of Persian, I have published an article on an Iranian poet in the international journal *World Literature Today*. In October 1991, I helped an English major write a paper that was accepted by the Popular Culture Association of the South; I wrote a companion piece, and we read both essays at the conference in Norfolk, VA. In late October 1991, I collaborated with three honors students in presenting "An Honors Approach to Poetry and the Fine Arts" at the National Collegiate Honors Council in Chicago, IL.

In Spring 1991, I had the opportunity to direct a senior honors project, a collection of original short stories. After much close work with the student, I wrote a preface that introduces the talented pieces. I have encouraged this student to send her work to a national contest for eventual publication. I include a copy of my preface in Appendix A.

A more recent example of collaborative scholarship is my association with two Bulgarian students who have read papers at a special session I moderated at the Southern Humanities Council Annual Conference in February 1992. One of the major conference themes was comparative views of the South, and I encouraged both students to write abstracts to accompany my proposal for a session on "The Literature and Sociology of the South from an East European Perspective." Our proposal was accepted, and I helped the students prepare their papers. As moderator, I also wrote a brief response to their unique observations of the South. Appendix A includes a copy of our proposal. Presently, I am helping both Bulgarian students to submit revisions of their essays to an international conference scheduled for Summer 1992, in Italy.

Student Evaluations

17 Appendix B includes student evaluations from all my classes at Columbia College as well as several from courses I taught at other institutions. My evaluations are consistently high in all categories, and I earn commendations from students about my enthusiasm, knowledge, standards, methods, helpfulness, and fairness. The college's evaluation forms rate faculty on several items, using a scale that defines performance as outstanding, superior, satisfactory, poor, or unsatisfactory. In 1991, I taught multiple sections of four different courses; my ratings are indicated in the following chart:

	Outstanding	Superior	Satisfactory	Poor	Unsatisfactory
Eng. 336	75%	22%	3%		
Eng. 277	86%	12%	2%		
Eng. 150	78%	20%	2%		
Eng. 103	77%	20%	3%		

Such figures are consistent in my evaluation since I began teaching in 1973. Students frequently score me in the upper 97th percentile or better in outstanding teaching.

18 Students' personal comments on evaluation forms are as generous as their ratings. Students refer to my *enthusiasm*: "Dr. Z makes learning a joy"; "Very energetic and exciting"; "He taught the subject with passion, joy"; "He has an uncanny and exciting way to talk to us"; "He keeps you attentive"; "Dr. Z [has] the capacity to motivate interest and creativity in his students"; "It was obvious that he loves what he does."

19 But effective teaching is more than showmanship, and students also praise my *high standards* and my emphasis on *scholarship*: "He knew the material extremely well"; "He…looked at the criticism before coming to class to help us understand"; "He could answer all questions accurately and effectively"; "We…were persuaded to do our best and be 'professional'. This caused us to work hard and be proud of our work"; "I know how to do a *tough* research paper now"; "Although he requires a lot of work, I learned a lot…in his class"; "Professor was well-prepared, knowledgeable of subject material, and fair in every aspect"; "Very professional."

Many students focus on my *teaching methods* and my experimentations with the portfolio assignment: "He welcomed and enjoyed our questions"; "Doesn't criticize our thoughts, but encourages us to explore"; "He always listens, offers guidance, gives second chances when needed";

"I have never had a professor take so much time to give students feedback"; "He took time with us in our conferences"; "He is the fairest and best one-to-one professor I have ever had"; "The portfolio method...is the most effective way for me and...others to *learn*"; "He used so many different methods of teaching that one always got through to me."

I expend a great deal of my energy as a teacher on *individual attention*, and students recognize my efforts: "He always made time for me"; "He is dedicated to his students. We all love him"; "He always told us why we got a grade and how we could improve....He always had a personal note to us about our papers"; "Dr. Z was there when I had a question or needed help—that's something great to say about a professor"; "He respects our answers...gives everybody a fair chance"; "He doesn't grade on what skills you should have but on what skills you actually have and [on your] willingness to...do your best"; "He taught...each student...one-on-one. He *cares* about your work and about helping you *learn*"; "I cannot think of any one professor that has left me with a greater thirst for knowledge....I only hope someday I may have as tremendous an impact on a young mind as you have had on mine."

19

Letters from Colleagues

20

I enclosed in Appendix C copies of letters from colleagues commenting on my commitment to teaching, my hours with students in conferences, my professional development and scholarship, my devotion to the college, my work with student activities, and my community service. One colleague who has observed me in the classroom and in conferences and who has reviewed my comments on students' papers writes, "He challenges his students to 'be professional'...he exacts high standards from them and refuses to let them get off lightly when they produce second-rate work. Students...sense his genuine respect for and interest in what they have to say." Another colleague who supervises student teachers and who has observed my work says, "John is the consummate professional, the man who gives his all to his career and to his friends....He asks for the best from his students because he always demands it of himself....John is, in a phrase, a 'master teacher.'" A colleague *outside* my department observes, "From day one of his joining our faculty, John has been energetic and enthusiastic as an active participant in student, faculty, and college functions." The *chair* of my department kindly remarks, "John is an exemplary teacher. His successful innovations in...teaching...have spurred forth his students and have inspired his colleagues to emulation. His enthusiasm in the classroom is contagious, so that even his most reticent students gain a new vision of what they may achieve."

21

Teaching Awards

Appendix D contains evidence of outstanding teaching awards for which I have been nominated or which I have received. While I was a graduate teaching assistant at the University of South Carolina in 1975, I was a finalist for the Amoco Teaching Award, a campus-wide prize for all teaching faculty. And in 1991, I was selected by both faculty and students for the Columbia College Outstanding Faculty Member Award. I also received the 1991 Sears-Roebuck Foundation Teaching Excellence and Campus Leadership Award. Currently, I am the college's nominee for the Governor's Professor of the Year Award, a statewide competition among faculty from all public and private institutions in South Carolina. In addition, I am a nominee for the 1992 Outstanding Teacher Award sponsored by the South Atlantic Association of Departments of English.

Syllabi, Reading Lists, Assignments, Handouts, and Exams

22

Appendix E includes copies of my syllabi for various courses I have taught over a number of years. I have added some syllabi for classes similar to ones I teach now at Columbia College. These are similar to ones I taught at other institutions to demonstrate my commitment to change and currency not only in my own scholarly development but also in my teaching. The English 201 course I taught between 1979 and 1983 in North Carolina, for example, is identical to the college's English 277. My syllabi reflect continual variety and flexibility in readings, methods, and goals, with increasing evidence of precision in detailing expectations and criteria for evaluation. The syllabi get better overall, though cluttered and lengthy with growing demands of assessment. Yet, the syllabi record progress in my teaching as I try to keep both myself and the courses fresh.

23

24   One noteworthy addition to some of my syllabi is the inclusion of a reading list, such as the bibliographies on selected authors for research projects in one class. Such lists reinforce the connection between scholarship and teaching, and provide a useful resource for students. In all classes, I suggest additional readings during discussions, and I plan to add reading lists to all my syllabi.

  Appendix F includes copies of representative assignments for freshman classes in which students need extra guidance. I have selected assignments from classes I taught several years ago, and from recent classes, in order to show development in my efforts to be more specific and helpful. For example, the dated sheet labeled "EH 102 Short Fiction Essay" is skimpy in outlining both the topics and the requirements; the "Final Exam Topics," dated and composed several years later, reveals more care and planning, more direction, more instruction; the English 103 and 150 sheets, used in different semesters more recently, also reveal greater detail and more emphasis on using the assignments to teach, not just to test. I have added other assignments that illustrate the value I place on providing models for students. The "Annotated Bibliography" and "Research Paper" sheets offer samples of the style and content of annotated citations and the methods of incorporating research into a critical essay; the assignments also stress the significance of good scholarship, reinforcing a major competency of all my courses. Of course, I provide students with samples of each kind of essay I ask them to write. Finally, the handout "Sample Portfolio Entries" models for students the active learning that comes from maintaining a serious, thoughtful portfolio.

25   Appendix G contains handouts I use in several classes. Since the portfolio is a major assignment in my classes, I include samples of "Suggested Topics for Out-of-Class Entries," a handout encouraging students to write on a variety of topics. Often embedded in the suggestions are vital issues that enhance students' learning and produce good writing. At the end of a semester, I often reread students' entries on suggested topics and group them according to the issues a student seemed most interested in exploring; then I customize the final exam topics for each student, referring her to selected entries in her portfolio. I add a "Checklist for Oral Reports," which focuses on important features of this particular project, and "Outline of Romantic Tendencies," which helps English 336 students in highlighting key concepts and in seeing a historical overview—skills often lost in rapid survey courses.

  In Appendix H, I have placed copies of objective exams I use sporadically, for I prefer essays as a superior means of assessing students' learning. Essays provide students with an opportunity to integrate knowledge; to express their critical thinking about subject matter; to organize, develop, and substantiate ideas. Essays also require students to engage the vital processes of writing, of communication, of invention, and expression of ideas in coherent form. Students must generate knowledge, not just react to it in objective responses. Evaluating essays takes more of the teacher's time than scoring quantitative tests, but I believe essays offer a more valuable index of students' learning.

Teaching Improvement

26   Just as I stress the importance of ongoing professional activity in my role as scholar, I value the imperatives of experimentation and improvement in teaching. The constant revisions in my syllabi and methods attest to my desire to improve teaching. Also, I have attended workshops and conferences focusing on the enhancement of teaching techniques and goals. In December 1988, I participated in a writing-across-the-curriculum workshop conducted by Dr. Henry Steffens of the University of Vermont. In February 1989, I attended the conference of the Georgia-South Carolina College English Association. In November 1989, I co-presented "Write to Think," a workshop on the use of journals at the meeting of the South Carolina Association of Developmental Educators.

Teaching Related Activities and Committee Work

  As part of my service to the community, I frequently extend my teaching to audiences outside of the college. For example, Appendix I contains a copy of a page from my vita which shows that I speak on literary and other topics to several community groups and civic clubs. Also in Appendix I, I include evidence of my membership in the college's speakers bureau and in the South Carolina Humanities Council. In addition, I participate as a teaching scholar in the South Carolina libraries' "Let's Talk About It: Reading and Discussion Program" funded by the National Endowment for the Humanities.

My committee responsibilities at the college involve me in work towards the improvement of teaching, too. I am a member of the Collaborative Learning Steering Committee, which has dutifully sought to enhance teaching by developing ways of incorporating interdisciplinary and collaborative methods into the curriculum. The committee also has taken on the charge of revising the general education program at the college in order to strengthen both teaching and learning. I am also a member of a special committee for reform and improvement of academic advisement.

Letters for Students

A valuable service teachers can provide for students is to write cogent letters of recommendation for scholarships, jobs, or other goals. Appendix J contains letters I have written in recent years at different institutions, demonstrating the continued, serious effort I make to help students.

Future Teaching Goals

1. I feel that because of my academic background, my record of excellent teaching, and my current and vital scholarship, I should teach more upper-level courses in my areas of specialization. I would like to teach modern American literature to majors. Perhaps I will have such a chance this year, for the chair of my department has already begun to press for sharing of courses and has offered his own upper-level courses to serve as a model to the rest of the department.

2. My strengths in comparative literature encourage me to develop more courses in diverse literatures. My department should offer advanced world literature courses for majors. I have published several pieces on works of foreign literatures, and I would like to teach culturally diverse literature in advanced courses. The college's growing emphasis on curriculum reform may change the English major in the next two years, and I hope to be a leader.

3. I would like to earn a teaching Fulbright in a Latin American country. Such an experience will enrich not only my scholarly background but also my teaching. I already have begun the application process.

4. I hope to find more ways of incorporating word processing technology into all courses. Currently, I build into composition classes days on which I accompany small groups to the Computer Lab in order to teach them basic skills. I would like to discover new ways of devising projects that encourage students to become more proficient with computers. A valued colleague has taught me to use a community computer journal in an honors course (an assignment sheet is attached to the syllabus for that course in Appendix E). I also plan to continue learning from colleagues and conferences.

27

Appendices

28

Appendix A: Address at the Faculty Convivium
Appendix B: Student Evaluations
Appendix C: Letters from Colleagues
Appendix D: Outstanding Teaching Awards
Appendix E: Syllabi
Appendix F: Representative Assignments
Appendix G: Sample Assignments
Appendix H: Examinations
Appendix I: Teaching Related Work
Appendix J: Letters for Students

INDEX

administrative support, 33. 34
advising students, 20
Angarano, Donna W., viii, 60
animations, 47
Annis, Linda, viii, 7, 9, 16, 23, 26, 27,157, 252
annotations, 50, 51
appendix, 7, 42, 47
areas for enhancement, 42
Arnold, Judith M., viii, 70
arrangement of materials, 14
articles, 14
assessment, 5
Auburn University, 60, 109
awards, 17
base line, 9
bells and whistles, 48
benefits, 37
Biology Department, 193, 214
bolster credentials, 18
Boyer, Ernest L., 38, 45
Branch, Charles, 64
Brown University, 24
buddy system, 10
burn out, 34
CD-ROM, 47
Chatterjee, Indira, viii, 78
checklist for evaluation, 43
choosing items, 4
Clark, Diane M., viii, 85
class discussion outline, 55
Classroom Observation Report, 32
Clemson University, 3, 93

collaboration, 39, 43
colleague evaluation, 14
College of Business, 109, 204
College of William and Mary, 3, 123, 150
color graphics, 47, 52
common questions, 19
communication, 26
computer literacy, 48
conference presentations, 5
consultant, 10
content and organization, 21
continual analysis and improvement, 22, 42
Council of Independent Colleges, 32
Counseling & Human Services, 167
course evaluations, 30
course innovations, 22
course portfolios, 40
course syllabi, 5, 52
Covey, Stephen, 205
Cronic, Daria T., viii, 93
curricular revisions, 5
curriculum vitae, 14, 50
date, 9, 255
department chair/head, 6, 10, 12, 35
display, 52
doctoral candidate, 210
Economics, 109
Eison, J., 20, 27
Electrical Engineering, 78
electronic course syllabus, 53
electronic curriculum vitae, 50

electronic mail, 53
electronic materials, 49
electronically augmented
    teaching portfolio (EATP), 46-48
English, 116, 123, 174
entering job market, 24
essays, 23
evaluation, 5, 9
evidence of instructional
    effectiveness, 30
evidence, control or
    corroboration of, 10
Exceptional Child Program, 132
exhibitions of students' work, 23
faculty acceptance, 26
faculty development, 43
faculty handbook, 35
Family Relations and
    Child Development, 223
fellowships, 25
Ferzola, Anthony P., viii,102
field-work reports, 23
finding a job, 253
Foundations and Special Education, 93
Fulwiler, Toby, 142
Geology, 150
Georgia Southern University, 3,116,
    132, 243
gerontology, 223
getting started, 24, 40
graded student essays, 5
graduate students, 18, 24
grants, 17, 25
Gropper, Daniel M., viii,109
Harvard University, 24
help to colleagues, 6
Hendrix, Ellen H., viii,116
highlights of ratings, 22
histograms, 52
Hobart and William Smith
    Colleges, 2, 193
home page, 47
honors, 5

improve teaching, 8,15, 25, 37, 39
improved student evaluations, 253
innovative instructional practices, 23
institutional support, 32, 39
instruction in laboratories, 20
instructional improvement, 15
instructional innovations, 5
interactive software, 47
Internet, 47, 55, 56
items appear consistently, 21
items for portfolio, 13
Kennedy, Colleen, ix,123
Kenney, Stephanie L., ix,132
laboratory reports, 23
Law, 183
Lieberman, Devorah A., ix, 46
Llewellyn, Robert R., ix, 141
lucidity, 7
Macdonald, R. H., ix, 150
MacQueen, R. M., ix, 159
maintaining revisions, 42
Marquette University, 17
material from oneself, 4, 49, 50
material from others, 5, 15
Mathematics, 102
Medical College of Georgia, 17
mentor, 10, 11, 20, 26, 38, 43, 252
merit pay, 17, 25
Millis, B., 7, 27
Morgan, Oliver J., ix, 167
multimedia, 47
Mura, Karen E., ix, 32,174
Music, 85
new faculty, 21, 35
newly designed courses, 35
nonprint materials, 6
O'Neil, M. C., 12, 27
off-campus activities, 6
Oklahoma State University, 223
outcomes of teaching, 40
Paul, Richard W., 143
peer visitation, 32
performance reviews, 6, 23

personal statement, 5
personalized product, 21
personnel decisions, 12, 16, 26
Philosophy, 141
philosophy of teaching, 8
Physics, 159
Political Science, 231
portfolio concept, 1
portfolio posters, 35
portfolio revisions, 37, 39
practicums, 23
pre- and post-testing, 23
preparing portfolio, 10, 25, 28
presentation software, 49, 54
products of good teaching, 53
products of student learning, 5
professional conferences, 23
professional development, 22, 31
promotion and tenure reviews, 25, 35
Psychology, 243
quantitative rankings, 52
reasons for portfolio, 34
reflective statement, 5,13, 22
Rehnke, M. A., 8, 27
released time, 25
reviewers, 47
revising a portfolio, 255
revising form and content, 38, 40
Rhodes College, 3, 85,141,159
Rodriguez-Farrar, 12, 27
Rose, Charles P., ix, 183
Rueter, John, ix, 46
Rutgers University, 3
Ryan, James M. , ix, 193
salary increases, 25
sample portfolios, 58
samples of student work, 14
scholarship of teaching, 41
Schön, D., 37, 45
screen applicants, 25
Seldin, Peter, v, 7, 9, 11, 12, 16, 17,
    20, 23, 26, 27, 33, 41, 45, 46, 57,
    157, 254

selecting and organizing material, 16
self-assessment questions, 20
self-evaluation, 5, 6
self-mentor, 20
self-paced learning, 55
self-reflection, 8
Shore, M. B., 12, 27
simulations, 47
Small Animal Surgery and
    Medicine, 60
Smith, Fred, 64
Southern Illinois University, 24, 210
Speech Communication, 210
Stanley, Kenneth L., x, 204
statements from colleagues, 5
statements on each item, 13
storing and critiquing, 47
student achievement, 30
student career choices, 6
student comments, 30
student evaluations, 14, 22, 23, 52
student excellence, 28, 29
student learning, 23, 40, 41
student presentations, 23
student publications, 5
subjectivity, 26
Sullivan, Maggie M., x, 210
Susquehanna University, 32, 33, 35,
    174, 214
syllabi, 13, 22, 23
table of contents, 8
teaching awards, 25, 252
teaching development, 5
teaching dossier, 2
teaching fair, 33, 34
teaching goals, 31
teaching improvement, 31
teaching journal, 74
teaching philosophy, 29
teaching portfolio process, 35
teaching portfolio workshop, 33
teaching positions, 17
teaching responsibilities, 4, 22

teaching scholarship, 31
teaching strategies, 8
teaching-related activities, 13
team-taught course, 34
technology, 14, 46, 48
terrible teaching, 20
Tobin-Janzen, Tammy, x, 214
Uniform Resource Location (URL), 47
University Libraries, 70
University of Colorado, 17
University of Nevada, 78
University of Scranton, 102, 167
updating a portfolio, 14
using the portfolio, 15
Valdosta State University, 204, 231
Valencia Community College, 3
videotape, 6, 47
Wake Forest University, 3,183

Washington State University, 17
ways to display, 46, 49
ways used, 25
weak teaching, 25
Weber, Joseph A., 28, 223, x
Western Michigan University, 70
Willis, Clyde E. , x, 231
Wilson, Janie H., x, 243
Wolf, K., 38, 45
workshops, 22
World Wide Web, 56
Wright, W.A., 12, 27
written legacy, 18
year-end self reports, 42
Zubizarreta, John, x, xiv, 6, 7, 9, 10,
    11, 14, 16, 23, 26, 27, 37, 41,
    45, 254

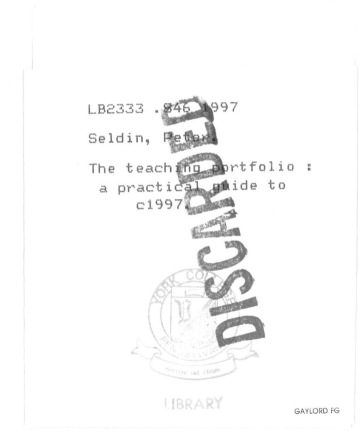